THE BOOK OF

MARGERY KEMPE

THE BOOK OF

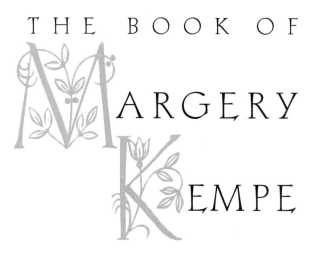

MARGERY KEMPE

A NEW TRANSLATION BY

JOHN SKINNER

IMAGE BOOKS
DOUBLEDAY

NEW YORK LONDON TORONTO SYDNEY AUCKLAND

An Image Book

PUBLISHED BY DOUBLEDAY

a division of Bantam Doubleday Dell Publishing Group, Inc.

1540 Broadway, New York, New York 10036

IMAGE, DOUBLEDAY, and the portrayal of a deer drinking
from a stream are trademarks of Doubleday, a division of
Bantam Doubleday Dell Publishing Group, Inc.

Library of Congress Cataloging-in-Publication Data
Kempe, Margery, b. ca. 1373.
The book of Margery Kempe / a new translation by John Skinner. — 1st ed.
p. cm.
"An Image book"—t.p. verso.
1. Kempe, Margery, b. ca. 1373—Biography. 2. Women authors, English—
Middle English, 1100–1500—Biography. 3. Christian pilgrims and pilgrimages—
Early works to 1800. 4. Mysticism—England—Early works to 1800.
5. Christian women—Religious life—England. I. Skinner, John. II. Title.
PR2007.K4A199   1998
248.2'2'092—dc21
[B]   97-37659
CIP

ISBN 0-385-49037-2
Copyright © 1998 by John Skinner
All Rights Reserved
Printed in the United States of America
May 1998
First Edition
Book design by Julie Duquet
1   3   5   7   9   10   8   6   4   2

For the Carthusian Novices, Brothers, and Fathers
of Saint Hugh's Charterhouse, England

INTRODUCTION

News of the discovery of *The Book of Margery Kempe* was broken in a letter to *The Times* of London on December 27, 1934, by the distinguished American medievalist Hope Emily Allen. "Previously," she wrote, "scholars had been forced to conclude that medieval old ladies did not write their reminiscences." Yet now the first known autobiography in the English language had come to light, having lain hidden for four hundred years in the library of an Old Catholic family, the Butler-Bowdons. And, moreover, this unique document was written by a woman.

Hope Allen herself had been visiting London when the manuscript was first brought to the Victoria and Albert Museum for examination. A friend describes Allen's reaction, "her eyes shining with excitement," as she told of the find; this was something a fortunate scholar handles only once in a lifetime. And her letter to *The Times* carries the same sense of discovery, for it was directed as much at the general public as at the rarified world of medieval scholars.

Up to this moment, little had been known of Margery Kempe, for only the barest selection of her extensive writings appeared to have survived. In 1501 these random fragments had been gathered together by Wynken de Worde, William Caxton's apprentice and successor. Printed as *A shorte treatyse of contemplation*, they were soon wrongly ascribed to "Margery Kempe . . . a devoute ancres." Already, Margery had been grouped with the fourteenth-century English mystics in the same category as Richard Rolle and Dame Julian, the anchoress of Norwich, her exact contemporary and the author of *A Revelation of Love*.

Now at last the public was informed; we have the whole story. And what a surprise: Far from being a typical holy woman, an anchoress vowed to celibacy, a dedicated solitary like Julian, Margery Kempe was a married woman who had borne fourteen children. Moreover, she had been a woman of substance who had briefly run the largest brewery in Lynn; then, on turning to religion, she had traveled hundreds of miles on pilgrimage to the Holy Land, to Rome, to Santiago di Compostela in Spain.

These were some of the early surprises. More were to come, chief among them the difficulty of understanding the true nature of Margery Kempe's spirituality and the underlying reasons for the constant conflict and disputes that marked her life. Margery's account of her spiritual awakening, her conversion from her sinful way of life, is full of conflict and recrimination. She seems to have been incapable of sustaining any kind of harmonious relationship with either friend or passing acquaintance. What was the purpose of this new way of life that caused her so much trouble? Was this really the way to become a saint? The difficulty in answering these questions that present themselves so forcefully as soon as we meet her is that Margery herself remains, as we shall see, an unsure witness.

Hope Allen went on to collaborate with an English medieval scholar, Professor Sanford Brown Meech, in editing the new find for the Early English Text Society, from which this new translation derives. They established that the original had been copied probably before 1450, not long after Margery's death. The copyist put the name "Salthows" on his handiwork; Salthouse being a village on the coast of Norfolk. Because the manuscript is also marked as having belonged to the Carthusians of Mount Grace in North Yorkshire, and the Carthusians were great copyists of such texts, it is generally supposed that Salthouse was a choir monk there. In addition, throughout the text a sometime reader has added his own short comments, and even some little sketches in the same red ink. Once again, as several of these comments refer to the Mount Grace community, this is assumed to be the hand of an unknown Carthusian monk. Such are the interesting details that would have rewarded the diligent Hope Allen.

But a gap of sixty years separates us from the novelty of these events, and it would be wholly unhelpful to parade Margery Kempe's book before today's readers simply as autobiography. For one thing, that genre had yet to be invented; and for another, it would be unrealistic to anticipate the literary skills necessary for such an accomplishment in a woman who could neither read nor write. All Margery set out to do was, as she says in her own preface, to record for "sinful wretches" (like herself) how God showed his mercy toward her and the workings of his grace in her soul. But again, if the genre is perhaps more properly to be described as the "diary of a soul," this is not to suggest that it matches the polish and sophistication of Saint Augustine's *Confessions* or of Margery's contemporary, Saint Catherine, who was writing at much greater length her account of yet another spiritual journey in faraway Siena.

It was not simply that Margery Kempe, like almost every woman of her day, was uneducated; the English language itself was still a spoken language. Its spelling was uncertain, its grammar and syntax still rudimentary; the very soil it sought to grow in was as yet undrained and, above all, still waiting to enjoy to the full the richly dunged matrix of its complex linguistic past. It would be another two centuries before the advent of printing and the rush of learning, when suddenly William Shakespeare would celebrate the fullness of that harvest crying out to be reaped. So it is that in Margery's book we must be content to listen to the repetitive echoes of common talk, as if we were merely listening to any chance conversation in the streets of fifteenth-century Lynn.

In one sense, given Margery's considerable skills as a conversationalist and even storyteller, it is surprising that her text is so impoverished in vocabulary while much of its structure remains obstinately repetitive. The reason for this might be as much pious intent, an awareness that the text should seem semi-sacred, as any lack of literary skills on the part of author and amanuensis. But in achieving a fresh version from the Middle English, it seems more important to offer today's readers a lively account by loosening the language, rather than adhering too tightly to the literal tautness of the Mount Grace version.

Since she herself could not write, Margery had to dictate what she wanted to say. She had two scribes. The first attempt to set down her book may have been by dictating her words to her son; he had lived for a long while in Germany, married a local girl, and then returned home with her, leaving their young daughter behind with friends. (There is only one drawback to this supposition, which has been closely argued: Her son died within a month of his return to England, leaving precious little time for such a labor.) Presumably at Margery's pleading, the first draft was then taken up by a priest with the intention of completing her task, only to discover that the manuscript was to all intents and purposes illegible— an indecipherable jumble of English and German.

After a delay of some four years, her new scribe virtually rewrote the book aided by Margery's memory and fresh dictation. And at this stage, ten further chapters were added, giving rise to "Book II." The question occurs, How much did this new scribe import his own sense of style and expression into Margery's story? As a priest, he might be imagined tailoring and shaping the story so as to enhance its purpose, to edify the faithful who would someday come to read it. (Margery had stipulated that she would commit her experiences to paper on the condition that they would be made public after her death. She could hardly have guessed that publication would not occur until the twentieth century!)

We can never be certain how much Margery's original narrative was molded by her scribe. But it is quite clear in certain vivid passages—such as those dealing with her heresy trials and the stormy crossing of the North Sea—that it is Margery speaking directly onto the page. Moreover, given that her second scribe was an educated cleric, he seems to have offered very little help in structuring her book. It would seem most likely to have been written down more or less as it came to her mind; that is to say, in a series of events linked not chronologically, as we might expect of a modern biographer or medieval cleric, but thematically, as the woman's mind may have been pleased to work and sort.

This elected manner of telling her story, with very little regard to the true sequence of events, presents a sometimes confusing and at worst misleading impression to the reader. At a first reading, it is easy to imagine that once Margery took up with the idea of becoming a pilgrim, her lifestyle changed into a continual traipse from one holy site to the next. In fact, her story may be divided into three distinct periods. The first was her marriage and bringing up her family in Lynn; this included her failed business enterprises, her conversion, and the beginnings of her "visions." Secondly, her pilgrimages: the eighteen-month journey to the Holy Land, and her return via Assisi and Rome; and after a gap of two years, at the conclusion of her journey to Santiago di Compostela, the succession of trials she endured when she was arraigned as a suspected heretic. And lastly, the final phase of her life, which she spent back at Lynn. Yet, not surprisingly, these remaining years continued to be punctuated by drama: her husband's horrific fall, followed by his death a year later; the great fire of Lynn; and the return of her son, followed by his own untimely death. Finally we hear how, on impulse, Margery set out upon her final journey, escorting her daughter-in-law home to Germany, only to stumble, almost by chance, on one last pilgrimage.

Margery Kempe lived in the last quarter of the fourteenth century and into the first half of the fifteenth. Since by deliberate choice, or by blind oversight, Margery chooses to remain silent on almost all the detailed background of her life, it may be helpful to offer a brief outline of the England of her day and, in particular, fourteenth-century Lynn.

In Margery's lifetime, England was prosperous, although sometimes swept by plague and common revolt. Her kings (Richard II, Henry V) were increasingly confident and in bullish mood. Margery would have heard of the English archers' exploits during Henry V's decisive victory over the French at Agincourt. Yet it would not have interested her a great deal. Closer to hand, she would also have witnessed the Peasants' Revolt: a serious nationwide uprising against the king's poll tax levied to fund his wars against the French. In East Anglia it came to a head when Geoffrey Litster and his cronies took Norwich by the scruff of its neck. Most in authority fled or fell to the mob, who would soon have taken control if not for the city's warring bishop. Calling his men to arms, bishop Henry Despenser soon rounded them up a little way outside Norwich. He heard their sins, which he was pleased to absolve, and then sent them on their eternal way.

In addition to such civil strife, the church was having to attend to considerable dissent among its members. The teachings of John Wycliffe, who died peacefully enough in a rural parish in 1384, were beginning to take insidious hold on ordinary folk; their clever mix of radical criticisms of church and state that empowered the common man was to prove a heady prelude to the upheavals of the Reformation. The Lollards, as they were known, held private prayer meetings away from church that grew increasingly popular, especially as members read aloud from their newly translated English bible. Their most prominent leader was Sir John Oldcastle, otherwise known as Lord Cobham. His rebellion was to prove a serious threat to the king and become the accidental cause of suspicion falling on Margery, which led to her heresy trials. Long after his execution, Oldcastle was rehabilitated by the reformers and deemed an early Protestant martyr. Indeed, Shakespeare's original name for Falstaff was in fact Oldcastle, but, after Protestant objections, he was forced to change it in favor of Sir John Fastolf, another Norwich worthy who served Henry V in France.

Into this busy scene, Margery Brunham was born, around 1373. Her background was secured in the merchant middle class: Her father, a wealthy burgess, almost certainly dealt in cloth, the staple source of wealth in that region. Five times he was elected mayor of Lynn, then known as Bishop's Lynn and today called King's Lynn. Six times over a period of twenty years, he was one of the town's two members of parliament.

Today East Anglia is something of a backwater, taking life as it comes and rejoicing in a rich, fertile land that yields the best cereal crops in the whole of Great Britain. But in Margery's day, it was wool that ruled. Sheep flocks teemed in every field, yielding their fleeces to the wool trade that plied through the ports of Lowestoft, Lynn, and Norwich to the Low Countries and thence to the rest of Europe. Raw wool was sold in great quantities to the Flemish weavers, but the local industry was also highly developed. The weavers of the little town of Worsted, just outside Norwich, lent their name to a cloth that was the envy of Europe. And even today London's tailors would not dream of cladding their city clientele in anything other than pure worsted. Yet the Norwich of Margery's day, second only to London in wealth and influence throughout the kingdom, is but a faded memory. The important historical and personal dates in Margery's lifetime are summarized at the end of this preface. This will perhaps help to clarify the sequence of Margery's life that is at times barely discernible from her own account. Indeed, the purpose of her writings remains overtly spiritual throughout the book. As much as we would have appreciated detailed descriptions of the Holy Land in 1413 or what it was like to join the mass of pilgrims crowding into Compostela from across Europe, little or nothing is offered. In part, as has been suggested, this is due to the strictly spiritual intention of her book; but it may also speak of Margery's inward-looking manner of life. At one point she apologizes for misspelling place names, but adds firmly that she did not go on pilgrimage in order to write down accurately the name of every town she passes through.

I am reminded of my own encounter with the English Carthusians with whom I stayed for two weeks in order to write a book about their way of life. I was able to join them on two occasions for their weekly walk, when the community spends the day outside the monastery walking on the Sussex Downs. It was striking how little any one of them had eyes for the outside world, the great whale-backed downs, a lazy heron lifting off the river at our approach. Instead the monks walked two by two, changing companions every twenty minutes, and each gave the other their courteous and complete attention. The outside world was no longer of any great interest to them except in the context of their new interior world of prayer and silence.

Coming to the crux of the matter: How genuine was Margery Kempe, the mystic?

Certainly, in one chief respect she disappointed even her own best intentions. She has failed to be recognized officially either then or since as a saint. Yet there are plenty of un-canonized heroes and heroines whose holiness has gone un-noticed by the process of formal canonization; Julian of Nor-wich is one.

The first important correction that must be made is not to regard as a genuine vision every conversation with our Lord that Margery reports in such detail. It seems clear that on a number of key occasions these conversations are contradic-tory and simply not to be trusted; for instance, where our Lord tells her to write an extremely sententious letter to the widow of Lynn (see footnote 38). Even more pertinent, when she reports our Lord pleading with her to be silent at her prayers, she has him saying that if she will not listen to him she should at least listen to what her confessor tells her! (See Chapter 88.)

Clearly Margery's method of praying was largely circum-locutory. (See at end, "The Prayers of Margery Kempe," her final say in this book: a method of prayer *certainly not* to be imitated!) Moreover, when she wasn't addressing God with such lengthy and creatively emotional speeches she seems to have used a vivid method of meditational recall much loved and practiced in her day. This prayer of active and affective imagination was popularized by Bonaventure and Bernard, as well as in England by Anselm and Aelred before them, so that it became the familiar pabulum of preaching throughout the Middle Ages. As a tradition of prayer, it was still influential in the sixteenth century when Ignatius adapted it to play a prominent part in his method of prayer and meditation con-tained in *The Exercises*, his famous composition of place. Thus, when Margery describes in close detail how she helped our Lady care for the infant Jesus in Nazareth, there is no ques-tion of her literally enjoying such extravagant visions; we are dealing with her own affective meditations upon which she appears to have spent many long hours, creating her own inner world.

And yet there is something special about her description

of her initial conversion vision (see Chapter 1), in which Christ comes to her wearing a mantle of purple silk and sits on her bed, saying: "My daughter, why have you left me, when I never for one moment went away from you?" Special, if only for the fact that it turned her life around. In psychological terms, what works is real. At the time, Margery was utterly stuck: This was her turning point. It is significant, too, that Margery places this encounter right at the very start of her book. And certainly this, together with her "mystical marriage" vision in Rome, seem to stand out apart from any other of her seeming "visions." Her strangely threatening encounter with God the Father, experienced in Rome, in which the Son must mediate his Father's message to a reluctant subject, would appear to be in the same category. It sounds quite distinct from mere affective meditation, not least because Margery appears plainly terrified and quite resistant to this new kind of direct immediacy with the Godhead.

Having made this distinction between the two kinds of experience that Margery describes—her meditations and her visions—one might ask what she herself did with such experiences. When Margery goes to Julian for advice on her way of life, she is given the classic answer: "Be careful that these are not contrary to God's glory and to the benefit of your fellow Christians."

It is Margery Kempe's propensity for upsetting all and sundry around her that has aroused most of the suspicion and criticism of her—both during her lifetime and since her book has come under the close scrutiny of more and more scholars. This process shows no sign of decline: A medievalist friend of mine in Oxford has lost count of the number of approaches he has had to decline from American students wishing to present their doctorate on some new aspect of Margery Kempe.

Let us hope that their many labors and diligent research will shine yet more light on a fascinating medieval lady. Mar-

gery will never be Saint Kempe, but the conundrum of her
patience in suffering her own simple foolishness is a wonder
to behold, and an example to us all. Like the Carthusians who
first copied her words and deeds, at the very least she took
God for real.

Margery's account of her life is written largely by association; she groups similar incidents rather than attempting any strict chronological sequence. In fact, her life may be simply divided into three main periods:

1. BIRTH, MARRIAGE, AND CHILD-REARING IN LYNN
   1327: *John Brunham,* first time elected mayor of Lynn.
   1373(c): *Margery* born; death of *Saint Bridget of Sweden.*
   1393: *Margery and John Kempe* married.
   1401: *William Sawtre* burned.

2. PILGRIMAGES AND HERESY TRIALS
   1413: *Pilgrimage to Jerusalem* following death of her father. Probably autumn as (Chapter 11) on Midsummer Eve she concludes her agreement with John. Then she waits three weeks to see Bishop of Lincoln and finally is interviewed by the archbishop of Canterbury in his garden at Lambeth.
   1414–1418: *Council of Constance* convoked by Pope John XXIII in 1413 and aimed at ending the Great Schism (when there were three rival popes); to set down reforms and deal with John Huss.
   1414: *Margery arrives in Rome,* stays on until Easter of 1415.
   1415: *Margery leaves Rome* (Chapters 37–42); *Margery sails home to England* on Saturday, May 20; *Agincourt:* On October 25 the English army of Henry V (outnumbered four to one) defeated the French. France was to be dominated by the crown of England for the next 100 years.
   1415: *Margery home to Norwich* (on May 21?).
   1417: *Margery sets out for Santiago* in spring (Chapter 44), repays her debts in Bristol, returns from Santiago in August.

1417: *Margery is tried for heresy:* Leicester (Chapters 45–49); visits York and then London (Chapters 50–55).

3. MIDDLE AGE AND FINAL PILGRIMAGE

1421: January 23: *Fire in Bishop's Lynn* (Book II, Chapter 2).

1431: *Margery's husband and son die* (Book II, Chapter 2).

1433: July 20: *Margery goes to Aachen* and venerates the four great relics (Book II, Chapter 7).

1434: *Margery visits Syon Abbey* (Book II, Chapter 10).

1438: Before Easter, *Margery is admitted to the Guild of the Trinity* at Saint Margaret's Church, Lynn.

1440(c): *Death of Margery Kempe.*

Margery Kempe's Introduction

ere begins a short account that will offer sinful
wretches both consolation and comfort as well
as some understanding of the high and inex-
pressible mercy of our sovereign Savior Jesus Christ. His
blessed name be worshiped and made known forever; for
even in our own lifetimes he has been so good as to show us
his majesty and kindness in spite of our unworthiness. All our
Savior's workings are to teach and guide us, and the grace he
works in every creature brings benefit to us all providing we
are not without his loving charity.

Therefore our merciful Lord, Jesus Christ, has allowed
this short account to be written down in order to glory his
holy name; for it touches on a few of his wonderful works —
how by mercy, by his kindness and in his charity, he stirred
and moved this sinful creature to return his love. How, at the
prompting of the Holy Spirit, I spent many years promising

vows of fasting and many other penances. And yet I always turned back at the least temptation. Indeed I was just like a reed bending at every least breath of wind and only standing upright again when it ceases to blow. This went on until our merciful Lord, Jesus Christ, took pity on his creature, the work of his hands. For he turned my health into sickness and my wealth to poverty; my good name into one constantly blamed by others, their love for me into hatred. For many years I had always been unstable and now I was overtaken by all these reverses; yet I still found myself steadily drawn and still stirred to enter the way of higher perfection, of which Christ our Savior in his own person was our supreme example. He trod it in sorrow, that same path of duty long before us.

Through the mercy of that same Jesus, I want to tell in some part the story of my life. Firstly, how I was touched by the hand of our Lord so that I fell seriously ill, indeed for a long period; I lost my mind, until our Lord by his grace restored me once more. But I will give more details of this later. Then too my worldly possessions, which were many and abundant at the time, were suddenly no more, threadbare and barren. Then I had to let go of pomp, and my pride was laid low and finally cast aside. Those same people who had once looked up to me were now the first to find the sharpest criticisms. Even my relatives and especially my closest friends suddenly turned into ruthless enemies.

I began to wonder at this amazing change, and I came seeking shelter under the wings of my spiritual mother, the Holy Church. I went in all humility to my confessor; I accused myself of all my failings and followed this with much corporal penance. In a very short time, our Lord visited me with many contrite tears. Day after day I continued to weep, so that many declared openly that I could stimulate my tears at will. But they merely belittled the work of God.

Soon, I became used to being slandered and put down in public, shouted at and reviled by everyone in sight, all on account of the grace and virtue brought by the comfort of the Holy Spirit. Then it became a kind of comfort and inner strength when I suffered any pain for the love of God and on account of the new grace he was working in me. It seemed to me that the more I had to put up with in the way of lies and complaints, the more I grew in grace and in consolation when I meditated on holy things and knew a higher contemplation than I had imagined possible. For I now began to make wonderful speeches and have intimate conversations with our Lord; and he would speak to me and tell my soul how I would be despised for his love; but that I must have patience and set all my trust, all my love, and all my affection on him alone.

Sometimes, the Holy Spirit would inspire me and I would know about many things still hidden but about to happen. But more frequently, while I was absorbed in these sacred speeches and conversations, I would weep and sob so much that people grew very alarmed. But how could they know how homely[1] and intimate our Lord was behaving within my soul? Yet it was hard even for me to tell of the grace that I was feeling; it seemed to come from heaven, to be well beyond the reach of my own power of reason. Besides, my body would be sometimes so enfeebled by the experience of such grace that I always failed to put into words exactly what I felt within my soul.

All the time, I went in fear and trembling of being deluded and deceived by my spiritual enemies. The Holy Spirit often prompted me to seek advice from many different priests who had experience in these matters; I went in search of doctors of divinity, bachelors, bishops — I even consulted more than one archbishop. I had conversations with several anchorites as well; I would tell them of my new way of life, about whatever graces the Holy Spirit of his goodness worked in both my

---

[1] This word, while still in familiar use in the United States, has fallen in disuse in the UK; more importantly, it is a word constantly used by Julian of Norwich to describe the intense mystical activity of God's love that she herself experienced. Margery is to visit Julian later (see Chap. 18).

mind and my soul. And all these wise and experienced persons to whom I confided my anxieties, agreed in their advice. Because of the grace our Lord undoubtedly showed me, I began to love him greatly; as to my interior promptings and stirrings of soul, I was also obliged to follow them, trusting that they truly came from the Holy Spirit and not from some evil spirit.

Some of these good priests were so convinced that my experiences were genuine that they went so far as to declare that they would wager their souls before God that I was truly inspired by the Holy Spirit. Some wanted me to have a book written that would tell all about my experiences and revelations; some offered to write it themselves, there and then. But I always refused. I knew in my soul that it was too soon to write anything down. And so it was some twenty years since the start of my first experiencing such feelings and revelations that I agreed to have anything written down. It was then that our Lord was pleased to bid me that I ought indeed arrange for them to be written and recorded: that is to say, the way of life I had adopted, my innermost feelings, and some of the revelations that had been shown me—all so that his goodness might be known to the world at large.

At first, I could find no one suitable to become my scribe; there were some who were qualified enough, yet they simply refused to believe what I had to say. Then I made an arrangement with a man who had recently returned from Germany. He was English by birth but had married a German wife and settled there with their young child. But because he knew me very well, and also, I trust, was moved by the Holy Spirit, he came home to England with his wife and all their worldly goods and lived with me until he had finished writing down all that I wanted to tell him. But it was barely completed before he suddenly died.

So then I turned to a priest friend of mine; I put the matter to him, and he agreed to read the manuscript. His verdict was that it was so ill-written that he could barely decipher it.

Apparently it was written down in neither English nor German, and the letters were inscribed like none he had ever seen, he told me. Finally, he declared that no one would ever be able to read a word of it, unless they had some special grace. Even so, he promised me that if he could possibly decipher it, he would make a fresh and legible copy.

But then so much evil talk began to arise about my weeping that this priest was afraid to be seen talking to me. And, for the same reason, he was reluctant to make a start on the book for about four years, although I continued to ask him to do something about it. After all this time, he then told me that he was unable to read it and therefore would not help me. He added that he did not want to risk his reputation on such work. And so he handed me on to someone who had been a close friend of my original scribe; he felt confident that this man would be just the one to decipher such appalling handwriting, not least because he had received several letters from the original scribe while he had been living in Germany.

And so I approached this man and asked if he would be willing to help me write a new version of my book, but on condition that it was kept secret as long as I lived. I made him an offer of a very large sum for his work. And so this man agreed to make a start. But the project was doomed from the beginning. He had not written half a page before he complained bitterly that he could not continue: The writing was unintelligible, the book itself without rhyme or reason.

It then transpired that the priest who had first promised to help me with this new transcription had a bad conscience. He knew all along that he had given his promise to write it all out again, provided that he could succeed in reading the original. Knowing that he had not yet tried his best, he asked me if it were at all possible for me to retrieve the book for him. I promptly did so and took the parcel back to my priest with a light heart. I told him that if he would give it a good try, I for my part would pray to God for him and win the grace for him not only to read it at last but also to write it all down again in good order.

He trusted in my prayers and began to study it a second time. And now it seemed to him a good deal easier than it had been before. He began to read it word for word as I sat with him; and sometimes, when there was a difficult passage, I was able to help him through.

But I should make one thing clear. This book is not written in the order of events so that one thing follows another exactly as really happened. But things are set down simply as and when I remembered them while I was dictating my story. There was such a long delay in committing everything to writing that I had forgotten the exact time and order of when things actually happened. Yet at the same time I made sure that nothing was written down that did not truly take place.

When my priest friend at last began to write my book, his eyes began to trouble him. Indeed, they failed so that he found difficulty in forming his letters, and he could not even see enough to mend his pen. Yet he could see everything else perfectly well enough. He tried spectacles—perched on the end of his nose—but that only made matters worse than before. He complained to me about his problem. I told him his enemy was envious of the good work he had in hand and would try anything to prevent it. I urged him to do as well as God's grace let him and to carry on. And when he returned to the book once more, he found he could see as well, so he declared, as ever he had before. He was as content working in the daytime or by candlelight.

And that is why, in the year of our Lord 1436, once he had completed a quire and added one more leaf, he agreed to write this introduction anew in order to give a fuller explanation of how this book came about. So that it was written after this short preface which now follows.

PREFACE

his brief account will tell of a person of high position, proud of her place in the world, who was then drawn to our Lord by great poverty as well as sickness, humiliation, and a great many insults and similar healing misfortunes, which she suffered in many places and in many different countries.

Some of these trials of which I shall tell are not related in the order they occurred but simply as and when I remembered them. I should explain: It was twenty years and more after I had left the world and steadfastly embraced our Lord before this book, an account of my trials and innermost feelings, came to be written. At first, a Carmelite friar[2] had vol-

---

[2] "A White Friar": this was Master Aleyn (cf. Chap. 9) who took an interest in Margery when she was injured by falling masonry in church. Monks were identified and popularly known by the color of their habits: Thus, Black Friars were the Dominicans, Gray Friars the Franciscans.

unteered to write my life story, if I so wished. But I knew in my heart that at that time it was too soon; it would be many years later before I knew it to be right.

As things turned out, my first scribe was a man who possessed little skill in writing, either in English or German. Which meant that it could be read only by those who were filled with God's grace; in addition to that, I was so slandered and blamed that very few people believed my account of all I had experienced.

In the end, a priest had a strong desire to read my account, but even he found it hard to understand and he struggled with this first draft over four years. But afterward, at my urging and prompted by his own conscience, he tried once more and found it much easier than before.

And so he started to write in the year of our Lord 1436, on the day after the feast of Mary Magdalene (July 23), helped out by some details I myself was able to offer him.

Book 1

1

hen I was twenty, or perhaps a little older, I was married to a well-respected burgess of Bishop's Lynn and, as such things usually happen, I soon found myself with child. All through my pregnancy, even up to the birth, I was constantly sick; so that when I went into labor I was so weakened that I despaired of my life and believed I would not survive.

At this point, I sent for my priest for I had something serious on my conscience that I had never confessed before. For I was always being tricked by my enemy the devil who deceived me by saying that so long as I was in good health there was no need to confess; I could do penance privately and God would in his mercy forgive me everything. And so I would often do hard penances, fasting on bread and water and performing acts of charity; but all the while I never disclosed my sin in confession.

But whenever I was sick or depressed in my mind, the devil would begin to whisper that I would be damned because I had not confessed and been absolved of that secret sin. So that believing I would not survive the birth of my baby, I sent for the priest, as I say, wanting to make my full general confession of all the sins of my life.

But when it came to the point of telling my sin that I had hidden all this time, my confessor grew impatient with me; he began telling me off in no uncertain way before I had a chance to explain what I wanted to say. At last I fell silent and would say no more, whatever he might try to do or say. As a result, what with the priest's sharp words and my own inner fear of damnation, I went out of my mind. For half a year, eight weeks, and a few odd days I was terribly disturbed and plagued by evil spirits.

All the while I saw, as I thought, devils opening their mouths as if to swallow me alive, their insides full of fire. They would sometimes grab at me or utter threats; they would pull me around in the daytime and at night throughout all this length of time. These devils would call out loud to me; they continually terrified me with their cries telling me to leave the church, deny my faith, abandon God, his mother, and all the saints in heaven.

These same devils also told me to deny all my good works and any small virtue I might have, also to turn aside from my father and mother and all my friends. Which is just what I did. I slandered my husband and my friends, even myself. I spoke many wicked and cruel things; I felt empty of any goodness or virtue; I was intent only on wickedness; I did and said just as the spirits tempted me. Many a time I wanted to kill myself and be damned in hell with them. And to prove it, I bit my hand so badly that the scar is visible to this day. More than this, I would tear and scratch myself, wounding my breast and around my heart with my nails, for want of any other instrument at hand. Left to my own devices, I would have done even more harm to myself, but I was tied and forcibly restrained by day and night.

I suffered in this way from these troubles and many other temptations for such a long time that people thought I would never recover or even survive with my life. Then one day, I was lying alone without anyone minding me; our merciful Lord Jesus Christ—he is always to be trusted, blessed be his Name—appeared to me although I had deserted him. He was in human form, yet most pleasingly beautiful, truly he was the loveliest sight that human eyes could ever gaze upon. Wearing a mantle of purple silk, he sat upon my bed; he looked at me with such a joyful face that I felt a sudden inner response as if strengthened in my soul. Then he spoke the following words to me: "My daughter, why have you left me, when I never for one moment went away from you?"

And as soon as he had spoken these words, I swear that I watched as the whole room opened up so brightly it might have been by lightning, and he rose into the air, not very fast at all but easily and gracefully, so that I watched him all the time until the air closed in once more.

Almost at once, I grew calm again and came to my senses. So that when my husband returned home, I asked him to give me back the keys to the larder so that I might get myself food and drink as had been my practice before I fell ill. But my servants and my nurses were against the idea, saying that if he handed over the keys I would be sure to give everything away. They still thought I was out of my mind.

Nevertheless, my husband, who was always kind and considerate toward me, told them to hand back the keys; and so I fetched myself food and drink, nothing too substantial since I still felt weak and unsteady. But now I was once more able to recognize my friends and members of my household, and everyone who came to visit. For many were curious to see for themselves how our Lord Jesus Christ had worked his grace in me—blessed may he be who is always close at hand when we are most in trouble. For when people think he is far away

from them, then in truth he is very near indeed with his
merciful grace.

Not long afterward, I was able to resume all my normal
duties, running the household and behaving in a sensible,
level-headed way. But I was still unclear what it was that our
Lord was really asking of me.

2

ince by God's mercy I had been returned to my
right mind, I believed that I was now bound to him
and so I decided to become his servant. Neverthe-
less, I would not be persuaded, neither by my husband nor
anyone else, to abandon my pride or my showy style of dress.
Yet I knew well enough what unpleasant things people said
about me; I wore the very latest head-dress and my sleeves
were slashed, so too was my cloak, to reveal all the many
colors I wore beneath. All this so that people would stare all
the more and think much of me.

And when my husband would try and talk me out of this
behavior, he got a short, sharp answer: I told him that I came
of a well-born family and, in fact, he should never have married me. I reminded him that my father had not only been the
mayor of Bishop's Lynn but also was alderman of the Guild
of the Holy Trinity. I insisted that I would maintain my family's standards whatever people chose to say.

The truth is that I was very jealous of my neighbors, especially if they could afford to dress as well as me. All the time,

I craved public attention and admiration; I had not learned any lesson from my long illness. Moreover, I was never content with all the worldly possessions God had given me but would always want more and more.

Then, out of pure greed, I went into brewing. For three or four years I was one of the best brewers in Lynn. At the end, though, since I did not really know the trade, I lost a great deal of money. Even with the best workers, skilled brewers many of them, things always seemed to go wrong. When the brew was going well, with a good head of yeast, suddenly it would go flat and the beer was spoiled. This happened time and again, until one by one my workmen walked out on me, either ashamed or in despair of things ever going right, they never said.

It was then that I remembered how God had punished me before—even though I had taken no notice; now it was happening all over again. But this time I was losing money; so I took heed and gave up brewing for good.

Then I asked my husband to forgive me for not having taken his advice sooner. I told him that my pride and sinfulness were the cause of all my troubles, and that although I had meant well, I would promise to change from now on. But this was not an end to my worldly enterprise. I settled on a horse-drawn mill. I bought two strong horses and hired a man to work them, grinding people's corn. I thought this would be a good line of business. But the venture had not long to run: shortly after we set up, on Corpus Christi eve, the unbelievable happened. My man was fit and healthy, the horses good and strong; they had always worked the mill perfectly well up until then. But now, when he took one horse from the stable and harnessed him to the mill, as he had done many times before, the horse refused to walk the rounds, no matter what his driver did. My man said he was sorry, he had tried everything he knew to make the horse pull. He tried leading him by the head, he tried beating him; then he spoiled and fussed over him, but nothing he did was any good. The

horse would sooner go backward than forward. So then my
man put on spurs, good and sharp, and rode astride the horse
to make him pull. But this was no better. When he saw nothing was any use, he put the horse back in his stable and fed
and watered him. The horse ate perfectly normally, as if nothing had happened. So then my man took the second horse
and put him in harness on the mill. And it was exactly the
same as his pair; he was not going to pull, whatever his driver
did.

At this, the man left his job and would not stay a moment
longer, as if to say that it was all my fault. And sure enough,
word soon went around Lynn town that neither man nor
beast was willing to work for me. Some even said I was
cursed, that God was taking public vengeance on me; some
said this, some said that. But some few men, who were wise
and whose hearts were nearer to the love of our Lord, declared it was a special mercy of our Lord Jesus Christ to call
me away from the vanity and proud ways of the world.

It was now, seeing all these troubles come at me from all
sides, that I recognized them as scourges by which our Lord
would punish me for my hidden sin. And so I begged God for
his mercy; and I left my pride behind, and my ambition and
all my desire for worldly success. Instead I did corporal penance and set out along the road to everlasting life. I will explain how this unfolded in the pages that follow.

3

ne night, as I lay in bed with my husband, I heard a sound of music so sweet and delightful that I thought I must be in Paradise. As soon as I heard it I got out of bed, saying: "Alas that I did ever sin, for it is so merry in heaven." For truly, the melody was so sweet to my ear that it surpassed any kind of music in the whole wide world without compare. And certainly, ever after, as soon as I heard laughter or music I would be overcome with tears of devotion and sighs in abundance for the great bliss of heaven; and I never gave any thought for the shame and contempt of this wretched world.

Having received this holy call from God, I could never put it from my mind—so much so that I would always be talking of it. Whenever I was in company I would suddenly say, "Heaven is such a merry place"; and anyone who knew how I had lived before and then heard me talk in this way of the joys of heaven would answer me, "Why are you always going on about heaven? You've no idea what it's like; you haven't gone there any more than we have!" In reality, they were angry and upset with me that I no longer joined them in speaking endlessly about worldly trivia as once I had.

And also from this time I had no further desire to have sex with my husband; indeed this burden of marriage seemed so abominable to me that I would sooner have eaten or sucked up ooze from the gutter than consent to intercourse, except that I was still obliged to remain obedient to my husband.

I therefore told him, "I am not allowed to deny you my body, but now all the love and affection in my heart is withdrawn from every earthly creature and set only in God." But he always wanted his way with me; and I complied but with much weeping and wailing that I could not live in chastity. I would often try to persuade my husband to be chaste, telling him how I knew only too well that our excessive lovemaking was displeasing to God. I argued that considering all the very great pleasure we had had in giving our bodies to each other, ought we not now, by mutual consent, desire to chastise and punish our bodies by refusing to give way to such lust anymore? My husband would agree in principle that this was a good idea; but that he would only do so when it was God's will. And so we went on as before, he using me, for he could never desist. But all the while I prayed God that I might live in chastity. And three or four years after matters had come to a head, only when it pleased our Lord, my husband at last agreed that we take a vow of chastity. But I shall, by Jesus' leave, write about this later.

It was also as a consequence of hearing this heavenly music that I began to do severe penance to my body. Sometimes I would confess two or three times in a day, especially of that one sin which I had hidden and kept secret for so long, the one I told about at the start of my book. I also began to make frequent fasts as well as vigils. For instance, I would rise at two or three in the morning and go to church; and I might still be praying there at noon or even stay the whole afternoon. On account of this strict way of life, many people slandered and criticized me. I also got myself a rough cloth (the kind that is used to dry malt in a kiln) and this I wore discreetly under my skirt, as secretly as I could manage lest my husband should spot it. And he never did know in all that time, though we lay side by side in bed each night, and I continued to wear it throughout the day. I even bore him children during this time.

Then came three years during which I had great difficulty

and labor with temptations. These I bore as best I could, meekly thanking our Lord for all his gifts. For indeed I was happier and more contented now in spite of all the criticism, mockery, and reproaches I received than I was before when I had received praise and admiration from one and all. For I knew full well that I had sinned grievously against God and deserved far more shame and suffering than any human action could mete out to me. And besides, contempt in this world is the right way ahead so as to win heaven, for Christ himself chose that same path. Moreover, all his apostles, the martyrs, confessors and virgins, and everyone who came to heaven, trod this road of tribulation; for I desired nothing so much as heaven itself.

At last my conscience was at peace since I believed I was now setting out along the way that would lead me to that place where I most wanted to be. And yet, all the same, I still had contrition and very great compunction—I was frequently given to tears and often sudden loud sobs would take me unawares—all on account of my sins and my unkindness to my maker. And many a time as well, our Lord would put me in mind of all those unkindnesses since my childhood. It was then that I began to realize my own wickedness so that I could only grieve and weep and pray the whole time to be forgiven in his mercy. My tears were so plentiful and constant that many folk thought I could weep and leave off at will; and so they decided I was a cheat and a hypocrite who wept in public simply for effect. There were very many—firm friends before I left the world—who would have nothing to do with me. But for myself, I thanked God for all he had done for me; all I wished for was his mercy and the forgiveness of my sins.

4

or the first two years after I had been called to our Lord, I had great peace of spirit and was free of all temptations. It was easy to put up with fasting; indeed to go completely without food scarcely troubled me. Equally, I loathed every pleasure the world had on offer; and I felt no rebellion of the flesh. My purpose was so strong that I feared not one devil in all hell; I also did a great deal of bodily penance. Indeed, I was convinced that I loved God more than he loved me. There I was, struck down by the deadly wound of vainglory, and I was utterly unaware. As an example, many times I knelt before the crucifix and begged him to loosen his hands from the nails and put his arms around me to show his love.

Our Lord Jesus Christ, seeing my presumption and by his mercy, sent me, as I have already said, three years of very great temptation. One of the hardest of these I am determined to tell in some detail. For it will serve as an example to those who come after that they should never trust in themselves nor take any pride in themselves, as I was fool enough to do. There is no doubt at all in my mind that our enemy of the spirit never sleeps but constantly probes our makeup and our personality; wherever he finds them at their weakest, at that point, our Lord allowing, he will set his trap. And then no man escapes by his own devices.

And so it was that for me he laid the trap of lechery; just as

I had thought all physical desire was dead in me. So for a long time now I was tempted to lechery, and there was nothing I could do. Yet I often went to confession, I wore my hair shirt; I did constant bodily penances and shed many a tear; I often prayed to our Lord to keep me safe and preserve me from falling into temptation. For I felt I would rather be dead than consent to sin. And through all this time, I had no desire to make love with my husband: it was all very painful and horrible.

It was during the second year of these temptations, on the eve of Saint Margaret, that a man I fancied told me just before evensong that he would give anything to sleep with me and have it off with me. He insisted that if he couldn't be satisfied now, then it would have to be another time — but it was not for me to choose. He was saying all this just to see what I would do. But thinking he really meant it, I said very little in answer. So we parted and both went our separate ways to evensong; and the church itself was dedicated to Saint Margaret of Antioch.[3] But I was so disturbed at what I had heard that I did not hear a single word of evensong; I could not even say my Our Father, nor think a single good thought. In that instant, I was in more turmoil than I had ever been.

The devil convinced me that God had abandoned me: Why else would I be so sorely tempted? I fell for the devil's words, and I began to give way, because I had no good thoughts of my own. That was why I was so certain that God had left me. So after evensong, I went over to tell him he could have his way, fully believing this was what he wanted. To my astonishment, he was completely evasive so that I couldn't understand him any more. And at that, we parted for the night. I was in such a state, tossing and turning all night long, that I scarcely knew what to do. There I lay alongside my own husband; yet

---

[3] The Legend of Margaret, a virgin martyr of the third or fourth century, who was one of the saints most venerated in the Middle Ages. She was said to have refused to marry the Prefect Olybrius and so suffered terrible trials and torments before being beheaded at Antioch.

to have made love with him would have seemed a detestable thought, although it was not sinful. Yet all the while I kept on thinking of sinning with the man who had tempted me while I was at church. At long last, because the temptation continued unabated and since I was so weak, I was overcome and made up my mind. I went off in search of my man to ask him if he would have me. He told me straight that for all the world's wealth he would not sleep with me; he said he would rather be chopped up small, just like meat for a stew.

I came away from him utterly confused and ashamed of myself; all I could see was my own weakness compared with his own strength of mind. Then I remembered the great grace God had given me, the peace of mind I had enjoyed for two whole years; how I had repented all my sins with many bitter tears and determined never to sin again but rather to die first. And now I realized how I had consented to sin with my own deliberate will. In that moment, I almost fell into despair. I thought I might be in hell itself for the sorrow I felt in my heart. I wondered if I was still worthy of his mercy for I had so willfully given in to such a sin; how could I ever serve God again, once I had proved myself so false to him.

Nevertheless, I often confessed my sins time after time, always performing whatever penance my confessor imposed upon me; and I abided closely to the rules of the Church. Such graces God gave me—blessed may he be—but he did not take away my temptation; rather it seemed to me that he increased it.

And therefore I thought he had forsaken me and dared no longer trust in his mercy. Throughout the following year, I was almost constantly troubled with horrible temptations of the flesh and by despair; my only consolation was that our Lord in his mercy, as I have to admit to myself, afforded me each day the best part of two hours during which I was able to grieve for my sins with many bitter tears. And afterward I was once more troubled by temptations to despair and felt as far away from experiencing God's grace as if I had never felt it at all. I found this so unbearable that I continued to wallow in despair. Except on the rare occasion when I felt the touchings of grace, my trials were so intense that I could no longer see how to bear them, so that I was in continual mourning and full of sorrow as if God had forsaken me for good.

5   The following five chapters appear not to belong in chronological order with those that follow. Their purpose appears to be an attempt at revealing the extent and nature of Margery's spiritual activity and so explain her numerous and urgent pilgrimages.

hen one Friday immediately before Christmas Day, as I was kneeling in Saint John's Chapel in my parish church of Saint Margaret's of Lynn, weeping my heart out and begging mercy and forgiveness for all my sins and transgressions, our Lord Jesus Christ, blessed be his name, overwhelmed my soul and said to me: "My daughter, why do you weep so bitterly? It is I myself that has come to you, Jesus Christ, who died for you on the cross, suffering cruel pain and torment. I, the very same God, forgive you all your sins. And you shall never go to hell or even purgatory; but when you come to pass out of this world, in the twinkling of an eye, you will have my bliss in heaven, for I am the same God who brought these sins to your mind and made you confess them all. Therefore I grant you true contrition until the end of your life.

"Therefore do exactly as I ask, do not hesitate to call me Jesus, your lover, for so I am your love and will be without end. And, my daughter, you have a hair shirt on your back; I want you to leave it aside, for I am going to give you a hair shirt for your heart which will be much more real and pleasing to me than all the hair shirts in the world. But as well as that, I want you to give up eating what you most like, meat. And instead you will eat my flesh and blood, that is Christ's own true body in the Sacrament of the altar. This is my will, daughter, that you receive my Body every Sunday[4] and I will give you so many graces that all the world will marvel.

"As for yourself, you will be eaten and gnawed at by worldly people just like rats eat stockfish.[5] But do not be afraid, my daughter, for you will overcome your enemies. And I myself will give you my grace so that you will be able to find an answer for every cleric and learned priest, words that speak the love of God. And I swear to you by my own majesty that I shall never leave you in weal or in woe.[6] I shall protect and help you so that not any devil in all hell, nor angel from heaven, no man on earth shall ever separate you from me: Devils in hell may not, angels in heaven will not, and man on earth shall not.

"And daughter, I want you to give up saying the rosary and think such thoughts as I myself put into your mind.[7] Be content with the thoughts that I will put into your mind. I am happy for you to pray your way, using many prayers, but only until six o'clock. Then you must fall silent and talk to me with your innermost heart; in return, I will give you high meditation and true contemplation. I also want you to go to the anchorite at the Preaching Friars;[8] tell him every secret I

[4] Such frequency among the laity was almost unheard of, twice a year being the norm; yet Margery would have heard of a similar practice of frequency in the life of Saint Bridget of Sweden. See Chap. 16 when Margery journeys to Lambeth to obtain special permission for weekly Communion from Archbishop Arundel.

[5] Fish such as cod, haddock, or hake would be dried hard in the open air without salt and so preserved.

[6] This phrase echoes the experience and utterances of Julian of Norwich in her *Revelations;* Margery will later meet and spend several days with her.

[7] Saying the rosary and reciting set prayers were—and still to this day—form part of the Roman approach to prayer. Significantly, Margery represents the awakening of the individual that was beginning to show at her time. One serious manifestation were the Lollards, a sect that believed in the individual's duty to address God directly without the necessary intermediary of church or priest.

[8] This unnamed Dominican priest was clearly a notable holy man in Lynn. He serves Margery well—both as her confessor and spiritual supervisor—and supports her through her many trials. (See Chaps. 18, 19.)

have revealed to you and all my words of comfort; and do whatever he tells you, for my Spirit will speak to you through him."

I went as bidden to the anchorite and told him all the revelations that had been shown me. When I had told him everything, the priest thanked God and with great reverence and tears in his eyes said: "My daughter, believe me, you are feeding from the very breast of Christ; you have been given a promise of your future place in heaven. But I warn you to take any such thoughts that God may give you as humbly and devoutly as you can; then you should come and tell me about them. And then, with our Lord's good grace, I may be able to help you discern whether they have come from the Holy Spirit or from your enemy the devil."

6

ome time later, I was making my meditation in the way I had been taught, simply lying quite still. I could not decide which way my thoughts should tend, so I said to our Lord, "Jesus, what should I be thinking?"

Our Lord answered me inwardly, "Daughter, think about my mother, for she is the source of all the grace that you receive."

Then the next moment, I saw Saint Anne and she was heavy with her child as if she were ready to give birth; and so I begged her to let me become her maid and servant. And presently, our Lady was born; and I determined to look after her until she was twelve years old. She was to have the very best food and drink as well as beautiful white garments and white scarves to wear upon her head. And then I told the blessed child, "Lady, you shall be God's mother."

The child replied, "I only wish that I could be worthy enough to be the servant of that woman who will conceive the son of God."

But I said, "Lady, if that grace falls on you, I beg you, allow me to remain your servant."

As I stayed in contemplation, it seemed to me, the blessed child went away for a while; but presently she returned and told me: "Daughter, I have now become the mother of God."

Then I fell down on my knees with great reverence and tears, saying, "I am not worthy, my lady, to be your servant."

Then I set out together with our Lady and Joseph, and I had with me a flagon of mulled wine, all spicy and honied. They journeyed to Elizabeth, mother of John the Baptist, and when they came together, they embraced with great reverence. And they stayed together with joy and great gladness for twelve weeks. And afterward, John was born, and our Lady took him gently into her arms and handed him to his mother, saying that he was to be a holy man, and so she blessed him.

Then as we were saying our farewells with tears of affection, I fell on my knees before Saint Elizabeth to beg her to ask our Lady that I might continue to serve her.

"Daughter," Elizabeth replied, "it seems to me that you perform all your duties very well."

And then I traveled with our Lady to Bethlehem, and there I procured lodgings nightly and made sure that our Lady was made welcome. I also begged for her fine white linen to swaddle the babe when he was born. And when her time came, I ordered bedding for our Lady and Son to lie upon. And next I begged food for our Lady and her blessed babe. And I bathed him with bitter tears of compassion and swaddled him, and I was reminded of the painful death he was to suffer for the love of sinful men. I whispered to him, "Lord, I shall treat you gently, take care not to bind you too tight. I beg you do not let me displease you in any way."

7

n the Twelfth Day after his birth, three kings appeared bearing gifts, and they worshiped our Lord Jesus Christ as he lay in his mother's lap. As our Lady's servant, I gazed in contemplation as all this took place, and all the while I wept copiously. And when I saw that they wished to take their leave in order to return to their homes, so much was my sadness when I saw that they could bear to turn from the presence of our Lord, that my tears almost tore me apart.

Now after this, an angel came and told our Lady and Joseph to go out of the region of Bethlehem and go to Egypt. Then I journeyed with our Lady; and each day as I found her a bed for the night, I was filled with many comforting thoughts and meditations, together with much high contemplation. Sometimes my tears would last some two hours and frequently longer without letting up, especially when I considered our Lord's passion, or my own foul sins, or the sins of people in general, or when I thought about the souls in Purgatory, about the poor and the suffering; for indeed I wanted to comfort them all.

Sometimes my tears came without restraint, and they could be very noisy; because all I wished for was the bliss of heaven, and it seemed to me that I must wait so long to go there. How much I desired deliverance from this wretched world.

Our Lord Jesus Christ told me with inner voice that I must stay and suffer the pains of love, "for I have chosen you to kneel before the Trinity to pray for the whole world, and many hundreds and thousands of souls will be saved by your prayers. Therefore, daughter, you have only to ask for what you want and I will grant your petition."

And I answered: "Lord, all I ask for is mercy and to be spared eternal damnation, I ask for myself and for everyone living in the world. Correct us here as you will, also in Purgatory; but of your high mercy keep us from damnation."

8

nother day, as I lay at prayer,[9] the Mother of Mercy appeared to me and said, "May blessings be yours, daughter, your place in heaven is prepared, before my Son's knee, both for you and for those whom you wish to be with you."

Then her own blessed Son asked me: "Daughter, who will you have as your companion?"

---

[9] Margery lay down to pray; see Chaps. 5 and 6. Perhaps being a big woman this was her most relaxed pose. All experts agree that we should not adopt a deliberately uncomfortable posture but rather one conducive to total bodily relaxation.

"My dear worthy Lord, I would like to choose Master Robert (Spryngolde),[10] my spiritual father."

"Why do you ask for him rather than your own father, or indeed your husband?"

"Because I may never thank him enough for all his goodness toward me and the endless trouble he has taken in hearing my confession."

"I grant you that wish for him; but your father, your husband, and all your children shall also be saved."

Then I said, "Lord, you have forgiven all my sins; now it is my wish to make over to you—as my executor—all my good works that you yourself perform in me. Whether I pray, or think, or weep, whether I go on pilgrimage, fast, or speak to any good end, it is my firm resolve that you give half to Master Robert in order to increase his merit with you, just as if he himself had done these things. And the other half, Lord, share among your friends and enemies: For I would have you alone as my reward."[11]

"Daughter, I will indeed become your ever faithful executor and I agree to all that you ask. Because of this great love you have shown to your fellow Christians, you shall have double your reward in heaven."

---

[10] This (again Dominican) priest, mentioned in Chap. 57, would seem to have been Margery's second confessor; her first, the anchorite, had apparently died while she was on pilgrimage to Jerusalem.

[11] This kind of bargaining based on a computed merit that can actually be exchanged in some kind of monetary fashion seems strange to modern Christians. But it would have been very familiar to Margery and been a constant exhortation in many of the sermons she listened to. Seeing that she clearly believed in the idea of storing up merit in order to enter heaven (preferably without Purgatory's painful passage), this was indeed "great love."

9

n another occasion, as I prayed to God asking him that I might live in chastity with the full permission of my husband, Christ spoke to me inwardly: "You must fast each Friday and go without both food and drink; then you shall have your wish before Whit Sunday, for I will suddenly quench all sexual desires in your husband."

Then, on the Wednesday of Easter week, when my husband wanted to make love to me, as was his custom, he came toward me; so I said: "Jesus, help me," and he suddenly had no means of touching me in any way at all. And ever since that day, we have never been together as man and wife.

Now it happened that one Friday before Whitsun Eve, as I was kneeling in my church of Saint Margaret's, Lynn,[12] hearing mass, I heard a loud and dreadful noise. I was immediately very afraid, for I had been terrified by people constantly saying that God would have his revenge on me. I was kneeling down, my head bent forward, prayer book in my hands; I prayed to our Lord Jesus Christ for grace and for mercy. Then, without warning, from the highest part of the church roof right up among the rafters, a piece of stone and a length of beam came crashing down, hitting me in my back and on

---

[12] Margery's church is still standing in King's Lynn (as it now is called). Although drastic reconstruction was needed when the steeple fell at the end of the seventeenth century, many details remain as she would have known them.

my head. The stone weighed something like three pounds, the beam was twice as heavy: I thought my back had been broken in two and I was convinced I would last but a little while longer. As soon as the accident happened, I called out loud, "Jesus, Mercy!" and at once all my pain was gone.

A good man named John of Wyreham witnessed the whole event and, supposing I had been gravely injured, came across and touched my sleeve. I remember his exact words: "Madam, how do you fare?"

But I was right as rain and in one piece, so I simply thanked him for his kindness; but secretly I was amazed that now I felt no pain whereas just previously I was in great distress. And in truth, afterward I felt not a twinge of pain for twelve whole weeks. Then the spirit of God spoke in my soul: "Take this as an important sign. If people will not believe this, I shall work even greater miracles still."

A well-respected doctor of divinity, Master Aleyn,[13] who was a White Friar, came to hear about this miracle, how it had pleased our Lord to save his servant from the malice of my enemy. And because of him, many other people also came to hear about this so that they greatly glorified God for his goodness to me. But there were still a good number of people who refused to believe what they heard; they said it was a sign of God's anger, his vengeance even, rather than any sort of sign of his mercy or favor.

---

[13] The Carmelite Alan of Lynn, some twenty-five years older than Margery, is known to have taken his doctorate at Cambridge; he wrote extensively on the mystical life. He became a strong supporter of Margery.

10

MARGERY BEGINS HER TRAVELS
AND PILGRIMAGES.

hortly after this happening, I was prompted in my
soul to visit certain places for my spiritual good,
inasmuch as I had been cured; but I was not free to
do so without my husband's consent. I asked him, and he,
believing it to be God's will, readily agreed to come with me
to whichever places I felt drawn. And our Lord Christ Jesus
assured me: "My servants are most eager to meet you."

And so it turned out. I was welcomed and made much of in
many different places, so that I began to grow anxious of
becoming proud and vainglorious. But our merciful Lord
Christ Jesus—blessed be his name—told me, "Daughter, do
not be afraid, I shall take away your pride. And those who
honor you, honor me; they that despise you, despise me, and I
will punish them. I am in you, and you in me.[14] And those
who do listen to you hear the voice of God. Daughter, if any
living person, no matter how sinful he might have been will
leave his sin and listen to what you tell him, I will show my
love for you by giving him whatever grace you promise I will
give him."

And now I set out with my husband first to York and from
there to several other destinations.

---

[14] Clear reference to Jr. 14:20.

11

t so happened on Friday—it was Midsummer Eve and the weather was very hot—as we were coming away from York. I was carrying a bottle of beer in my hand while my husband clutched a cake against his chest, when suddenly he asked me this question: "Margery, supposing a man came along with a sword, and he said he would cut off my head unless I made love to you, tell me truthfully, for I know you never lie, would you let him cut off my head or else would you let me love you, just like I did in the old days?"

"Sir, why bring that up? We've managed well enough to be chaste for eight weeks now!"

"Because I want to know what you really feel."

And then I told him the sad truth: "In all honesty, I would rather see you killed than we went back to our old unclean ways."

"You are not a good wife to me," he replied.

So I asked him why he had failed to make love to me over those past eight weeks, since we had slept side by side in the same bed night after night. He declared he was scared even to touch me, that was why he no longer made love.

"Well, sir, you had better mend your ways and ask God for mercy: Didn't I tell you three years ago that your need for sex would wither all of a sudden? Now the time has come; so I hope I shall have my way. Good sir, I beg you to grant me what I ask of you: I will pray that you be saved by the mercy of our Lord Jesus Christ, and then in heaven you may have greater reward than if ever you had worn a hair shirt or chain coat for penance. I beg you, let me take a vow of chastity before whichever bishop God chooses."

"Certainly not," he declared, "because now I may make love to you without sin, but then I would be in mortal sin."

So I said, "If it is the will of the Holy Spirit, I pray to God that you agree; and if it is not the will of the Spirit, I pray God you never agree."

At that, we went on our way toward Bridlington; and as it grew hotter and hotter, I was getting more and more anxious for my safety. Until at last we came to a wayside cross. My husband sat down beneath it and called me over, saying: "Margery, do what I want, and I will do whatever you wish. The first thing is that we still sleep together in the same bed, just like we've always done. Second, is that you pay all my debts before you go off to Jerusalem. And the third thing, that you eat normally with me on Fridays as you always used to do."

"Certainly not, sir," I answered. "I will never allow myself to break my Friday fast as long as I live."

"Very well," he declared, "then I will have you again."

I asked him if I could first say my prayers, and he was kind enough to agree. So I knelt down there and then beside that cross in the field. And this was my prayer, which brought many tears with it: "Lord God, you know all things. You know for these past three years I wanted desperately to keep chaste for you, and now at last it would be possible. Yet I do not dare, out of love for you—because that would mean breaking my vow of Friday fast which you yourself bound me to. Blessed Lord, you know well enough I will not go back on my vow since it is your will; but I am in great trouble unless I find the answer in you. So, blessed Jesus, let me know your will, then I will follow it and fulfill it with all my strength."

Then our Lord Jesus spoke to me very sweetly and told me to go back to my husband and ask him to let me have what I wanted: "And tell him he can have what he wants. Daughter, the only reason I made you fast was so that you could have your way more quickly. And now you may have your way, I no longer need you to fast. Accordingly, I bid you in the name of Jesus eat and drink whatever your husband chooses."

Then I thanked our Lord for his grace and wisdom; and straightway went to my husband and told him: "If you please, sir, you shall give me what I want and I will answer your request. Promise that you will no longer come into bed with me, and I will pay all your debts before I leave for Jerusalem.[15] Give me back the freedom of my body, so that you waive all your marriage rights from now on as long as you live; and for my part, I will eat and drink with you at your pleasure every Friday."

At this my husband agreed, with the words: "May your body be at God's disposal from now on as freely as it has been at mine."

Whereupon I thanked God greatly and rejoiced that I had been granted my cherished wish; so that I suggested to my husband that we say three *Paternosters* in honor of the Trinity for the great grace we had received. Thus it was that we knelt beneath that cross, and afterward we ate and drank together in a spirit of great joy. All this happened on Friday, Midsummer Eve, 1413.

And afterward, we journeyed to Bridlington as well as many other places, where we spoke to God's servants, anchorites and recluses, and very many good people who loved our Lord such as scholars of holy reputation, doctors and bachelors of divinity in every kind of place. And to some of them in particular, I was able to manifest my innermost feelings and my secret contemplation, just as I had been bidden, in order to find out whether there might be any deception in them.

---

[15] John Brunham, Margery's father, died earlier this year; his considerable wealth would have enabled her to pay off her husband's debts and afford the considerable outlay for her forthcoming journey to the Holy Land.

12

ur Lord sent me to a number of different religious houses, among them a monastery where I was made welcome for love of our Lord. But there was one monk there, a man of senior office, who despised me and treated me with contempt. In spite of his antagonism, at meals I was always invited to sit next to the abbot, and often during the course of the meal I spoke out aloud a few pious words now and then, which God had put into my mind. And the monk who disliked me was present with all the others listening to what I had to say. And as I continued to speak, I felt that I was beginning to win him over, so that at length he began to take a liking to everything I had to say.

And when the meal was at an end and I was in church, he came across and spoke to me: "I have heard that God speaks to you. I beg you find out whether or not I shall be saved, and which of my sins have offended God the most; I am not prepared to take you seriously unless you are able to tell me my sins."

I told him directly: "Go and hear mass, and I will see if my tears can win you grace." He did as I said; and I found myself weeping in a most extraordinary manner for his sins. And when mass was over, I prayed to our Lord Christ Jesus, "Blessed Lord, what kind of answer am I to give this man?"

"My dear daughter, tell him simply in the name of Jesus that he has sinned lecherously and also by despair and in holding on to worldly possessions."

"Oh, gracious Lord, it is going to be hard for me to tell him that; he will humiliate me publicly if I put so much as a foot wrong."

"Do not fear; speak out in my name, in the name of Jesus; what I have told you is the truth."

At this, I asked our Lord Jesus Christ a second time, "Good Lord, shall he be saved?"

"Yes," our Lord replied, "but only if he gives up his sinful ways and listens to your advice: Tell him to confess—also to resign the position he holds outside the monastery."

When the monk came back, he asked me directly: "Margery, tell me what are my sins."

But I replied, "Sir, I would ask you not to talk to me about them; I promise you, if you do as I say, you will be saved."

"But I will not believe you unless you tell me my sins."

"I understand, sir, that you have committed sins of the flesh, of despair and holding on to worldly possessions."

At this, the monk stood quite still; he was utterly taken aback. Yet after a moment he insisted, "Tell me then whether I have sinned with married women or with young girls."

"Sir, with married women."

Then he repeated his question: "Will I be saved?"

"Yes, sir, but only if you do as I tell you. Grieve for your sins and I too will help you grieve. You must make your confession and turn aside from your sins. Resign the outside office that you hold, and God will give you his grace because of his love for me."

Then the monk took me by the hand and, leading me into a fine parlor, he brought me a generous meal; finally, he gave me gold to pray for him, whereupon I took my leave.

Later, I visited the monastery once more and learned that my monk had indeed resigned his outside position, just as I had told him, and had also abandoned his sinful ways. He had been appointed sub-prior, and thanks to God's grace he was well disposed and a disciplined monk at last. He welcomed me warmly and blessed God for the fact that we had ever met in the first place.

13

'n another occasion, I visited the monastic church at Canterbury, and I was weeping so much that they condemned me out of hand and complained bitterly about my behavior. But I continued my weeping almost all day long, morning and afternoon for the sake of all the monks and priests as well as for lay people. So public were my tears that my husband kept his distance, pretending he did not know me; and so I was left alone and did not see him for the remainder of that day.

There was an old monk, who I was told had once been treasurer to the Queen before he had taken vows; he was a man of great influence whom many feared. Taking me by the hand, he spoke to me, saying: "What have you to say about God?"

"Sir," I replied, "I like both to hear about him as well as speak of him," and I told him a scripture story.

The monk answered, "I wish you could be shut away in a house of stone, then no one could speak to you."

"Well, sir," I told him, "you should speak up in support of God's servants, yet you seem all too ready to oppose them. May God change your ways."

Then a much younger monk declared, "Either you have the Holy Spirit, or else there is a devil within you. For what you have just spoken is from Holy Scripture and not your own words."

So I answered him by saying, "Sir. Would you let me tell you a story?"

At this, the crowd began to say to the monk, "Let her have her say."

So I began: "Once there was a man who had sinned grievously against God; and when he had confessed, his priest as part of his penance told him to hire men who should chastise and correct him for all his sins. And in return he must reward them in silver for their pains. And one day, he was among a group of important men, just like you good people, God save you all, and he stood among them, just as I am standing with you now; and they all despised him, just as you all despise me. But the man was smiling all the while and laughing as if he found their words pleasing. Their spokesman said, 'Why are you laughing so, you poor fool, when we all despise you so much?'

" 'Well, sir, I have every reason to laugh. For days on end I have had to pay out good silver to hire men to criticize me so as to do penance for my sins. But thanks to you, I can keep my purse shut today.'

"It is quite true what I tell you, good sirs. When I was back home where I come from—day after day weeping and grieving—I was put down because I did not have any of the shame and scorn that I deserve. But now I must thank you all for the very profitable morning and afternoon that I have enjoyed among you. May God be thanked for it."

Then I went out of the monastery; but they followed, shouting after me, "You will be burned! Lying Lollard. Here is a cartload of briars! We've got a barrel ready to burn you in!" It was evening now, and as I stood outside the gates of Canterbury, crowds of strangers began to gather and they continued to stare at me, not knowing what to make of this disturbance.

People started to shout out: "Grab her! Burn her!" And all I could do was to stand stock still. My whole body trembled and shook violently, and no one came forward to take my side or offer to help me. And I had no idea where my husband had disappeared to.

But soon I began to pray silently to our Lord in this manner: "I came here, Lord, for love of you. Blessed Lord, help me, have mercy on me."

And when I had finished the heartfelt prayer to our Lord, along came two very good-looking young men who asked, "Are you neither Lollard nor heretic?"

And I replied, "No, sirs, I am no Lollard nor heretic."

And they asked me which inn I was staying at; but I told them I did not know which street. I told them that I believed my husband and I were meant to be staying at the home of some German. So these two young men, treating me most kindly and insisting that I pray for them, led me safely back to my inn where I found my husband.

And on our return to Lynn, I learned that many people had slandered me in my absence, telling all kinds of untrue stories about the things I was said to have done on my travels.

But after all this, I enjoyed great peace of soul for a long time; and each day I knew high contemplation in prayer, holding many holy talks and colloquies with our Lord Jesus Christ both morning and afternoon. I also shed many sweet tears in my devotions; indeed these were so plentiful that it was a marvel that my eyes were able to suffer it all, or that my heart could endure without being consumed by the fire of such love.[16] I truly felt that my heart glowed from such holy talk with our Lord as we spoke together many times. For instance, he might say to me, and he did so frequently: "My dear daughter, love me with all your heart, for I love you with

---

[16] The Mount Grace copy has margin notes in red throughout the manuscript. Alongside this account by Margery of her mystic prayer are the words "R Medlay v. was wont so to say." Richard Methley was born in 1451 and was a renowned mystic at the Yorkshire charterhouse. He left a brief diary of his own mystic experiences covering a short period of a few months.

all my heart and with all the power of my Godhead; for in my sight you have always been my chosen soul as a pillar[17] of my Holy Church. I always gaze on you in mercy; for you would never be able to endure the hatred and contempt that lie ahead for you without the support of my grace."

14

From then on, I found much joy when I was criticized simply because I loved God. It gave me great pleasure and comfort when I was blamed and scolded for openly loving Jesus; that is to say, when I condemned sin and praised goodness, or when I insisted on repeating gospel texts that I had heard in sermons, or when I went to the trouble of consulting wise priests.

Sometimes I would try to imagine what death I might die for love of Christ. For the love of God I could almost find enough courage to face any kind of execution, yet dying itself still made me fearful. Aware of this weakness in myself, I would begin by picturing the simplest death; I would see myself being tied head and feet to a stake and then having my head struck off with a sharp ax, all for the love of God.

Then our Lord put these words in my mind: "Daughter, I thank you for being ready to die for love of me, for when you entertain such thoughts you earn such a reward in heaven as if you had in truth suffered such a death. Yet no one is going

---

[17] Again the Carthusian reader has carefully drawn in the manuscript's margin a little column topped by a cross.

to kill you, no fire will burn you, you will not drown at sea, no wind will harm you, for I will never forget that you are written in my hands and in my feet; and I am glad that I suffered those wounds for your sake. I will never turn from you in anger: I will love you always.

"Never fear, even if sometimes the whole world seems to be against you; it is because they fail to understand you. I promise your very soul that if it were possible to suffer my pains again as once I did, I would be willing to suffer all that pain just for you alone, rather than have you separated from me forever. And therefore, daughter, just as you see the priest take a baby to the font and immerse it in the water so as to wash away its original sin, in the same way I shall wash you in my precious blood to rid you of all your sins.

"And although I sometimes take away your inner feelings of grace so that you can no longer pray, cannot even weep, do not be anxious, for truly I am a hidden God within you; for in this way, you have nothing to be proud of. For then you recognize that tears or spiritual converse with me are sent to you by God alone. They are his free gifts—no one ever earns them—and he gives them to whomever he pleases without in any way robbing you.

"Receive them humbly therefore and be thankful when I send them; put up with it patiently when I withdraw them and go on seeking until you receive them once again; for tears of remorse, spiritual awareness, and compassion are my highest gifts, the most sought after I can give on this earth.

"And what more could I possibly do for you (unless I were to take your soul out of your body and bring it to heaven, which I will not yet do). Remember whatever befalls, where God is, there is heaven also: God is in your soul with many an angel surrounding you and guarding you night and day. For when you set out for church, I go with you; when you sit at table, I am at your side; you go to bed and I come too; even when you leave town, remember that I journey with you.

"Daughter, there was never a child so pleasing and attentive to his father as I will be to you, helping and keeping you at every step. The workings of my grace are rather like the way I made the sun do its task. As you well know, sometimes the sun shines out brightly and then everyone enjoys its warmth, but another day it is hidden behind the clouds, unseen all day long, yet its heat and brightness are still there. In exactly the same way I choose to deal with you and all those many souls that I have specially chosen.

"It may be that you do not always weep as you would like, yet my grace is still in you. That is how I show you that you are my true daughter, yes and mother also, and sister, wife and spouse. See what it says in the gospel where our Lord tells his disciples: 'Everyone who does my heavenly Father's will is mother, sister, brother to me.' So as long as you try to please me, you are my very own daughter; when you weep and mourn at the pain of my passion you are my true mother having pity on her child; when you grieve for the sins of others and their trials and sufferings, you are a real sister; and when you mourn that you are kept from the bliss of heaven, then you are my own true spouse and wife, for a wife's place is at her husband's side for she finds no true joy away from his company."

15

ow that I knew at last that our Lord had forgiven me all my sins, as I have already re-
counted, I had a great longing to see for myself the place where he was born. And I wished especially to
visit the place on earth where he had suffered his passion and
where he died. And I wanted to visit as well all those holy
places where he spent his life on earth as well as those he
came to after his resurrection. And while I longed greatly to
make this journey to Jerusalem, our Lord also bade me go to
Rome and to Santiago di Compostela. For two whole years I
would gladly have set out, yet I had no money to make any of
these journeys. So that I prayed to our Lord and asked him:
"Where shall I get money enough to make these journeys to
such Holy Places?"

Our Lord responded, "I shall send you sufficient friends
from various parts of England who will help you. And remember, my daughter, I will travel with you to every country
you come to and there I myself will care for you. I shall take
you there and bring you safely home again: No Englishman
shall die in any ship you take. I shall save you from the power
of all evil men. And, my daughter, I want you to dress overall
in white, no other color, that is my special wish."

I complained at this, saying, "Dear Lord, can't you see, if I
dress differently from the run of decent women, people will
start talking about me, saying that I am a hypocrite, and they
will laugh at me all the while."

"That is certainly true, my daughter, yet the more ridicule you bear for my sake, the more I am pleased."

After this, I dared not do anything other than as I was bidden. And so we set off on our journeyings, my husband and I—what a good man he was to me, always so gentle and accommodating. And although sometimes—panicking for no reason—he would leave me on my own, yet he would soon come back; and he would always try to speak out in my defense as much as he dared, given his fear of other folk. While everyone else who traveled with me betrayed me sooner or later; in the main, they accused me falsely of things I had not done, which must have been the work of the devil.

Such was the case with one man whom I fully trusted. It was his idea that we should travel together, and I accepted at once. I was pleased with this arrangement as he would be able to support and look after my needs. Moreover, he had lived for a considerable time with my anchorite confessor; and I knew him to be a good judge of character since he was not only a doctor of divinity but was known by everyone as a holy man. So it was that this manservant asked permission to travel with me entirely at his own prompting. And I also took my own maid with me; and everything was fine so long as no one spoke out against us. But our Lord permitted the enemy to lead people on so that they criticized me for my tears and called me a hypocrite and a deceitful person; they even threatened to burn me. As soon as this began the manservant, who was meant to be so trustworthy, turned on me with a stream of verbal abuse, declaring finally that he would no longer travel with me. This led my maid, who seemed to find discomforts at every turn, to rebel against my authority, frequently refusing to accompany me into an unfamiliar town so that I must go alone.

Yet I could always rely on my husband, who stayed at my side when everyone else deserted me. He came with me wherever our Lord instructed; he always believed that everything was for the best and that all would be well since God had willed it.

It was during this round of travel that he came with me to see the bishop of Lincoln—Philip Repyngdon was his name.[18] As it turned out, we were obliged to wait three weeks before we were able to see him as he was away from his palace. When at length he returned and learned that a woman had been waiting to see him for such a long time, he sent for me at once to discover what I had to tell him. When I came before him and greeted him, he welcomed me warmly, saying he had wanted to meet me for a long time, adding that he was very glad I had come. I therefore asked if I might speak to him privately in order to manifest my spiritual life to him; and he set aside a convenient time for this.

And on the appointed day, I was able to tell him about my meditations and holy contemplation as well as other hidden matters concerning both the living and the dead which our Lord had shown my soul. For his part, he was grateful to hear it all and gave me as much time as I needed to say whatever I pleased. He gave his approval to all my spiritual sentiments as well as endorsing my visions, which he declared to be important and holy experiences, inspired by the Holy Spirit. And he strongly advised me to write my own account of them. But I replied that it was not God's will that they be recorded so soon; and indeed they were not written down for at least another twenty years.

And then I came to the point and asked him, "My Lord, if you please, I am urged from within my soul that you should clothe me with the mantle and ring[19] and that you should dress me overall in white. For I have learned by a revelation that if you clothe me like this on earth, our Lord will clothe you in heaven."

And so the bishop answered, "I will grant your request provided your husband agrees to it."

---

[18] Bishop of Lincoln, 1405–1419. At Oxford as a young man he had fallen under the influence of Wycliffe. His support was so public that it led to his excommunication; but abjuring Wycliffe, he was soon reconciled. He later became chaplain to Henry IV and finally cardinal.

[19] That is, to take a formal vow of chastity before the bishop.

And I replied, "My Lord, I beg you send for my husband and hear what he has to say."

So my husband was called and the bishop asked him, "John, is it your will that your wife should take the mantle and ring, and that henceforward you both shall live together in chastity?"

"Yes, my Lord," he answered, "and in token of that chastity we now both vow, I hereby offer my hands into yours," and so saying, he put his hands between those of the bishop.

And the bishop concluded his dealings with us for that day; his manner had been welcoming throughout and he had treated us most warmly.

A few days later we were invited to eat by the bishop; and I saw for myself that before he sat down to the meal he himself gave thirteen poor men a loaf of bread as well as thirteen pence to each one. And, when I learned that he did the same thing every day, I was so moved that God should give the bishop his grace to perform such a charity that my many tears were obvious to all his household, so that they wondered what was amiss.

We then sat down to eat, a large and important gathering of divines, priests, and squires. Yet even among such a company, the good bishop was kind enough to have special dishes sent from his high table over to me. And as we ate, several divines began to ask me many a searching question; but by the grace of Jesus I was able to reply to them all. Indeed, my answers pleased the bishop greatly while my interrogators were astonished at my prompt and accurate replies.

When the meal was over, the bishop called me into his parlor to deliver his final words: "Margery, you and your husband requested me to give you the mantle and ring, and I have taken advice about this. I am persuaded not to profess you in so solemn a manner without further deliberation. You tell me that, by God's grace, you intend to go to Jerusalem. Pray to him that it may wait until your return; for by then you will have proved yourself and become recognized."

The following day, I went to church and prayed to God with all my strength of soul for guidance in this important matter so as to know what answer I should give the bishop. And our Lord answered me in this way: "My daughter, tell the bishop that he is more afraid of what the world has to say than of the love of God. Tell him that I would have approved of him granting your wish just as I allowed the children of Israel to borrow the goods of the people of Egypt and leave with them. So, daughter, tell him that if he will not do it now, it will be done later on, when it is God's will."

But when I delivered my message to the bishop exactly as I had been told, he made a further excuse. He asked me to go to Archbishop Arundel of Canterbury, saying that as I was not of his diocese he had no jurisdiction to cede to my request for mantle and ring. But as I saw it, this was merely the clever advice of his officers who had taken a dislike to me.

Finally I told him, "My Lord, I will indeed go to the archbishop of Canterbury for I have many different reasons to do so. But I will not put this matter to him, for that is not God's will."

As I took my leave of the bishop of Lincoln, he gave me twenty-six shillings and eight pence to buy clothes, and asked me to pray for him.

16

hen I traveled with my husband to London, for the archbishop was staying at Lambeth at the time.[20] We entered the great hall in the afternoon, and there we found a great many clerics, employees of the archbishop, and numerous others, both gentleman squires as well as yeomen. They were all very casual, and I was very shocked to hear their language. The swear words were extremely offensive and most of their exchanges were completely mindless. I felt bold enough to challenge them outright by telling them that unless they stopped their swearing, which was a gravely sinful habit, they would be damned.

At once, a cockney woman came forward dressed in a coarse skin coat, and challenged me with a stream of abuse. She shouted in a really spiteful way: "I wish you were over at Smithfield,[21] then I would donate a bundle of firewood to have you burned. I'd like to watch while you died!"

I was silent and did not even answer her. But my husband was terribly upset at hearing this outburst against me. And so, after waiting further, I was called to meet the archbishop

[20] Lambeth Palace, just across the river from Westminster, was in Margery's day and remains the London residence of the archbishop of Canterbury. Thomas Arundel, 1353–1414, was consecrated archbishop in 1396. He had fallen out with King Richard II and suffered banishment but returned to crown his successor, Henry IV, whose chancellor he became. He was a fierce opponent of the Lollards and presided over the trials of three of their number before condemning them to be burned alive.

[21] William Sawtre, a priest from Lynn, had been condemned as a Lollard and burned publicly at Smithfield some ten years before.

who was outside in his garden. After the usual courtesies, I came straight to the point and asked him if he would be kind enough with his jurisdiction to allow me to choose my own confessor and to have permission to receive holy communion every Sunday.[22] I made it clear to him that this would be conditional upon my being rightly disposed and in a state of grace and added the further request for a letter to the purpose under his seal that would be valid throughout his entire province. His manner was open and friendly, and he granted my request in full without any hint of the least payment or charge against his secretaries drawing up and sealing the declaration.

I was encouraged by his open generosity and, feeling in my heart that I had his confidence, I began to tell this holy bishop about my way of life and the graces God had performed in both my mind and soul. I did so purely to see what he would say and wondered whether he would find my frequent tears excessive or my contemplation suspect.

I was able to tell him why I wept so, and also the precise way our Lord spoke in my soul. He listened carefully and declared that he could find no fault in any of this; on the contrary, he endorsed my way of life and expressed himself glad that the great mercy of our Lord had been so manifest in our times—blessed indeed is his Name.

At this, I plucked up my courage and told him that his household needed to be put in order. I tried to express myself as politely as I could. "My Lord, Almighty God who is Lord over us all did not give you your power and jurisdiction so that you might tolerate people to behave like this in your service. Such men are traitors to him for they put him to death again every day by constantly uttering such terrible oaths. Since you yourself will have to answer for them, you should either make them change their ways or dismiss them from your service."

---

[22] Margery was seeking a rare privilege; normally, the faithful would receive communion only once or twice in the entire year.

He received this humbly and with charity, permitting me
to unburden myself. His response was very reassuring, and I
took it that matters would be put right. And so we went on
talking until after dusk, and presently the stars began to appear in the sky overhead. At length, I took my leave of him
and my husband did the same.

Afterward in London many good people wanted to talk
with me; and frequently when I spoke about the love of God
they were moved to tears. Both I and my husband were made
very welcome and could have stayed on in that city for as
long as we pleased.

But now it was time to return to Lynn. And arriving there,
I went at once to my confessor, the anchorite at the Dominican priory, to tell him about my journey and how I had gotten
on in my travels around England. He was very pleased to see
me safely home again, and declared that my success in completing so many expeditions was in itself a miracle.

But taking me into his confidence, he declared: "I have had
to listen to a great deal of evil gossip about you while you
have been away. Indeed, the truth of the matter is that I have
been advised to avoid you and not to see you any more. I
have even been assured of the patronage of several influential
men, as soon as I have given you up. But I have told them:
'The woman I knew as she set out upon her journey was
upright and God-loving and quite clearly led by the Holy
Spirit. I have no intention of deserting her, no, not for any
other woman penitent in the whole of England. Indeed there
is no one apart from Margery with whom I would rather be
associated.' "

21²³

hen I first began to have revelations,
our Lord told me simply: "Daughter,
you are to have a child."

At which I replied at once, "But what shall I do about
caring for it?"

Our Lord answered me, "Daughter, do not worry about
that; I shall see that your baby is looked after."

"Lord, I am unworthy to hear you speak directly to me like
this: I still make love to my husband and that upsets me
greatly and makes me feel guilty."

"But that is why it is not sinful, instead it brings you reward and fresh merit. Be sure that you will not have any less
grace for that; for I want you to blossom with every spiritual
fruit."

"But that kind of life is only for your holy virgins!"

"True, daughter, but I love wives just as much; especially a
wife who, if she had her way, would live chaste and always
tries to do my will. To be a virgin may be more perfect and
holier than being a widow; yet I love you, daughter, as much
as any virgin living. None can prevent me loving whomsoever
I wish and as much as I wish; and remember, daughter, love
vanquishes every sin. So ask me simply to give you love. No

---

23 As she has already told us, Margery's sense of chronology is distinctly lacking. It seems
logical to bring her Chapter 21 forward at this point to make more sense of her unfolding story.

gift is so holy as the gift of love; nothing is to be desired more than love, for love can win what it wills. And so, daughter, you cannot please God more than by dwelling continually on his love."

And so I began by asking our Lord Jesus how best to love him. He replied: "Remember your sinfulness and think of my goodness."

I answered him: "I am more unworthy than anyone to whom you have ever offered your grace."

"Daughter, have no fear. I take no heed of what a person was but what they will be. Since you despise yourself, you will never be despised by God. Think of the story of Mary Magdalene or the life of Mary of Egypt[24] and of Saint Paul as well as many other saints, and all of them are now in heaven. Them that are unworthy, I make worthy; them that sin, I make holy. In the same way, I have made you worthy of me so that I love you once and for all time. And mark this, there is no saint in heaven that you may care to speak with and he will not reply. For whoever God loves, they also befriend. And when you please God, you also please his mother and all the saints in heaven. Daughter, I call to witness my mother and all the angels and saints in heaven that I love you with all my heart and I will never let go of my love for you."

Then our Lord spoke to his mother: "Blessed Mother, tell my daughter yourself how much I love her."

While I lay quite still, I could not help weeping and sobbing as if my very heart would burst to hear these sweet words our Lord had whispered in my soul.

And at once, the Queen of Mercy, God's own mother, also spoke intimately to my soul: "My dear daughter, I bring you good news that is the literal truth—I come to bear witness for

24 The legend of Mary of Egypt, popular in the Middle Ages, told of a young Egyptian girl who left home to become a prostitute in Alexandria. After seventeen years, she was prompted to travel on pilgrimage to Jerusalem—paying her way by offering herself to the sailors. Not daring to enter the holy shrines, she was told by an icon of the virgin to go into the desert "where she would find peace." There she lived for many years doing penance; and when her clothes wore out, her hair covered her body. She was discovered by the monk Zosimus who covered her with his cloak and promised to bring her Communion the next day. But on his return, she was dead.

my sweet son Jesus before all the angels and saints of heaven who love you greatly. For, daughter, I am your mother, your lady, and your mistress who will teach you how best to please God in every way."

And so it was that she taught and instructed me; so marvelously, in fact, and in detail so sublime and holy that I was shy of telling anyone apart from my confessor the anchorite. He had obliged me under seal of obedience to manifest everything, even my most secret thoughts; and I did as he asked me.

17

ong before all this took place, when I was still having children and in fact had just recently given birth, our Lord Jesus Christ told me that I would have no more children; and then he told me that I should make my way to Norwich.

But I said, "Ah, dear Lord, how am I to get there? I am feeling very faint and weak."[25]

"Have no fear. I shall give you all the strength you need. I want you to go to see the vicar of Saint Stephen's.[26] Tell him

---

[25] We cannot suppose she gives birth one day and walks out the day after. Margery has just had her last child; this is the start of her new life, and she is understandably nervous. She was to travel many hundreds of miles on pilgrimage and in seeking out holy persons; but on this journey, her first sally from her home town, she shows great reluctance. Lynn to Norwich is a mere forty miles.

[26] The saintly Richard Caistor, vicar 1402–1420, was a man of considerable learning, who wrote extensively (including the popular hymn "Jesu Lord That Madest Me") and was well known for his Christian goodness. Later, his tomb was instantly a place of pilgrimage (see Chap.

that I greet him warmly and that he is a highly chosen soul of mine; say that his preaching greatly pleases me. Then I want you to tell him all the secrets of your soul, and my counsels that I reveal to you."

Then making my way to Norwich, I entered his church. It was a Thursday and the vicar was walking up and down with another priest who was his confessor. (And this same priest was still alive when my book was first written down.) And I too was dressed all in somber black.

I greeted the vicar and asked if, that same afternoon after he had eaten, I might come and talk with him on the love of God—perhaps for one or two hours. At once, he flung his hands up and blessed himself: "Bless us both! How could a mere woman spend as much as one hour let alone two talking about the Lord God. Why, I shall not eat a thing until I find out what you can say even for one hour speaking only of our Lord."

Then he sat down in the church straightaway; and, sitting sideways to him, I began to tell him all the sayings which God had revealed to my soul. Next, I went on to tell him about my whole way of life starting from childhood, in as much detail as I was able to recall. I told him how unkind and ungrateful I had been to our Lord Jesus Christ; I spoke of my proud attitude and vain behavior; how I had resisted God's laws and been so envious of my fellow Christians; how at length I had been punished—all in Christ's good time—with many trials and terrible temptations; then after all this, how I had been fed and comforted by holy meditations, especially when I brought to mind our Lord's passion.

And even as I was still talking about the passion of our Lord Jesus Christ, I became aware of a terrible discordant noise that soon became unbearable. So much so that I collapsed as it were in a faint; and there I lay trying all the while

---

43): He left all his goods to the poor, refusing the usual custom of making provision in his will for masses for the repose of his soul. The beautifully decorated church of Saint Stephen still stands in Norwich today.

to put the noise out of my head yet finding myself powerless to do so. Then suddenly, in a leap of faith, I knew how much joy there is in heaven, where there is such bliss that at its very least it outstrips any joy that might be found in this life. This act of faith gave me new strength within, and I was encouraged once more to tell the vicar everything I had been shown about the living and the dead and in particular about my own soul.

I told him simply how sometimes it was our heavenly Father who spoke in my soul, as plain and sure just like a close friend might in any conversation. Another time, it might be the Second Person of the Trinity, or again all Three Persons, the One God, speaking in my soul words of faith and love — that is to say, how I should love him, worship him, and dread him. I explained that this contemplation was so high that no book I had ever heard of — not Hilton's book, nor Saint Bridget's book, nor *Stimulus Amoris* nor *Incendium Amoris*[27] nor any other book I had ever had read to me — spoke so eloquently of God's love that I felt to be at work in my soul.

Sometimes, too, our Lady spoke in my mind; or it might otherwise be Saint Peter, Saint Paul, Saint Katherine,[28] or whichever saint I happened to become devoted to; these all made themselves known in my soul, teaching me how I could best love and please our Lord. Such conversations were frequently so intimate and moved me so much by their sacredness that I would fall down, writhing and contorting both my body and face; with loud sobbings and great floods of tears I

[27] Walter Hilton, who died in 1396 an Augustinian mystic, was a popular writer even while living. His Ladder of Perfection gives a lucid account of the stages of purification the soul must undergo in order to come to the spiritual Jerusalem. Richard Rolle (pronounced, with a fully resonant native Yorkshire O, "roll") had died fifty years earlier; mystic and poet, he led the hidden life of a hermit. Although *Incendium* is written in Latin, Rolle was one of the first to write in English. All these books, including the *Stimulus* of the pseudo-Bonaventure, Margery tells us — in Chap. 58 — were read aloud to her by a priest.

[28] Saint Katherine of Alexandria of Catherine wheel fame: She refused marriage to the emperor since she was already a bride of Christ. Reputedly, fifty philosophers confronted her to convince her of the futility of Christianity. When they tried to break her on the wheel, the contrivance split apart, injuring bystanders; so that finally she was beheaded. No early references in martyrologies exist, but Katherine's legend had become immensely popular by the Middle Ages.

would cry out "Jesus, have mercy!" and sometimes even "I am dying!"

It was because of all this that so many people slandered me, refusing to believe that it was the work of God. They preferred to think some evil spirit tormented my body; while others said I had some strange bodily affliction. But in spite of all their complaints and protests, this holy man, who was vicar of Saint Stephen's church in the city of Norwich, a holy man who God had raised up and shown to be holy by so many marvelous signs, from now on he was always on my side, supporting me against all my enemies. Once I had fulfilled God's wish to manifest to him my way of life in all its detail, he believed explicitly that I was in touch with God's will and that the grace of the Holy Spirit was with me; for he it is who breathes where he will.[29] And though we may hear his voice, we may never know in this world whence it comes or where it goes.

And after this first meeting with the holy vicar, I would always confess to him whenever I came to Norwich and he would give me Communion with his own hands.

There was one later occasion when he stood by me. I had been summoned to appear before the bishop's officials because a charge had been lodged against me by envious people. Choosing the love of God against any loss of face in this world, my good vicar came along with me to attend my examination, where he was successful in saving me from my accusers.

I had a revelation that he would live for a further seven years before dying at peace and in great grace; and sure enough, so it turned out.

---

[29] A reference to Jesus' words to Nicodemus, Jn. 3:8.

18

nd once again, I felt within my soul that I must go to another priest who had a good and holy reputation in order to manifest my soul—just as I had done before to the good vicar of Saint Stephen's. This was a White Friar by the name of William Southfield,[30] a member of the Carmelite monastery in the same city of Norwich. Following upon this impulse, I came to the friar early one morning. I talked with him in a chapel for a good while; for I wanted to know if there was any way in which I could tell if I was deceived by any of my experiences.

But the good man would only hold up his hands as I told him all my spiritual feelings, saying "Jesus have mercy" and "Thanks be to Jesus." And when he had heard me out, he said, "Sister, have no qualms about your way of life; it is simply the Holy Spirit working his grace mightily in your soul. We must all thank him, and you, too, with all your heart for his goodness. He breathes his grace in you as a help and comfort for the rest of us and also he deals likewise with others like yourself. It is in this way that we are saved from

[30] William Southfield, like Richard Caistor, was a priest with a reputation for holiness; it was said that he had received visions including visitations from our Lady. Margery does not tell us specifically if these two meetings took place one after the other; her mentioning them together would merely seem to be her way of linking similar incidents in order to record them accurately. Whether or not: Her need to pour out her soul to every available wise person shows how isolated she feels in her chosen way of life. Her presenting problem here is "discernment of spirits," whether it is God or the devil talking to her. She spends "many days" with the lady anchorite Julian of Norwich, who gives her a simple reply (see later in this chapter).

many troubles and perils which we deserve to suffer because of our sins, were it not for such good souls living among us. Blessed be God Almighty for his goodness.

"Therefore, sister, my advice to you is that you simply allow yourself to receive God's gifts in all humility and without fuss. Offer the Holy Spirit no obstacles; do not resist his goodness, for he can give his gifts wherever he wishes, bringing his good to the unworthy, offering sinners forgiveness. For his mercy is always at our disposal, only we can bar his way by our sins; for he does not stay in somebody who is in debt to sin. Indeed he flees all falsehood and pretense; what he asks of us is a humble, sorrowful heart that is intent on good will. As the Lord declares in Isaiah: 'My eyes are upon the man of humbled and contrite spirit, who fears my word.'

"My sister, I feel absolute confidence in our Lord that you have this attitude, either in your will or your heart—preferably in both. Remember that our Lord does not deceive those who put their whole trust in him; I hope you are one of those who seek and want only him. And so you should believe with all your heart that our Lord loves you and is working his grace within you. I will pray that God may increase this working in you and continue it for his everlasting glory by his merciful grace."

Hearing his words gave me enormous comfort, peace of soul, and rest in my whole body. I felt my faith immensely strengthened.

And finally, I was told by our Lord to go to an anchoress in the same city (Dame Julian).[31] She welcomed me; and I was able to tell her of the grace that God had put into my soul; of my compunction for past sins, of my contrition, the consolation I received in my devotions. I told her equally of my compassion for Christ when I meditated, how I had enjoyed

---

[31] "Then she went to Dame Julian of Norwich, and the anchoress gave her counsel about her revelations" is written in red by the Carthusian monk of the Mount Grace. This indicates that Julian's reputation as a mystic was well known among the Carthusians; but did their library contain a copy of her *Revelations*?

the grace of contemplation. I also described some of my many conversations with our Lord and the words he had put into my soul. I also told her in detail of the numerous and wonderful revelations; for what I wanted to learn from this anchoress was whether I had been deceived by them. For I knew she was an expert in this very field, so I knew she would offer me very good advice.[32]

When she heard about our Lord's wonderful goodness, the anchoress thanked him with all her heart for visiting me like this. Her advice was that I should remain always obedient to God's will, carrying out with all my strength whatever prompting he put into my soul. But I must always be careful that these were not contrary to God's glory or to the benefit of my fellow Christians. Because, if this were the case, then such promptings were not those of a good spirit, but rather of an evil spirit.[33]

"The Holy Spirit can never urge us to do anything against charity; for if he did so, he would be acting against his own self, for he is the sum of all charity. And so it is that he leads a soul to chastity, for those who live chaste lives are named as temples of the Holy Spirit;[34] and the Holy Spirit grounds a soul, making it steadfast in true faith and right belief.

"But the sort of person who is forever in two minds, dithering at every turn, he is full of doubts—just like a wave at sea, pitched up and thrown over by the wind. No one like this is likely to receive the gifts of God.[35]

[32] The irony here is not easily lost: Julian's own unique *Revelations of Divine Love* were to preoccupy her in her anchorhold for over twenty years before she was able to discern some meaning and commit them in writing to posterity. One can only marvel at Julian's patience and humility in hearing Margery out. The two women could not be more different.

[33] Here is the central question of spiritual direction: How can we be sure this idea is "God's will"? Julian's reply is very sane and based on the gospel: Do nothing against the love of God or your neighbor. Her words that follow—and Margery's quotation would appear to be a genuine record—offer us the only historic account of Julian's mind apart from her own writings.

[34] Julian quotes Paul (1 Cor. 6:19), who speaks against fornication; and he goes on to reason that "you are not your own property: You have been bought and paid for; so use your body for the glory of God." Paul is speaking out against consorting with prostitutes; he is not condemning Christian marriage as something flawed or second best. Neither, it seems, is Julian.

[35] Once again, Julian's advice flows from her familiarity with scripture—see James's letter, Chapter 1.

"Whatever creature who knows these signs should believe firmly that the Holy Spirit dwells in their soul. And moreover, when God gives a creature tears of contrition, compassion, and devotion, they ought to know that the Holy Spirit is present in their soul. It is as Saint Paul says, the Holy Spirit who prays for us, expressing our pleas in ways that we could never put into words. He means that the Holy Spirit makes us ask and pray, mourning and weeping with tears that are too plentiful even to count. No evil spirit could ever effect these signs: Saint Jerome tells us that human tears torment the devil even more than the pains of hell. God and the devil will always be at odds, they shall never be able to live in the same place together. And remember, the devil has no hold over our human soul.

"Holy Writ says as much: The soul of a just person is the seat of God. This is who I trust you are, my sister, and I will pray that God gives you perseverance. Put all your trust in God and don't be afraid of the world's chatterings. For the more contempt and shame and insults you have from the world, the more you rise in the eyes of God. Patience is all you need: Remember our Lord's saying, 'Your endurance shall win you your lives.' "

The anchoress and I had a great deal to say to each other about all these sacred and holy matters. Dwelling on the love of our Lord Jesus kept us absorbed for the many days we spent together.

Over a period of time, I was able to reveal my way of life to many trustworthy priests as well as to learned doctors of divinity, some who were religious and others secular priests; and they all of them were of the opinion that it was the grace of God himself that was with me. They went on to reassure me that there was no reason to be afraid of self-delusion in my way of life. And so they all advised me that I should persevere, indeed their greatest anxiety was that I would lose heart and fail to keep to my way of perfection. They realized that I had so many enemies speaking slander against me, that they felt I might not be able to bear it all without very special grace and an invincible faith.

But there were others, those who had no means of knowing about my way of life except from what they saw or what they heard from others, who spoke really badly about me. Their evil lies caused me much distress and increased animosity from people in every quarter.

In spite of all this, my confessor in Lynn, the Dominican anchorite I have told of, vowed in his soul that he was certain my intentions were honest and to be trusted, for he could find no deception behind them. And he it was who prophesied that on my pilgrimage to Jerusalem my maid would cause me a great deal of trouble, and that our Lord would test me sorely to the very limit.

And when I heard him say this, I begged him, "Good Father, whatever shall I do when I am so far away from my home if even my maid turns against me? I would be without any physical support, and I wouldn't know where to turn for spiritual comfort. I could never hope to find a confessor like you."

His reply was, "Don't be afraid of anything, our Lord himself will come to your aid. His comfort is better than all the rest. I promise you, when every friend you have has left you, he will send you a hunchbacked man to be your guide and take you wherever you want to travel.[36]

As matters turned out, it was exactly as my anchorite prophesied, even down to the last detail, as I hope I will be able to describe faithfully later on.

But for that moment I said to him, making the most of this opportunity to air all my grievances, "Good Father, what am I to do? The priest I confess to when you are not available is always so very fierce on me. He never seems to believe in my

---

[36] Margery's physical fears were fully justified. The medieval pilgrims had to find their route and make their way safely across often hostile terrain and in foreign places where they were at constant risk. For a woman traveling alone, such risks would become intolerable; Margery needed to belong to a group of pilgrims and travel safely with them. This was to prove difficult.

feelings; he won't set any store by them; instead he belittles them as insignificant trifles, almost jokes about them. And that always ends up hurting my feelings; for to be honest, I like him very much and really want to follow his advice."

I was surprised at the anchorite's reply: "It's no wonder, daughter, he can't take your feelings for real. He remembers you as a sinful woman, and he finds it hard to credit that God would be on such intimate terms with you in so short a time. For myself, I believe in you after all our conversations and would not for the world be as hard on you as he is. But for your own good, God has made him like a scourge for you. It is just like a blacksmith who takes his file to the iron so as to make it shine bright and clear, when before he touched it, it appeared coated with rust and dull to the eye. The sharper he is with you, the more brightly your soul will shine before God's eyes. But my task before God is to be your spiritual father, someone who is here to comfort you and make you strong. Be humble, meek, and thank God for both him and for me."

19

Before I set out for Jerusalem, our Lord sent me to a well-known lady to speak in confidence and pass on a message he had for her. For her part, the lady would speak to me only with her confessor present; and so I told her that I was happy at this arrangement. So when her confessor arrived, all three of us went into her chapel together. And there, with great trepidation and many tears, I told her, "Madam, our Lord Jesus Christ has asked me to tell you your husband is still in Purgatory; and although he will be saved, it will be a long time before he gets to heaven."

This lady was greatly displeased by this, saying that her husband had been a good man; she flatly refused to believe that he was in Purgatory. But her confessor sided openly with me. He said that what I was saying could very well be true; and he backed me up by telling several pious stories that he knew.

Later this same lady sent her daughter and one or two other members of her household to the anchorite who was my special confessor, to tell him to give me up or otherwise he would lose her as his friend and patron. The anchorite told these envoys that he certainly would not forsake me, not for anyone on earth. He told them that when anyone asked about my way of life and for his own opinion of me, he said at once that I was God's own servant, adding that I was the tabernacle of God.

My confessor told me himself about this incident; wanting to bolster my faith, he said: "Even if God were to take away from you his gift of your tears and all possibility of talking directly to you, you must still believe that God loves you. You can be sure of getting to heaven because of these gifts you once had; for tears of love are the greatest gift God can give us on earth. Anyone who truly loves God should be thankful to him for you."

On another occasion, a widow came to me and asked if I would pray for her husband to find out if he still needed help.[37] And, as I began to pray for him, it became apparent to me that his soul would be thirty years in Purgatory—that is, unless he had some better friends on this earth. And so I was able to tell the widow this; and I suggested, "If you give three or four pounds for masses to be said and as alms to the poor,

---

[37] The medieval view on Purgatory was straightforward and practical. Most wills provided for masses to be said, candles lit, and prayers said for the repose of the departed soul.

you will please God greatly and your husband's soul will be alleviated."

But the widow hardly listened to my advice, and the matter was ignored. So I approached my anchorite and told him in general terms of the experience I had had. He interpreted it as coming from God and declared that, whether or not the man's soul had need of it, such actions were good in themselves and should be carried out. Encouraged by this, I then told him the details, in the hope that my confessor would be able to find an occasion to speak with the widow. But for a long while, I heard no more on the subject.

But afterward our Lord Jesus Christ said to me once more, "Those prayers and good works I asked you to have done for this soul have still not been done. You should ask your confessor about it."

I did so right away; and he confirmed that nothing whatever had been done. And I said outright: "My Lord Jesus Christ has told me as much just now."

When this affair was at its height, I was preoccupied while at my prayers with wanting to know what to say to the widow. And I was told in my soul that I should tell her to leave her present confessor and, in order to please God better, she should go to the Dominican anchorite at Lynn and tell him in detail about her way of life.

I passed this message on to the widow, but neither she nor her confessor would believe a word of it. They would only believe me, they said, if God would give her the same graces as he gave to me. But then she declared flatly that I must not cross her doorstep again. When I was bold enough to suggest that she was bound to feel a certain love and affection toward her present confessor, she retorted that it would be a good thing for me if my love and affection were turned in the same direction.

Then, at our Lord's command, I had a formal letter drawn up to send her. I dictated it to a master of theology and had it sent to the widow. Among other things it stated that this

widow would never have the grace I had; and that I would
never again visit her house, which would please God
greatly.³⁸

And again our Lord spoke to me: "It would be worlds
better for her if she set her love on the same things as you do.
I tell you to go to her confessor and say that since he refuses
to believe your message, that they will be parted sooner than
he can tell. Whether he likes it or not, outsiders will hear
about it before he does. Daughter, let this teach you how hard
it is to get someone to go against their own wishes."

Twelve years later, things turned out as I had said. But
it cost me great sadness, even torment to have been our
Lord's go-between in this matter. But all the time, my love
of God grew, and I grew more confident than I had ever been
before.

20

I was hearing mass one morning, which was being celebrated by a pious young priest. As he held the host up
high over his head at the elevation, I saw the host
shake and flutter to and fro, just as a dove might flutter her
wings. And again, when he held up over his head the chalice
containing the precious blood, it also moved rapidly back-

³⁸ Margery is clearly out of her depth here: It is quite unclear why our Lord should wish
such a letter to be written; in simplest terms, it has very little point. One is curious to know what
prompted the master of theology to connive with Margery, apparently not pausing to question
her motives.

ward and forward as if it might have fallen from his hands. When the consecration was over, I was amazed at the way the sacrament had vibrated and moved; I felt curious to witness him consecrate on another day, to see if this would happen again.

But our Lord Jesus Christ said to me, "You will not see it happen again like this; just be grateful to God that you witnessed it this once. My daughter, even Bridget never saw me do anything like this."

Therefore I questioned in my mind, "But, Lord, what can it all mean?"

"It means vengeance."

"My dear good Lord, what vengeance?"

"There is to be an earthquake," came our Lord's answer. "Mention it to whomever you please in the name of Jesus. For I promise you, daughter, that I speak to you as truly as I spoke to Saint Bridget. And I am telling you that every word in her book is the truth; and through you it will come to be recognized as true. For you will succeed, daughter, in the face of all your enemies. The more they envy you for the grace I give you, the better I shall love you. Because, whatever people say, I know you better than you know yourself. You think I am very patient with people's sins, and you are right. Yet if you could see those sins as I do, you would wonder even more at my patience. And you would sorrow all the more for these people's sins."

Then I replied, "My dear Lord, what is there I can do for these people?"

Our Lord answered me, "You do enough already."

So I prayed, "Merciful Lord Christ Jesus, all mercy, all grace, and all goodness belong to you. Have mercy, then, and pity and compassion on them. Show them your mercy and let them know your goodness; help them all by sending true contrition. For never let them die in their sins."

Then our merciful Lord told me, "I am rightful, my daughter, I can do no more for them than I do now. I send them preachers and priests to teach them; I send pestilence and war, I give them famine and hunger, now they lose all they have, or they fall sick and suffer many other trials. Yet still they do not believe in my word nor do they recognize how I visit them. Therefore I tell them, 'I caused my servants to pray for you, yet you despised their deeds and their lives.' "

22

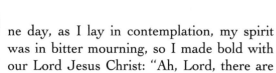 ne day, as I lay in contemplation, my spirit was in bitter mourning, so I made bold with our Lord Jesus Christ: "Ah, Lord, there are maidens dancing for joy in heaven even now. What is to become of me? I am no longer a virgin, and this sad loss of mine is forever with me. I sometimes wish that I had been killed as soon as I was lifted from the font at baptism; for then I would never have been able to offend you—my virginity would have been yours for good.

"Ah, dear God, I have failed to love you all the days of my life; I have run away from you, yet you have run after me. I used to fall into utter despair, but you prevented me."

"My daughter, how many more times must I tell you: Your sins are forgiven. You and I are now joined in love for all time. My love for you is very special: I promise you will have extraordinary grace in heaven; and at your departing I shall come to you, together with my mother and my holy angels, the twelve apostles, Saint Katherine, Saint Margaret, and Saint Mary Magdalene and many another saint who is in heaven. They praise me continually for all the graces I give you and they honor me, your God, your own Lord Jesus.

"So have no fear about the great pain of dying, for you shall have what you desire, to fix your mind on my passion and not your own pain. Have no fear of the devil from hell, he has no power over you. He is more afraid of you than you are of him. He is angry with you; your tears cause him more torment than all the fire in hell. And he sees you winning many souls with your tears. And I have already told you that you will have no more Purgatory than the slanderous words of this world. I myself have punished you, according to my scheme of things, with all the fear and dread of evil spirits you have felt awake or as you slept during all these years.

"Therefore I will save you at your end by my mercy; they will have no power over your body or soul. And I confess it is a great grace and a wonder that you are still sane, given all these troubles you have had to put up with.

"It is true, daughter, I have chastened you with the fear of the Godhead, frightening you often like a hurricane or storm at sea; and so you felt that my vengeance might overwhelm you because of your sins. It was I that tested you with many a tribulation, with griefs beyond number, and countless sicknesses; you have even been anointed at death's door, yet it was my grace that saved you. Therefore, my daughter, you have nothing more to fear. With my very own hands, those same hands that were nailed to the cross, I shall lift your soul from your body and bear it with joy and great harmonies, with sweet scent and fragrance, to offer you to my Father in heaven. There you shall at last see him, to dwell face to face without end.

"My daughter, you will be so welcomed by my Father; by my mother too, as well as by all the saints in heaven; for you have given them to drink so many, many times from the tears of your eyes. All my holy saints will cheer your homecoming. You will have your fill of every kind of love that you ever dreamed of. Then you will count blessed that time you were made, bless too the body of Him who has so [dearly]³⁹ bought you again. He shall rejoice in you, you in him—without end.

"My daughter, I am promising you that same grace that I offered Saint Katherine, Saint Margaret, also Saint Barbara⁴⁰ and Saint Paul: If any person living, from now until the Day of Judgment, shall ask a favor in your name, believing that God loves you, they shall have that boon or something even greater. And so those who believe that God has loved you shall be blessed forever. All the souls of Purgatory shall welcome your homecoming, for they have their own special reason to know how well God loves you. And those still on earth shall rejoice in God for you, who will work so much grace in you that all the world will know that God loves you. You, who have been despised for love of me, shall be honored for that same love.

"Daughter, when you come to heaven, you will be able to ask for whatever you wish; and then I shall give you your desire. Have I not told you before, you are special among God's lovers; and so yours will be a special place in heaven, you shall have a special reward and singular honor. And most of all, since you are still a virgin in your soul, I shall take you by your right hand in heaven, my mother by your left, and then you shall dance, dance in heaven with all those other maiden virgins. And I will call you by your name, dearly bought, my own beloved darling. I shall whisper to you, my

³⁹ The word appears in red, a marginal gloss by the Carthusian monk who was clearly carried along by Margery's meditation. He was perhaps taken aback at Margery's boldness in identifying her death with that of Christ: yet she was correct.

⁴⁰ Saint Barbara's story grew popular in the late Middle Ages: Shut in a tower by her father so that no man might see her, she became a Christian. Frustrated, he handed her over to the magistrate who duly condemned her to death; whereupon her father was suddenly struck down by lightning. Saint Barbara became the patron of those at risk from sudden death, especially miners and, later, gunners.

own beloved spouse, 'Welcome, with every imaginable joy and gladness, dwell now with me nevermore to leave, without any end; but dwell with me in joy and bliss, which no eye can see, nor ear hear, nor may tongue tell, nor yet heart think: all this have I ordained for you and for all my servants who wish to please me and love me as you do.' "

23 The following disconnected moral anecdotes, or spiritual tales, would probably have provided Margery with an endless flow of pious conversation when she sat at table with strangers who had invited her to a meal.

There was once a vicar who approached me and asked me to pray for him. He said that he wanted to learn whether he would please God more by resigning his parish and benefice or by carrying on his cure; he said that he felt he did no good among parishioners and no longer knew how to care for their souls.

Later when I was praying and this was on my mind, I felt Christ speak in my spirit: "Tell the vicar to hold on to his benefice and carry on caring for his people; he must take care with his preaching and look after them individually; sometimes he should bring others in to talk about my laws and commandments, so that it is not always his full responsibility. And if they do not mend their ways, his reward will not be any less for that."

I passed this message on as I had been told; and the vicar persevered in his parish work.

And another time, I was praying in my own parish church of Saint Margaret's. I was in the choir and there a corpse had been brought to lie, a woman, and her husband was at her mass to make the customary offering for the repose of her soul.

And our Lord spoke to me: "Listen to me, daughter, the soul of this woman's body is in Purgatory. And her husband who is fit and well enough now will soon be dead."

And it all came about exactly as I had experienced in my revelation.

Again, on another occasion, I lay at my prayers[41] in the choir of Saint Margaret's when a priest came across to me and asked me to pray for a woman who was about to die. And as I began to pray for her, our Lord spoke: "Daughter, it is vital to pray for her; she has been a very wicked woman and it is true that she is about to die."

So I asked him, "Lord, for love of me, please save her soul from damnation." And then I began to weep many tears for her poor soul. And our Lord was pleased to grant mercy on her soul; yet he bade me continue to pray for her all the same.

On another day, my confessor came to me, asking me urgently to pray for a woman who lay at death's door, or so it was said; yet our Lord told me that she would recover and thrive. And so it turned out.

There was a good man—he was always helping the poor—who was a close friend of mine; and he became ill for many weeks on end. People were very concerned for him, because they thought he would not pull through; his every joint gave

---

[41] Margery appears to have prayed laying flat on her back. Did she choose the choir as a more discreet place to follow her devotions? More and more the opinion swings in favor of her belief that what is felt by each individual to be the most comfortable posture for prayer should be readily adopted.

him acute pain throughout his body. Our Lord told me in my soul, "Daughter, don't be anxious for him: He's going to recover and get over it very well indeed."

And so it turned out; for he lived for many a long year after that and was prosperous into the bargain.

Another good fellow was a dyer by trade; and he was also lying sick. When I was asked to pray for him I was answered in my mind that he would linger on a little while more and eventually succumb to his illness. And this is exactly what happened, for he died a little while later.

Another respectable lady, a close friend of mine, a holy woman in everyone's eyes, was extremely ill. Most of her friends and neighbors expected her to die at any moment. But while I was at prayer, our Lord told me, "She will not die for another ten years; soon you will have reason to celebrate, and then you will have many a good long chat, just like in the old days."

And so it turned out to be the case; this holy woman lived on for many a long year.

There were many other revelations that came to me in my heart; to write them all down would simply get in the way of telling of more important things. I have detailed those above simply to show what simple, domestic care our Lord Jesus has toward us all in his mercy; I was not trying to demonstrate any virtue of mine.

I could write many other presentiments such as these, about the living and the dying; some of them were to be saved, others were to be damned, and they afforded me great pain and affliction. Indeed, I would have chosen to suffer any physical pain rather than be party to such experiences. If I

could have escaped them, I would, for I greatly feared being
led astray by the tricks of my spiritual enemies. I had the
greatest trouble sometimes when such feelings simply did not
match up to common sense; and at such times my confessor
feared I would despair. And then at last, after a great deal of
trouble and trepidation, it would become clear to my soul
how to interpret my innermost feelings.

24

The same priest who later came to write down my
story wanted to test my state of soul before agree-
ing to the task. Accordingly he began to ask me
many questions over a period of time, all about the future.
That is to say, he wanted to know the outcome of something
that nobody could possibly predict at that present moment. I
was very reluctant to go along with this test, especially, for
instance, when he asked me to pray to God and find out when
our Lord would next visit me with his consolations—and, if
so, what would happen; for then he expected me to tell him
openly how I felt. Failing this, he said, he would be unwilling
to settle to the task of transcribing my book.

In part, I was persuaded to go along with this because
otherwise there was no way he could be persuaded to work
for me; and so I did as he asked and told him my inner
feelings, what I sensed was going to happen, whenever he
chose to put me through this test. It was his way of making
sure of me. The difficulty arose when sometimes he failed to

trust me; but that only got him into trouble, as in the following incident.

A young man, who was unknown to him, came to the priest and complained bitterly about how poor he was and how so much bad luck had come his way; he had his own theory why all this had happened to him and revealed that he had been ordained as a priest. There had been a brawl with a gang who had attacked him; he may possibly have over-reacted in defending himself, and yet it seemed to him that he could easily have been killed by them. The result was that one member of the gang, possibly even two, had been struck down by him; and, as a result, they were both either dead or likely to die. As a consequence, he had fallen into an irregular way of life as he feared that he could scarcely exercise his ministry without a dispensation from Rome. He had left his friends and fled to our part of the country for fear of being arrested on account of the two deaths.

The priest was all too ready to believe the young man's story; for one thing he had plenty of charm, he was good-looking, well-spoken. And he dressed and behaved like a priest. As a consequence, his listener felt extremely sorry for him and wanted to help him out in a practical way. So he approached a well-to-do burgess of Lynn. He was not only a man of compassion, but he was quite capable of becoming mayor of the town, save for the fact that he had been seriously ill for a good long time. The priest explained the situation to the sick man and his wife, who was a kind woman, fully expecting that they would be willing to give him a generous sum in this cause, for they had done so more than once in the past.

Now as it happened, I was visiting them when the priest called on his business. So I could not help overhearing him as he set out the young man's case, and very persuasive it seemed. Yet as I listened, I felt very strongly against the young man. So I pointed out that they had any number of neighbors living in poverty, all of whom they knew about, who had equal need of their help and relief. Would not it be better and more charitable, I urged, to give help to those they knew to be good folk, indeed their own neighbors, rather than reach out to strangers whom they had no knowledge of. Plenty of people seemed credible enough in their words and outward appearance: yet God alone knew what went on in their souls!

The good man and his wife judged what I had to say as sound sense and said they would give him nothing. The priest was very put out by this. Later on, he took me to one side and went to great lengths about how I had thwarted him so that now he had failed in his purpose to help the young man. He said that he still believed his story, and that the young man had continued to behave himself admirably.

I answered him, saying, "Sir, God alone can say what he did or did not do; for myself, I have never even cast eyes on him. But I think I know what he's up to. My advice to you, sir, is to let him find his own way of sorting out his affairs as best he can. Don't become involved with him, because he is out to fool you."

The young man carried on seeing the priest, ingratiating himself and declaring that he had several reliable friends elsewhere who would look after him right away, if they did but know where he had got to; adding that these same friends would be mighty grateful to anyone who helped him out of his present need. The priest swallowed all this and in the end was quite happy to lend him some silver shillings to tide him over. Next, the youth told the priest that he would be away for two to three weeks, but that he would be back promptly and pay back the money. The priest took his promise at face value and sent him on his way with his blessing against the day of his promised return.

After the youth had left, once more I had a certain premonition from our Lord that we would soon know him for a dishonest fellow who had gone for good. I wanted to know whether I was right or not and so asked the priest where that

young man he had thought so well of had gone. The priest
replied that he had merely gone away for a short time, adding
that he was perfectly confident of his return. I declared that I
was equally sure he would never show up again; nor ever did
he. And soon the priest was only too sorry he had ignored my
sound advice.

A little later after this affair, another scoundrel, this time
an old man, offered the selfsame priest a breviary for sale; he
assured him that it was in good condition and he could have it
for a very reasonable asking price. Again, the priest consulted
me and asked my prayers to see whether or not it was God's
will that he should purchase the book. While I prayed, he
bargained with the man and kept him sweet. And presently
he came back to me to hear my verdict.

Once again I counseled caution: "Sir, don't buy any book
from him; he's not to be trusted. If you do a deal with him,
you'll soon regret it."

So the priest began by asking the man if he could have
another look at the breviary. He hadn't got it on him, came
the reply. Very well then, but how had he come by it?

It seemed that the old man was executor to a priest, a
relation who had wanted him to dispose of it.

"Father," the priest addressed him, in respect to his years,
"why are you offering this book to me, rather than to anyone
else—there must be countless other priests who might be interested. And some of them, I feel sure, would be able to give
you a far better price than myself. We've never met before
and yet you come and single me out!"

"That is true, sir," came the reply, "you are quite correct.
It's just that I feel well disposed toward you; and besides it
was the wish of the former owner that if I were to spot a
young priest whom I judged to be of sober and honest ways,
he should be preferred against any other man. Moreover, I
ought to offer it at a lower price and ask him to pray for me.
That is why I came to you rather than to anyone else."

He was asked where he lived.

"A mere five miles away, sir, in Pentney Abbey."[42]

"I go there regularly, why have I never seen you?"

"No indeed, sir, I have only been there a short while—but now they are kind enough to provide my food each day, thanks be to God."

The priest asked if he might have sight of the book and see if they could come to some agreement.

"Sir, I hope to be back again next week. I'll bring it along with me. I promise you will have first offer, that is if you take a fancy to it."

The priest thanked him for his kindness, and so they parted; but he never saw the man again. And so once again the priest had proof positive that my intuitions were well-founded.

25

This would seem a suitable point in my story to tell in some detail a truly remarkable example of following my intuition, although in fact it took place long after events that are still to be related.

In my prosperous hometown of Lynn, the parish church of Saint Margaret had two chapels of ease that were fully licensed for administering all the sacraments save baptism and the churching of women by the prior of the Benedictines from the cathedral of Norwich. All three churches were adminis-

---

[42] An Augustinian abbey founded in 1135 some seven miles southeast of Lynn. Only the gatehouse still stands.

tered by a vicar and three of his brethren, all Benedictines, resident in Lynn.

Now a group of parishioners, wishing to secure the same status for their chapels of ease as the parish church of Saint Margaret's had, secured a bull from an ecclesiastical court in Rome. As a result, there was a great deal of bitterness and litigation as this pressure group pursued its aim to secure the right for baptism and churching independently of the parish church. The congregation of the chapel of Saint Nicholas, which was indeed a particularly fine church, had secured, some time back—in fact when my own father was mayor of Lynn—a papal bull that would have given them their font. But this itself had been the cause of a long-running dispute as it was conditional on "causing no derogation" to the status of Saint Margaret's parish church.

And so that matter was now started up all over again. Days were spent pleading the substance of the bull, and whether or not, if a font were installed at Saint Nicholas, the parish church of Saint Margaret's would suffer any appreciable loss. The Saint Nicholas group were men of substance, merchants in the main, not short of money with which to press their case; they even enjoyed the wide support of several lords. What a pity it is that money so often speaks louder than the truth.

In spite of their seeming strength, the prior, John Derham, who was a poor man, stood up to them; he was supported by his friends and those who took the honor of their parish church to heart. But as the matter remained in dispute, it began to wear down both parties, not least because no end seemed to be in sight.

And so finally, the whole affair was laid before the Bishop of Norwich, William of Alnwick. He was a just man, yet one who brooked no compromise; certainly he persecuted the Lollards in his diocese relentlessly. But in this matter he worked diligently to find a compromise that would restore the peace. He went a long way to offer the Saint Nicholas faction much of what they wanted, hedged around with certain conditions, so that their opponents feared they would at last secure a font and so make their chapel equal in status to the parish church.

And at this point, the priest who would later become my amanuensis came to me, as was his wont, and asked me how I felt in my soul about the affair—should they have their font or no?

I gave him my reply: "Do not be anxious, sir, for the understanding I have in my soul is that even if they had a bushel of gold nobles, they would not be able to buy what they want."

"Ah, but mother," said the priest, "have you not heard that my Lord Bishop of Norwich has already offered them their font, under certain conditions; they've even been given time to deliberate whether they wish to say yea or nay. Now I hardly think they are going to say no; they'll be only too glad to grab it with both hands."

Meanwhile I prayed to God that his will should be done. And insofar as I began to see more clearly, as the matter was revealed to me, I felt bold enough to ask our Lord to refuse their cause and make their boasts come to nothing. And so it turned out, according to our Lord's will, that they took exception to the conditions and eventually refused them, preferring instead to rely on the support of their lords and the law itself. And in the end, because they wanted to gain everything, they lost it all.

Blessed be God! The parish church remained with its dignity undiminished, just as it had been these past two hundred years and more; and my own revelation about the affair was proved sound and true.[43]

---

[43] Saint Nicholas, founded in 1146, remains to this day a chapel of ease.

26

ow, at length, it was time to set out on pilgrimage to all those Holy Places where our Lord had once lived and died and which had featured in my revelations several years before. Accordingly, I asked my parish priest, Master Robert Spryngolde, to announce from the pulpit that if any man or woman held any debt against my husband or myself, they should come forward and make themselves known to me before I left so that, God willing, I would settle up with each to their complete satisfaction. And this I was able to do.

Having done this, I took leave of my husband. I also said my farewells to my confessor, the anchorite, but not before he had given me ample forewarning of the trials and sufferings I would encounter on my journey; for he told me that every one of my traveling companions would desert me, but that a man with a hunchback would become my guide and, with our Lord's help, lead me safely on my way. And all of this came true, as I will presently record.

It was now time to take my leave of Master Robert, and as I did so, I asked him to give me his blessing. And I also said good-bye to other friends of mine. Then I made my way to Norwich to make an offering at the cathedral which is dedicated to the Trinity; and from there I went on to Yarmouth and gave another offering at the shrine of our Lady before boarding my ship.

We sailed on the late tide that night and by the following morning had reached Zierikzee, which is a sizable town. God in his great goodness gave me many tears of contrition for all my sins, and at other moments tears too for the sins of others. And whenever I brought to mind our Lord's sufferings, my heart was overcome with tears of compassion. Each Sunday, whenever time and place allowed, I would receive Communion, which always occasioned me to weep and sob so violently that very many people exclaimed how great was the workings of God's grace in such a lowly servant as myself.

For four whole years before leaving England I had eaten no meat and taken no wine. But now on account of my journey my confessor had directed me firmly under obedience that I should both eat meat and drink wine once more. And for a little while, I did as I was bidden. But then I begged my confessor to excuse me from eating meat, and allow me to do as I desired for whatever length of time he judged right.

But in no time at all, feelings ran against me throughout our company that I no longer ate meat, and they made sure that my confessor too would be annoyed with me. But they were even more irritated by my continual tears, and the way I would speak openly all the while about the love and goodness of our Lord, both at table when we ate together as well as in other places.

They never thought twice about criticizing and condemning me in public; they said they were not prepared to put up with me as my husband did when I was back home in England.

My reply was simple: "Our Lord God Almighty is as great a lord here as he is in England; and I have just as much reason to love him here as back home—blessed may he be."

But when I said this, my traveling companions grew even more angry with me than before; and their anger and unkindness caused me great distress for they were known as good people and I very much wanted to be called their friend, providing this would bring no offense on God. At one point, I took one of them aside and said: "Do you realize how much shame and hurt you are causing me?"

His reply came like a sword: "I pray to God that the devil's death may claim you swiftly and soon." He added a further stream of cruel and wounding words that I would rather not repeat. And then a few days later, some of the party whom I most trusted, including my own maidservant, turned against me. They declared that I should no longer accompany them and that they would take care of my servant to save her from being prostituted in my company. Finally, one of them who was looking after my money gave me a single noble and angrily told me to shift for myself as best I may; and everyone agreed that I could no longer stay with the party. And they left me that same night.[44]

The next morning, one of the group who got on well with me came and asked me to apologize to everyone and tell them that I would behave myself with extra care, if only they would allow me to travel with them as far as Constance.

I went along with this and so it was agreed, but it only led to more trouble and even greater distress. As the journey continued so too did their torments. They cut my gown so short that it only came down just below my knees. They made me wear some kind of apron made of white sackcloth so that people would take me for a fool and think nothing of me. While at table, they made me sit below everyone so that I scarcely dared open my mouth.

And yet in spite of all their malice, wherever we went I was given more respect than they were. For example, wherever we stayed overnight our host would always go out of his way to cheer me up in front of everyone. Sometimes he would even send me food that had been prepared for his own table; and naturally this greatly annoyed my traveling companions.

[44] Most of the friction between Margery and her pilgrim company arise from their diametric views of what it means to be a pilgrim. As is evident from Chaucer's account, the medieval pilgrimage bore some resemblance to a modern package holiday. It was a lifetime experience that cost good money; to enjoy the journey was only right. Margery's attitude of unrelenting piety was bound to set her outside the group.

As we neared Constance, we heard repeated rumors that we would be very fortunate not to be set upon and caused great physical harm. And presently we came to a wayside church, so I went in to pray for our safety. I prayed with all my heart and with many tears and weeping that we might be delivered from these unknown enemies.

And our Lord said in my spirit, "Have no fear, my daughter, your party will come to no harm all the while you are with them." And true enough, blessed may our Lord be in all his works, we went safely on our way until we reached Constance.

27

s soon as we had arrived in Constance, I had word that an English friar[45] was in the city. Taking advantage of the fact that he was not only a master of divinity and a well-respected scholar but also the Pope's legate, I made my full confession to him, telling him my life story from its very beginning right up to that moment.

And after my confession, I went on to tell him all the aggravation I was having with my traveling companions. I

[45] Margery's arrival in Constance would have coincided with preparations for the forthcoming Council, called to address the threefold papal schism and combat the accompanying tide of laity-driven reform. This description fits a major figure in the Council, the Carmelite Thomas Netter, provincial of the English Order, confessor to King Henry V, inquisitor of England, and a fierce antagonist of the Lollards. John Huss was to be offered safe conduct from Bohemia to answer before the Council; it would condemn him and hand him over to be burned.

spoke to him also of the grace of contrition and compunction given me by God, of the many consolations received at my devotions as well as the different revelations our Lord had shown me. And I revealed to him my continual fear of being deluded and led astray by my spiritual enemies, and how I only wished to escape from them so that they became a thing of the past rather than having to stand up to them every day.

When I had had my say, this distinguished and learned priest was able to find words that gave me great comfort. He declared that all he had heard was most surely the work of the Holy Spirit; so he bade me solemnly obey such promptings and take them as coming from God's hands when it so pleased him; he said I was to put away my doubts because the devil had no power to work such things in a soul. As to the difficulties with my companions, he promised that he would lend me his support.

Some time later, when it suited their arrangements, my company invited him to dine with them. This shrewd scholar warned me ahead that I should sit at table and behave in front of him just as I would if he were not present.

When they came to dine, everyone took the place they fancied once their guest of honor had been seated first. I myself sat at the lower end of the table in my usual place and spoke not a word. It was just as if he were not there.

Soon the legate spoke up and asked me, "Why are you not more cheerful?"

But I sat without answering him, behaving exactly as if he had not been there—just as he had told me. And when the meal was at an end, everyone started to complain about me to the legate. They declared that there was no way I could remain a member of their party unless he ordered me to eat meat just as they did, and unless I agreed to stop my tears and cease going on so about being holy.

At this, the good and learned priest declared, "I shall certainly not order her to eat meat when, if she abstains, she is better able to love our Lord. Now let us suppose that one of you had taken a vow to walk barefoot to Rome: I would not dispense you of your vow all the while you were able to fulfill it. Nor will I tell her to eat meat when our Lord gives her strength to abstain. As for her tears, I have no power to stop them—they come as a gift of the Holy Spirit. As regards her conversation, I will ask her to hold her peace until she meets with people who will listen to her more readily than you."

At this they grew terribly angry. They said the legate could look after me; as for themselves, they would have nothing more to do with me. And so he agreed to this arrangement and took me in his care just as though I were his own mother. He took charge of my money, which was around £20—although there was a further £16 that they quite wrongfully hung on to. They also refused to let my maid come along with me, in spite of her having given me her word before we set out that she would stay by me under any circumstances.

The legate then saw to all my arrangements, as I say, just as if I were his own mother; for example, he saw to the business of changing my English money into foreign coin. Meanwhile, I went off to church so that I might pray to our Lord to find someone who could be my escort on the journey. And now our Lord spoke to me, saying, "I promise you that you shall have a good companion to guide you on your way."

Not long after this, an old man with a long white beard approached me. He explained that he came from Devon, and then went on: "Madam, since your companions have abandoned you, will you invite me, for God's love and our Lady's, to come along with you and be your guide?"

I asked him for his name.

"William Weaver is my name."

And so I begged him, naming God and our Lady, to help me in my time of need. I promised to reward him generously; and so we struck our bargain.

Finally, I saw the legate and told him how our Lord had arranged everything so neatly. Thanking him, I took my leave; and I also bade farewell to my party who had so unkindly turned me out, as well as my maidservant who had broken her promise to me.

I confess that all this was done with a long face and a heavy heart: I was in a strange land whose language I did not speak. Moreover, I was now with a strange man whom I had only just met. And even as we set out, he suddenly said to me, "My worst fear is that you will be abducted, and all because of you I will be beaten up and lose everything—coat and all."

"Don't be so silly, William," I told him firmly, "God is going to look after us only too well."

Yet as each day passed, I could not put from my mind the story in the gospel when the woman is taken in adultery and brought before our Lord. And I prayed all the time with these words: "Good Lord, you drove her enemies from her; see off all wicked men and preserve my chastity. Please let me never be defiled; if I am, Lord, I vow that I will never return again to England."[46]

But as each day came and went, in fact we met very many wonderful people. No one had a bad word to say to me, but everyone received us both very hospitably; they gave us food and drink, and good wives in houses where we lodged would sometimes even give up their own beds to make me comfortable. And as we made our way, our Lord visited me with great spiritual consolation.

In such a way did God look after us until we came to Bologna. And shortly after we arrived, my former companions who had deserted me also turned up. And when they heard the news that we had arrived ahead of them in Bologna, they were incredulous. One of their number came to me and suggested I ask the company to take me back with them once more. And so I made an approach.

"If you want to travel with us, there must be a completely new agreement: You are not to speak of the gospel in our

---

[46] The danger of rape must have been very great. Pilgrims—like migrating birds—flocked together for safety. Now that Margery was guarded only by an old man, she must have felt acutely vulnerable.

hearing, and at mealtimes you have got to join us in our merrymaking."

I gave my agreement to these conditions, and so they received me once more into their company. And so from Bologna we proceeded to Venice; and there we waited for thirteen weeks before the first pilgrim ships sailed with the arrival of early summer. And on Sundays, I received Communion at a very large convent where the nuns welcomed me very warmly. Here too our Lord Jesus Christ visited me with much consolation and many tears, so that the good ladies of that house were amazed.

And so it happened after hearing mass one Sunday, as I sat at table with my companions I repeated a text from the gospel on which the homily had been based. My companions at once said that I had broken my undertaking. And I agreed with them, saying, "Yes, sirs, you are quite right. I can no longer keep my agreement with you, for I must speak about my Lord Jesus Christ even if the whole world had forbidden me."

So I had no option but to take to my room and eat alone for the next six weeks. As a result I fell so ill that I thought I would die; yet our Lord suddenly made me well again. And all this while my maidservant left me quite alone; the very mistress she had sworn to serve, she neglected, preferring to cook meals for the entire company and wash all of their clothes.

28

To add to my distress, my companions not only excluded me from their table but quietly went ahead with their sailing arrangements. They purchased casks for their wine supply and bought their bedding, without any thought for me. As soon as I learned what they had been up to behind my back, I too went to the same merchant and also bought my bedding. Then I went back to them and let it be known that I fully intended to sail in the same ship that they had decided upon.

But later that evening, as I was at my prayers our Lord warned me that I should avoid that ship; he indicated instead another vessel, which turned out to be a galley, saying I should use that for my safe passage.[47] When I happened to mention my change of plan to some of the company, they passed on word to the rest of the party. As a result, they dared not set sail in the ship they had first decided upon. They promptly sold off their wine casks; suddenly they appeared quite content to join me in the galley. Much against my better judgment, I continued in their company; and now, for their part, they dared not do otherwise than travel with me.

[47] The pilgrim's journey from Venice was an ancient trade route that hugged the coast, putting in frequently both for provisions and as a precaution against any sudden and unexpected storms. Once along the coast of Dalmatia and through the Greek isles, they would put in at Crete; thence to Rhodes and on to Cyprus, perhaps reaching Jaffa, the nearest port for Jerusalem, after a journey lasting a month or longer.

When it was time to prepare our beds, I discovered they had locked away my bedding; and then a priest, who was traveling with us, took one of my sheets, declaring that it really belonged to him. Then I called upon God to witness that it was mine. But at this, the priest swore a solemn oath on the book he held up in his hand that I was telling lies; he said he despised my sort and went on ranting at me.

I had to put up with similar unkind treatment all the way to Jerusalem. At length, just before we landed, I did my best to come to terms with them, saying: "Sirs, I beg you out of your charity, make your peace with me, for I am at peace with you. Please forgive me if I have annoyed you during our journey together. And if someone has wronged me in any way, may God forgive them as I also do."

When we landed in the Holy Land, we were taken on donkeys to Jerusalem. And so it was that when I first set eyes on Jerusalem, I was astride an ass; I was so moved that I thanked God from the bottom of my heart, and I prayed of his mercy that just as he had brought me safely here to see the earthly city of Jerusalem, so he would grant me his grace to see the city of bliss above, the heavenly Jerusalem. And at that moment, I knew in my heart that our Lord Jesus Christ would one day grant me my desire.

I was filled so full of joy and consolation at speaking in this way with our Lord that I was in danger of falling from my ass, such was the sweetness and grace that I experienced in my soul. But two pilgrims, who I learned later were from Germany, came to my rescue and made sure that I did not fall. One of them was a priest, and it was he who put spices to my lips as a comfort, for he believed that I was getting sick. That was how I was helped so very kindly on my way into Jerusalem; so that when we arrived I felt I had to explain myself. "Sirs," I told them, "don't be annoyed by my weeping here in this holy place; for this is the very land where our Lord Jesus Christ lived and died."[48]

We visited the Church of the Holy Sepulchre, the very center of Jerusalem. We were let in at evensong on our first day, and we stayed at prayer until evensong on the following. There were friars[49] looking after the church; and once everyone was settled, they presently lifted up a cross and processed from one holy spot to the next. And so as we pilgrims were led to the very places where our Lord had suffered his pains and his passion, each man and woman carried a candle, and the friars were able to give us a running commentary on what our Lord had suffered at each point. And I began to weep and sob; it was as if I were watching our Lord with my own eyes suffering his passion at that very moment. At the same time, in my soul I saw him most truly in my contemplation; seeing all this caused such compassion for him. And when at last we came up to Mount Calvary, I fell down, no longer able to stand or even kneel; and there I lay, writhing and struggling in my body. I reached out wide with my arms and cried aloud as though my heart would burst. For in the city of my soul I saw truly and freshly as if for the first time how our Lord was crucified. I could hear, as well as see face to face—that is, with spiritual insight—our Lady's grieving, Saint John's and Mary Magdalene's mourning, together with all those countless other lovers of our Lord.

So great was my compassion that it became for me a bitter pain of loss not to share to the full our Lord's own, true pain. I was quite unable to prevent myself from crying out loud, a kind of roar it was, even though it might have been the death

---

[48] Margery sums up very simply the traditional motive for pilgrimage, to see the very spot where it all happened. At this level, pilgrimage is an affirmation and renewal of faith in the incarnation of the Word made Flesh.

Far more complex were the motives behind the warring incursions of the crusaders that had spanned 200 years two centuries earlier. Muslims' memories were still fresh and bitter. As a consequence, in medieval times Christian pilgrims were still only admitted to Jerusalem under severe controls; pilgrims were literally locked into the Church of the Holy Sepulchre, session by session.

[49] The Franciscans had been zealous guardians of the holy places since Saint Francis himself had sojourned in Jerusalem for almost a year in 1220.

of me. This was the very first time I had ever experienced this sort of crying aloud in contemplation. And it was to be with me now for many more years; and there would be nothing I could do to prevent it, notwithstanding the contempt and rebukes I should suffer on account of it. My cries were so earsplitting, so sudden that people were taken unawares, save for those who had heard me cry out before and knew what it was about.[50]

Afterward, whenever I had these kind of attacks, which were most frequently occasioned by the mere mention of our Lord's passion, they sapped my physical strength so that I became quite weak. I might catch sight of a crucifix, or even happen to spot a man who had a wound, or it might even be a beast in the field that was wounded; or if a man beat a boy in my sight, or lashed his horse or any animal with his whip— any such sight or sound even would bring to mind our Lord himself being beaten or wounded, as vividly as the man or beast I could see before me with my own eyes. And there was always the same sense of reality, whether it happened in the country or in town, whether I was alone or surrounded by others.

Once I had experienced these first cryings aloud in Jerusalem, I had them again and again; they also happened to me when I was in Rome. But when I first returned home to England, they seldom came—perhaps, say, once a month. But after a while, they became increasingly frequent, once a week, then presently a daily occurrence. On one particular day I can remember having fourteen; on another day, seven. It occurred whenever God pleased to visit me in such a way; thus sometimes they would happen in church, sometimes as I was walking along the street, at other times when I was in my room, or in the fields outside. It was always when God chose to send them; I never could guess the time or the place. But

---

[50] The Carthusian who annotated the manuscript at Mount Grace notes in the margin the names of two recent monks who would also cry out, and he traces a line to the word "weak" below.

they never came without an overwhelming sense of the great sweetness of consolation and the highest contemplation.

As soon as ever I got the first inkling that I was about to cry out, I would try as hard as I could to hold it in, so that people should not hear me or get annoyed. This was because some people declared openly that I was tormented by a wicked spirit; others thought it was some kind of illness; some said I was drunk on wine; some simply cursed me; others wished I would fall into the harbor, or said I should be pushed out to sea in a bottomless boat; everyone seemed to have their own idea. But there were others, more spiritually aware, who loved and looked up to me. Some very learned men gave their opinion that our Lady would never have cried aloud in such a way, indeed no saint in heaven; but little did they know how I felt, nor could they guess how hard I would strive to stop myself from making any noise at all.

After a while, I worked out my own method. When I knew I was about to cry out, I would hold on to it as long as I could, doing everything to resist or suppress a shriek that was coming. But all the while it would well up, more and more until the moment that it would simply burst out from me. It seemed to me that when my body could no longer stand my inner stress and was overpowered by the wordless love that would boil up from my very soul, then I would sometimes fall down and call out with an unbelievably loud shriek. I felt that the more I struggled to keep it in, the louder would I cry when it came to the surface.

And this is what it was like when it first happened to me on Mount Calvary: I had a very real inner vision as if Christ hung before my very eyes, visible in his manhood. And when, given this grace by the great good mercy of our sovereign savior Christ Jesus, I saw so plainly his precious tender body all rent and torn by the scourges, more full of wounds than ever a dovecote was full of holes, hanging on the cross, his head crowned with thorns, his blessed hands, his tender feet nailed to the rough wood, the rivers of blood flowing plentifully from his every limb, the grisly, grievous wound in his precious side pouring out blood and water for love of me and for my own salvation, then I fell right down and cried aloud, my body twisting and turning fantastically in every direction, my arms outstretched as if I would have died. How could I prevent myself from calling out or hold my body still at such a moment, since the fire of love was burning so in my soul with the purest pity and compassion.[51]

Why should it come as a surprise that I cried out like this and behaved in such an extraordinary way, when one can see with one's own eyes both men and women every day of the week crying, raving, wringing their hands, behaving as if they had lost their wits; and yet they know very well how much they displease God. And why do they behave in such a way? Some of them because they have lost their worldly wealth, others for love of their family or because they are wrapped up in their worldly friends, but most because they are slaves to unbridled lust and illicit love.

If someone advises them to stop their weeping and complaining, they answer simply that they cannot. They will tell you that they loved their friend so much, for he was so kind and gentle toward them, that they may never forget him. How much louder would they complain if this friend of theirs were violently arrested before their very eyes and taken before a judge to be abused in every way before being unjustly condemned to death, especially the shameful public execution that our merciful Lord suffered on our behalf. How would they bear such a thing? I have no doubt they would cry and roar and seek revenge as best they could; otherwise people would think that they had abandoned their friend.

[51] This vivid description of Margery's experience has similarities to some few of the revelations witnessed by Julian of Norwich. Margery likens Christ's wounds to being inside a dovecote —a large walk-in building with countless nesting ledges or holes; Julian speaks of Christ's wounds bleeding in an equally lifelike simile: "The sheer flow of blood was like drops of water coming from thatch eaves after a heavy shower of rain . . ."

Both Saint Bernard and Richard Rolle use the dovecote metaphor in a similar vein; Margery could have heard this repeated in a sermon or had Richard Rolle's "Meditations on the Passion" read to her.

How can anyone feel that degree of excessive grief for the death of someone who has often sinned and offended against his maker. This offends God and makes a scandal for all true Christian souls. But at the same time, the death of our Savior —by which we are all restored to new life—we let slip from our minds. Such unworthy and ungrateful wretches we are! Nor can we even manage to support those who know our Lord's secrets and are filled with his love; instead we would rather mock and oppose them at every turn.

29

My companions and I came now to the grave where our Lord had been buried; and as I entered that sacred place and saw its low roof lit by the flickering candle in my hand, I fell down as though I would die from such sorrow. Presently, I managed to get up again, yet I was sobbing and weeping still; it was as if I had just seen our Lord buried right before my very eyes. Deep within my soul, I thought of our Lady, how she had mourned and shed tears when her son had died. I felt I shared all her sorrows as my own.

Wherever the friars chose to lead us in that holy place, I was continually weeping and sobbing in an alarming manner; but I was especially moved to see the spot where our Lord was nailed to his cross. Here I cried out loud and wept without any restraint, for I could not help myself. We were also shown a marble slab where Jesus was laid after he had been taken down from the cross; here too I wept with tender compassion in memory of our Lord's own Passion.

Later, when I received Communion on Mount Calvary, I wept again, with many sobs, and cried out so loudly that it was amazing to hear such a noise. I was so overwhelmed with holy thoughts, meditations, and contemplation on the passion of our Lord, and enjoyed such holy commerce with our Lord in my soul, that later I was quite incapable of telling anyone about them; they were so high, so holy. Our Lord visited me with many similar graces throughout the three weeks that I spent in Jerusalem.[52]

One day, rising early, we visited the high hills outside the city, and our Franciscan guides showed us the place where our Lord had carried his cross upon his back and where he had come face to face with his mother, and where she had then fainted and fallen down; and he too had fallen three times.[53] Here we passed the whole morning and then were taken to Mount Zion; I was greatly moved and wept a great deal, feeling deeply our Lord's own Passion. It was upon Mount Zion that our Lord washed his disciples' feet, and then a little way off where he celebrated the Last Supper with them.

I was very anxious to receive Communion in that same holy place where our merciful Lord Christ Jesus first made sacred his precious body in the form of bread and gave it to his disciples. And so it was with such great devotion that I shed many tears and was taken with violent sobbings—for at this place you receive a plenary remission of all your sins. It is the same in the Church of the Holy Sepulchre, where they have four such places of plenary indulgence: the first on Mount Calvary; the second at the grave where he was buried;

---

[52] The city in Margery's day was controlled by a resolute Muslim presence. Although the Franciscans had achieved exclusive supervision of the Church of the Holy Sepulchre (their convent was adjacent), Muslim guards escorted pilgrims in convoy from Jaffa to Jerusalem for a fixed tariff. Further money changed hands as they entered the church.

[53] Margery is talking about the Via Dolorosa, the traditional route of Christ's passage to Golgotha.

the third at the marble slab where his precious body lay after it was taken down from the cross; and the fourth at the hole where the holy cross was planted. And there are very many similar places of indulgence all over Jerusalem.

And when I arrived at the very place where the apostles received the Holy Spirit, our Lord gave me great consolation. Next, I visited the place where our Lady was buried.[54] And as I knelt upon the stone floor hearing one mass and then a second, our Lord Jesus Christ spoke to me: "My daughter, you do not come to this place in need of anything other than your reward and merit, since your sins were already forgiven before you came. I tell you that you are come here to increase your merit and reward. I am well pleased with you, my daughter, for you are obedient to Holy Church. You obey your confessor and follow his advice, and it is he who, by the authority of Holy Church, has absolved you of your sins and dispensed you of the penance due; you have no need to go to Rome, to journey to Saint James of Compostela, unless you yourself want to go. But all the same, daughter, I command you in the name of Jesus to visit these very places and do as I say. Remember that I am above Holy Church, and I myself shall go with you and keep you safe always."

Then it was our Lady's turn to speak with me, in my soul: "Daughter, you are well blessed, for my son Jesus will flood you with so much grace that all the world will sing your praises.[55] Be not ashamed, dear daughter of mine, to receive these gifts which my son will give you. Never be ashamed, dear daughter, of him who is your God, your Lord, your love. Was I ashamed of him—how could I be, my own sweet son, as he hung there upon his cross? Was Mary Magdalene ashamed, when she wept and cried for love of my son? As

---

[54] Margery refers to the Chapel of the Apparition—the apparition of the Angel Gabriel before Mary—which is in the Church of the Holy Sepulchre.

[55] It is at such moments in Margery's narrative that one doubts her reliability. This passage closely shadows Mary's own encounter with the Angel and the subsequent canticle Magnificat. Is Margery telling us a simple home truth: that we are all invited in the same way as Mary, mother of Christ, to host him?

you, daughter, will share our joy, so also will you learn to share our grief."

This was simply a part of my sweet conversation with our Lady; there was a great deal more that I may never repeat.

Later, I rode on an ass into Bethlehem. And when I came to the church and saw the crib where our Lord was born, I experienced great consolation and conversation in my soul, as well as my usual sobbings and tears that were accompanied by great spiritual uplift. As a consequence of this, my companions would not let me eat with them, and so I took my meals all by myself.

At this point the Gray Friars, the Franciscan fathers who had guided us to all the places of pilgrimage, took me in with them and welcomed me into their own refectory to save me from eating my meals alone. One of the friars had inquired of a member of our group whether that was the Englishwoman they had heard about who spoke with God. And when I heard of this, I remembered the truth of the words our Lord had spoken to me before I left England: "Daughter, I shall make all the world marvel at you, and there will be many men and women who shall come to me because of their love of you, and they will honor me in you."

30

ne day during our stay, my party planned to see the River Jordan, but they would not let me accompany them. So I prayed to our Lord asking that I could go with them. And he told me to go along with them whether or not they had invited me. I shall always remember that day; when we reached the River Jordan, it was so hot that I thought my feet would be scorched by the ground we stood upon.

After this, we went on to another pilgrim site, Mount Quarantine, where our Lord had fasted forty days and forty nights. The mountain was very steep and so I asked my fellow pilgrims if they would help me on our climb. But they flatly refused, saying it was so steep that they themselves could scarcely climb it. I was very depressed when I realized that I could not climb this holy mountain. But at this very moment, a Saracen happened to come along, a man of striking appearance. Seizing my chance, I slipped a groat into the palm of his hand and mimed to him that I would like him to help me up the mountain. At once, the Saracen took me firmly by the arm and helped me right up to the very top of this mount where our Lord had fasted forty days. After such a stiff climb, I was now exceedingly thirsty, but again I got no sympathy from my fellow pilgrims. Yet God, in his great goodness, moved the Gray Friars to take pity on me. They gave me something to drink and made me comfortable; and all the while my own countrymen remained indifferent.

All this while I was gradually becoming more strongly rooted in the love of our Lord and found myself more ready to face the shame and criticism I suffered for his sake wherever I went; this was because of the grace God gave me in my weeping, sobbing, and crying out loud, a grace that I could never escape when it pleased God to send it. Invariably I discovered that my feelings turned out to be true, and all those promises God had made to me before I left England, and at other times besides, came true just as I had expected. As a consequence, I grew more confident in continuing to receive such messages and conversations, and more bold in seeking their occasion.

When I came down safely from this mountain, all according to God's will, I went on the place where Saint John the Baptist was born. And a little later I saw Bethany, the home of Mary and Martha, and I saw the grave where Lazarus was buried and from which he had been raised from death to life again. And I also visited the chapel where our blessed Lord appeared to his blessed mother before all the others on Easter Day.[56] And I stood on the spot where Mary Magdalene was when Christ said to her in the garden, "Mary, why are you weeping?" And there are so many other places that I saw, more than I can write about here; for I spent three whole weeks in Jerusalem and in the surrounding places. And I experienced great devotion all the time I was in that holy land.

The friars at the Church of the Holy Sepulchre were especially welcoming toward me. They gave me a great number of important relics. They even pressed me to stay on with them, had I wanted to do so, such was their belief in me. The Saracens too made a fuss over me, accompanying and escort-

---

[56] The Chapel of the Apparition is situated in the Church of the Holy Sepulchre to which Margery must have returned. The ancient tradition that Christ's first appearance was to his mother is summed up by Saint Ignatius in the Exercises at the beginning of the Fourth Week: "Although this is not mentioned in scripture, still it is considered as mentioned when it says that he appeared to many others, for scripture would have us use our common sense, since it says, 'Are you also without any understanding?' "

ing me wherever I wanted to go.[57] Indeed, my experience of
the local people was that they were good, gentle folk, in sharp
contrast to my own countrymen.

When I finally came to leave Jerusalem and had arrived at
Ramla, which is halfway to the port of Jaffa, I wanted to
return to Jerusalem once more. I recalled the great grace and
spiritual consolations I had enjoyed there; and equally I had a
wish to gain more forgiveness. But then our Lord told me that
I must go to Rome, and afterward I must go home to England.

He reassured me, saying: "Daughter, whenever you recall
in word or thought your experiences, saying, 'Blessed be all
those Holy Places in Jerusalem where Christ suffered bitter
pain and passion,' you shall enjoy the same pardon as if you
were there in person witnessing it all again with your very
own eyes; and it will be exactly the same for everyone else
you chose to name."

We sailed back for Venice and on the voyage very many of
our party felt seasick, so that we began to grow anxious
whether they would survive. Yet all the while our Lord told
me, "Do not fear, daughter, no one will die on this ship that
also carries you."

And so it turned out true, just as my feelings had led me to
hope: Our Lord brought us all safe and sound to Venice. Yet
there, once again, my fellow countrymen deserted me. Off
they went without me, and I was left all alone. Some even
said to my face they would not keep company with me, not
even for a hundred pounds.

And when they had left me, our Lord Jesus Christ, who is
always at hand in the hour of need especially with those who
trust his mercy, spoke these words of comfort: "Do not be
afraid, daughter, because I will provide for you very well and
bring you to Rome in safety and see that you arrive home in
England without any villain molesting you. As I told you

[57] Poor Margery is giving herself a false importance: The local Moslems insisted on escorting pilgrims wherever they went—and charged their fee for the service.

before when you were in England, I would like you to dress yourself in white."

This announcement made me very unhappy and made me full of doubts, so that I boldly replied within myself: "If this is truly the spirit of God speaking in my soul, which I am able to verify by taking advice from the Church, then I will do as you ask me. If you bring me in safety to Rome, even if all the world mocks me, I shall wear white for love of you."

"Set out on your way, daughter, in the name of Jesus, for I am truly the spirit of God; I shall help you with your every need, I shall go with you and support you in every place you come to. Never mistrust me; you never found me misleading you, for I have never bidden you do anything that is not to God's honor and profit to your soul if you should carry it out; believe me, I shall pour great grace into you."

At that very moment I happened to glance up and caught sight of a wretched man sitting beside the road; his back was badly deformed by a great hump. All his clothes appeared to be patched, and I guessed he was about fifty. I went over to him and asked, "Good sir, what is the matter with your back?"

"It was deformed by an illness I suffered," came his reply.

Then I asked him his name and where he came from. He told me that he was called Richard and that he came from Ireland. Then I recalled my confessor the anchorite's words, as I recorded earlier, who had told me in England, "Daughter, when your companions have left you by yourself, our Lord will send you a man with a hunchback and he will escort you wherever you want to go."

So my heart was lifted and I spoke to him with great cheer: "Good Richard, will you be my guide as far as Rome? I will pay you well."

But his answer was gloomy: "No thank you, madam. I know very well that your own fellow countrymen have left you, but it would be very difficult for me to escort you. They would have been well armed, with bows and arrows and the like, so as to defend themselves—and you too, if you had still been in their number. But now then, as for myself, all I have for a weapon is a cloak full of patches. I go in fear and dread of being robbed by some enemy; and at the first sight of you, they would snatch you away and rape you. I would not dare become your escort—not even if you gave me a hundred pounds! I wouldn't want you to be ruined because of me . . ."

So I tried to cheer him up by saying: "Richard, you mustn't be afraid. God will look after both of us in perfect safety. And besides, I have two nobles to give you for all your pains."

This did the trick and he agreed to become my guide and companion for the journey.

Now soon after we set out upon our way, two Gray Friars came along, and there was a woman with them; they were also on their way back from Jerusalem. The woman led an ass that had a chest strapped upon its back which contained, as I presently learned, a statue of our Lord.

Then Richard had an idea: "Why don't you go along with these two Carmelites and the woman? You would be far safer with them. And I can meet up with you each morning and evening to make sure you are all right. That way I can get on with my game of begging my way along the road."

I agreed to this idea and joined company with the two Franciscans and the woman. No one in the party could understand a word that I spoke, but even so they shared their food with me every day and, as for lodgings, they insisted that I be cared for somewhat better than themselves. As a result, I felt more than usually obliged to pray for them. And as for Richard of the hunched back, I saw him regularly each morning and evening when he kept me cheerful company just as he had promised.

Now the woman who had the statue of our Lord in her chest would take it out whenever we entered any town of consequence. Then she would place it in the lap of well-to-do ladies who would dress it in fine shirts and kiss it just as if it had really been God himself. At the sight of their worship and devotion, I was overcome with sweet consolation and delightful meditations, which resulted in my bursting out into tears and loud cries again. What moved me most was that before, when I was in England, I had meditated deeply on the birth and childhood of Christ; so that now I could only thank God inasmuch as these people had as much faith as I in what I could see with my very eyes, while before I had seen it only inwardly.

When these kind women saw me weep and sob and cry out loud, so powerfully that I seemed at times to be overwhelmed, they would find me a comfortable, soft bed and lay me there; and they would comfort me as best they knew, all for love of our Lord. Blessed be his name!

31

efore I set out on pilgrimage from England, our Lord had bidden me to have a ring made and on it the words *Jesus est amor meus* inscribed. I thought so much of this ring that it was virtually priceless; I know I would never have parted with it, not even for a thousand pounds, and so I gave a great deal of thought about how to keep it safe on my travels. It was not merely that it had been made at God's bidding, but also the fact that I wore it to please him alone. And by coincidence, I had just decided

never again to wear a ring when God made his desire known
to me.

I happened to be staying the night in the home of a generous and hospitable man. Many of his neighbors came to meet
me, as word had gone through the village of my reputation
for perfection and holiness; and so to please them, I showed
them the cord I had purchased giving the measurements of
our Lord's tomb. They examined this very devoutly, and, being grateful for seeing it, they thanked me warmly. Later on, I
went up to my bedroom where I hung my ring beside my bed
on the purse-string that I normally wore about my neck. The
following morning, when I came to look for my ring it was
missing—it was nowhere to be found. This upset me greatly,
and at once I complained to the good wife of the household in
this manner: "Madam, my precious wedding ring—I call it
my Jesus ring—is gone!"

The good wife understood at once what I meant and asked
me to pray for her. At the same time, her expression immediately changed and she began to look guilty. So, taking a candle, I began to look all around my bed where I had slept the
night, while the good wife of the house grabbed a second
candle and busied herself in similar fashion. And at length I
found the ring on the floorboards; and I was able to break the
news to the good wife with great relief. Then, at my suggestion, the good wife begged my forgiveness: "Good Christian,
pray for me!"

Soon after this incident, I traveled on to Assisi. There I
happened to meet an English Franciscan whom I knew had
considerable reputation as a scholar. I was able to talk to him
at some length and tell him about my way of life, my inner
feelings, my revelations, and the grace that God worked in
my soul with his holy inspirations and sublime contemplations; and, above all, how our Lord himself would seem to
converse with me in my soul. This distinguished scholar declared that I owed God a very great deal; he insisted that he
had never heard of anyone alive in the whole world who was

on such homely terms with God, loving and talking directly to him, as I was. I could only thank God for all his gifts; no merit on my side deserved his goodness.

It was while I was staying there that I saw in the lower church of Assisi our Lady's headscarf which she herself wore here on earth; it was surrounded by many lighted candles and I was moved to devotion. I wept, I sobbed, I cried with a great many tears and an abundance of holy thoughts. I was also present there on Lammas Day[58] when the great pardon of plenary remission may be gained, so that I was able to obtain grace and mercy and forgiveness not only for myself but for all my friends and my enemies and the souls in Purgatory.

There I saw a lady who had come from Rome to gain the indulgence. Her name was Margaret Florentine; she was accompanied by many knights of Rhodes, many gentlewomen; but my eye was especially taken by her beautifully turned-out horses.

Seizing the moment, Richard of the hunched back went across to her and asked if I might return to Rome with her, and himself also; he explained that in this way, we would be safe from thieves. It must have been God's will, for at once this gracious lady received us as one of her party and agreed that we could accompany them to Rome.

When we arrived in Rome, my former pilgrim companions who had turned me out of their company had already arrived. When they heard tell that a woman answering my description had reached the city, they were astonished to learn that I had got there safely.

And then I went and bought my white clothes, so that now I was dressed all over in white just as I had been bidden to do years before: What had been revealed in my soul then was now fulfilled to the letter.

---

[58] Loaf Mass Day or August 1, when traditionally in the Middle Ages the first corn was made into a loaf and consecrated at the first mass in thanksgiving for harvest.

The Portinuncula Indulgence, associated with Saint Francis, was named after the little village two miles outside Assisi where the saint had his first call to serve Christ.

Then I was directed to the hospital of Saint Thomas of Canterbury in Rome[59] and there I stayed. Each Sunday I received holy Communion with great tears, violent sobbing, and loud cries; yet I was held in high esteem by the dear master of the hospital and by all his brethren. But then, through the workings of my spiritual enemy, there came a priest who was held to be a holy man in the hospital (as well as other places in Rome); he had been one of my pilgrim company and was also a fellow Englishman. Holy he may have been, but he succeeded in saying such terrible and slanderous things of me that I was thrown out of the hospital and, as a result, was deprived of both confession and my weekly Communion there.

32

hen I realized how alone I was, thrown out of the company of these good men, I was deeply miserable. Worst of all was the fact that, having no confessor, I could no longer go to confession whenever I wished. So, with much weeping and many tears, I prayed to our Lord that in his mercy he would provide for me, but solely in a way that pleased him.

Presently, I summoned Richard of the hunched back and asked him to go across to the church opposite the hospital on an errand. I told him to inform the priest of my way of life

[59] The hospice for English pilgrims had been founded some ten years before Margery was born; it is now the English College, the Roman seminary for aspiring English bishops.

and what trouble I was in, that I was constantly in tears since I might be neither shriven nor receive Communion; and to assure him that I had compunction and contrition for my sins. And so Richard went to tell the priest all about me: how our Lord gave me contrition and compunction to the accompaniment of many tears and especially how dearly I wanted to receive Communion regularly every Sunday, yet knew no priest who might hear my confession. Convinced by Richard's account of my genuine compunction and contrition, the priest said that he would be perfectly satisfied if I came in the name of Jesus and simply said my *confiteor* to him. (He was unable to hear my full confession since he himself could not understand English.) He would then be happy to give me Communion with his own hands.

But then our Lord sent Saint John the Evangelist to hear my confession: I said *benedicite* and he replied *Domine*. Although I experienced this in my soul, seeing and hearing him with my inner understanding, yet it was just as if I was confessing to another priest face to face. I told him all my sins and all my troubles, with many a sad tear, and he listened to me gently and kindly. And finally he gave me a penance for my transgressions and absolved me from my sins with sweet and humble words. As I heard them, my trust in our Lord's mercy was greatly strengthened; then Saint John told me that I could receive the sacrament at the altar, in the name of Jesus. And I saw him no more.

When he had gone, I prayed fervently throughout the whole mass, saying, "Lord, to show me that you are not angry with me, give me a well of tears so that I may receive your precious body with every kind of tears of devotion in your honor as well as to increase my own merit; for you are my only joy, Lord, and my only bliss, my comfort and all the treasure I have in this world, for I would have no other worldly joy, but only you. And therefore, my dearest Lord and my God, never leave me."

Then our blessed Lord Christ Jesus answered me in my

soul, saying, "My beloved daughter, I swear by my high majesty that I will never leave you. And remember, daughter, the
more shame, contempt, and rebuke you suffer for love of me,
the more I love you. I behave like a man who is deeply in love
with his own wife; the more other men envy her, the more
beautifully he will dress her, if only to spite them. I will behave in the same way with you. In everything you do, daughter, you cannot please God more than by believing that he
loves you. For if it were possible for me to weep with you,
daughter, I would weep with you, since I feel so deeply for
you. A time will come when you will be only too grateful, for
you will be living proof of that saying: 'Happy the man who
sits in his chair of happiness to tell of his chair of woes.' And
this will happen to you, daughter, and all your tears and sorrow shall turn to joy and bliss which will never pass."

33

n another occasion when I was in Rome, I
attended mass in the church of Saint John
Lateran. And as I heard mass, it seemed to me
that the priest who was saying it was a good and devout man.
I felt strongly moved in spirit to speak with him, so I told my
Broken Back to ask the priest if he would see me. But since
the priest did not speak English, he was unable to understand
anything I wanted to tell him. Equally, as the only tongue I
spoke was English, we had to communicate through an inter-

preter. And he was able to tell us each what the other was saying.

But then I begged the priest to pray, in the name of Jesus, to the blessed Trinity, to our Lady, and to all the holy saints in heaven that he would come to understand my language and all I had to say, through the grace of God. And I urged him also to ask others he knew who loved our Lord to petition the same gift of grace.

The priest, German by birth, was a good man, and a capable and learned scholar as well. He was in high standing because he held one of the most important offices of any priest in Rome.

Wanting to please God, he took my advice; he prayed daily as devoutly as he could, and he also persuaded others devoted to our Lord to pray with the same intention. They prayed like this for thirteen consecutive days. And then the priest came back to me to see if their prayers had been answered. He understood exactly everything I had to say to him in English, and I could understand all that he said. But he was totally unable to understand the English that others spoke; even though they might be saying the selfsame words as mine, he never understood unless it was myself who was speaking.

I made my general confession to this priest, telling him, as near as I could remember, everything from my early childhood right up to that same hour; and I received my penance with great joy. After confession I went on to tell him the secrets of my revelations and about my lofty contemplations: how I often thought of his Passion and that sometimes, when God gave me compassion, it was frequently so great that I could hardly bear it and I would fall down; and how, at such times, I would weep bitterly, have violent sobbings and cry out so loudly and horribly as to make people afraid and scared of me, thinking that I had an illness or that a spirit troubled me or that I was nothing but a shamming hypocrite, good at deceiving myself.

This priest had great faith that it was God working in me;

and if ever he was uncertain, our Lord, speaking through me, would send him signs of his own failings and mistaken behavior—all of which was known only to himself, but which our Lord revealed to me, telling me to pass it on. By this means, he knew full well that my feelings were genuine.

From then on, the priest would always welcome me with great courtesy and deference; I felt as if he might have been my own mother or a sister, for he promised that he would always support me against my enemies. And he stood by his word all the time I was in Rome; and in consequence, he had to put up with a good deal of hurtful gossip and much other trouble besides. And he even resigned the office he held in order to support me in my sobbing and loud crying; what a contrast to my English compatriots who, not content with deserting me, continued their animosity toward me. They upset me at every opportunity, insisting that I must never sob or cry out loud. They were incapable of believing that I was unable to help myself in the matter; instead they spoke out continually against me and the good man who had now become my ally.

My priest friend was so struck by my sobbing and crying out loud—it was particularly public on Sundays when I received Communion in a crowded church—that he determined to prove whether or not it was a gift of God, as I maintained, or if I was merely shamming, as my enemies said. One Sunday he arranged to take me to a church when the masses had all finished. We were alone there save for one other priest who was about to say mass. When I was just about to receive Communion, I suddenly burst into tears and cried out so loudly that my priest was astonished. He was sure that it was the loudest shriek he had ever heard, he told me. And he declared that he was now convinced that it was indeed the workings of the Holy Spirit. He felt it impossible to believe I could feign such behavior.

After this he was never again embarrassed to take my side and speak up for me. Inevitably, my detractors then turned

on him; but he said he was content to suffer such things in
God's good cause. And indeed many people in Rome began to
look up to him as a result; and they began to invite me out to
meals where they made me very welcome, always begging me
to pray for them.

The English group remained stubborn as ever, encouraged
by one particular priest in their company. He stirred up many
people against me by spreading false and evil gossip; he was
particularly incensed by my white clothing which, he pointed
out, others more holy than myself did not wear. But the real
reason for his hatred of me was that I refused to be bound by
him any more. I knew in my soul that it would be fatal to let
him have any further influence over me.

34

When this good German priest had been
my confessor for only a short time, I
began to suspect that my enemy, the
English priest, had been talking to him about me. This was
because one day he asked me outright if I was willing to obey
him or not.

I replied simply, "Yes, sir."

"I mean will you do exactly as I say?"

"Very willingly, sir."

"Then I instruct you to leave aside your white dress and
wear black clothes instead."

I did just as he bade me, feeling confident that I was pleasing God by my obedience in the matter. But then it was the turn of the women of Rome to torment me: They wanted to know if a highwayman had stolen my clothes. I told them simply, no.

Some little while later when I was still visiting other Holy Places, I came face to face with my enemy, the English priest. He was unable to conceal his delight that I had abandoned my white dress, and said at once: "I am glad to see you going about in black again. Just like your old self."

I saw what he was getting at and told him, "Sir, our Lord would not be offended if I were to wear white; in fact he wants me to dress that way."

But the priest retorted, "Now I know you have a devil inside you, I can hear him speaking to me loud and clear."

"Ah, please, kind sir, drive him out of me, for God knows how much I want to do my best to please him as much as possible."

At this, the priest lost his temper and poured out a great tirade against me.

When he was done, I said, "Sir, I hope and trust I have no devil inside me. If I did, I suspect he would make me very angry with you. But I have to confess to you that I don't think there's anything you could do that would make me the least bit cross." At this he looked crestfallen and slunk away.

Then I knew our Lord was telling me: "My daughter, take no notice of anything he says to you. If he were to trot off on pilgrimage to Jerusalem once every year, I still would not care for him. Every time he opens his mouth against you, he speaks against me; for I am in you, and you are in me. It is true that I have to put up with many hurtful words, but then I have always told you that I would be crucified in you again by many a sharp word; for you will be slain in one way only, by suffering all these sharp words. As for this priest who is your enemy, he is nothing more than a hypocrite."

When I was staying in Rome, my good confessor also ordered me under holy obedience, but partly as a penance, to

look after a poor woman who was living there. I cared for her
for six whole weeks, looking after her as well as if she were
our Lady herself. She had no bed of her own, and her only
covering at night was a tattered cloak. She was covered with
vermin which gave her great discomfort. I fetched fresh water
for her and also brought her firewood to keep her warm; I
was able to beg meat for her and even a little wine. When this
turned out to be sour, I would drink that myself, keeping any
good wine for the old woman.

35

n November, on the feast of the dedication of Saint
John Lateran, while I attended mass at the Church of
the Holy Apostles in the holy city, the Father of
Heaven spoke to me: "Daughter, I am well pleased with you.
For you firmly believe in all the sacraments of Holy Church
and all that is involved in them; but I am especially pleased
that you believe so firmly in the manhood of my own Son and
that you have such tender compassion for his bitter Passion.

"Daughter," the Father continued his discourse, "it is my
will that you be united, indeed married, to my Godhead. To
you I will reveal my most secret counsels; and with me you
shall live without end."

I was so awestruck at this that I fell silent in my soul: I
feared the Godhead with a reverent dread. Never before had
I had any such discourse with the Godhead; for all my love
and affections had been fixed upon the manhood of Christ.

Him I knew somewhat: From him I would not be parted, not for anything.

My feelings for the manhood of Christ were so intense that sometimes if I saw a mother carrying her child along a street in Rome, once I realized it was a boy that she carried in her arms, I would cry out with a great roar and weep aloud, just as if I were looking at the Christ child himself. If I could have had my way, I would have taken those baby boys there and then from their mothers' arms so as to kiss them in place of Christ. And when I saw a handsome man, it would cause me great pain to look directly at him: I would half wonder whether he were not the same who was both God and man. And since handsome men were frequently to be seen in the streets of Rome, I would go about weeping and sobbing bitterly. But although people were puzzled at my behavior, they never guessed the true reason for it.

Perhaps it was not very surprising then that I fell silent when the Father told me I was to be wedded to the Godhead. But now the Second Person, Christ Jesus, whose manhood I so loved, said to me: "What have you to say to my Father, Margery,[60] about these words he is speaking to you? Are you not pleased for this to happen?"

Again I was incapable of answering the Second Person. All I could do was to weep so much that I was amazed myself; all I wanted was to continue having him to myself and never be separated from him. And so the Second Person of the Trinity answered his Father for me, saying, "Father, you must forgive her, she is still young in wisdom and does not know how to answer for herself."

And then the Father, taking me by the hand, as it were in my soul's depths, led me before the Son and the Holy Spirit; and there were present also the Mother of Jesus, and all twelve apostles, and Saint Katherine and Saint Margaret and numerous other saints as well as holy virgins and a multitude

---

[60] This is the first time that Margery records her Christian name being used in place of the more formal "my daughter."

of angels. And the Father spoke to my soul, saying: "I take you, Margery, for my wedded wife, for fairer, for fouler, for richer, for poorer, so that you will always be ready and compliant to all that I bid you. And, daughter, never was there any child more ready to please its mother than I shall be toward you—both in weal and woe, I shall be there to comfort you. To all this I give you my word."[61]

And then the Mother of God and all the saints who were spiritually present to me prayed that we might have great joy together. While I thanked God with utmost devotion and many tears for this comfort he gave my soul, at the same time I judged myself utterly unworthy of any such grace; yet I was overwhelmed with many consolations in both soul and body. Sometimes, for instance, I would smell a scent so sweet that it seemed to surpass any earthly sweetness I had ever known before. Yet this sweetness was indescribable, except to say that I felt I could have lived on that alone should it have lasted.

At other times, I would hear with my own ears tunes and melodies that were so loud and real to me that I would be unable to hear what people were saying unless they raised their voices to me. These melodies were my daily experience over a period of some twenty-five years before this book came to be written. They would occur above all when I was at my prayers; I heard them many times while I was in Rome, just as clearly as when I had been in England.

With my own eyes I would see white things flying all about me on every side, as thick as those specks you see in a sunbeam. I found their delicacy a delight and a comfort to me; the brighter the sun shone, the more clearly I could see them. These, too, I saw many times and in many different places, in church as well as at home, when I sat at a meal or when I was at prayer; now outdoors when I was walking in the fields or even in a busy town, walking or sitting I would still see them.

---

[61] Saint Teresa of Avila's account of her own mystical marriage (150 years later) is somewhat similar; but clearly Margery's memory of her own marriage vows has colored her account.

I was frequently afraid of what they might be, for I would catch sight of them at night and in the daytime. But my fears were stilled by our Lord saying, "This is a sign, daughter, in which you must believe that God speaks to you. For where God is, there is heaven; and wherever God is, there are many angels. So God is in you, and you in God. You have no need to fear these signs, for they tell of the many angels that surround you. And they are there to keep you day and night, so that no devil may have power over you, no evil man harm you."

After this comfort, whenever I saw them coming I would repeat the words: *"Benedictus qui venit in nomine Domine."*

Our Lord gave me a further sign that lasted some sixteen years, growing stronger all this time, and that was a flame of fire. Wonderfully warm, delightful, and comforting, it never grew less but always more apparent: Even in the coldest weather I could feel the heat burning in my breast and especially in my heart—it was just like someone reaching out and feeling the warmth of a good log fire.

Once again, I was nervous when first I felt this fire of love burning in my breast; but our Lord answered me in my mind, saying: "Daughter, do not be afraid, for this is the heat of the Holy Spirit; and it will burn away all your sins, for the fire of love quenches all sins. And by this sign, you will know that the Holy Spirit is in you. You are familiar with my saying that where the Holy Spirit is, there also is the Father; where the Father is, there is the Son. And so, truly within your soul, you have the Holy Trinity. This is why you already love me so well; yet you shall have greater reason to love me—you shall hear what you have never heard, see what you never saw, feel what you have never felt before.

"Daughter, you may trust in the love of God as surely as God is God. Your soul may be more sure of the love of God than of your own body; for your soul will depart from your body, but God shall never part from your soul. Together they are one without end. And so, daughter, you have reason to be merry as much as any lady in the whole wide world. If only you knew, daughter, how much you please me when you willingly allow me to speak in you, you would never do otherwise. For this way of life is holy, and your time could never be better spent. Attending to me like this is far better than your wearing a coat of mail in penance, or a hair shirt, or fasting on bread and water. And if you were to say a thousand *Paternosters* every single day, you could never please me as much as when you are silent and allow me to speak in the still ground of your soul."

36

asting, daughter, is good for those who are only beginners, as well as penance in moderation, especially when advised or enjoined upon them by their confessor. And to say the rosary regularly is equally good for those who can do no better. This is not perfect; yet it is a good way along the road to perfection. For I tell you, daughter, those who go in for much fasting and performing great penance want it to be thought that theirs is the very highest way of life; so also those who devote themselves to many devotions would have it said that theirs is the best way; and those who give alms with abundant generosity would also like that to be considered the best.

"How often have I told you, daughter, that meditation, weeping, and high contemplation is the best manner of life on this earth. More merit in heaven will be yours for a single year of thoughtful meditation than a hundred years of mouthing vocal prayer. But you will not listen but carry on endlessly telling your beads, not caring whether I like it or no. But I am never displeased whether you think, speak mentally, or speak out loud: I am always pleased with you, whatever you do.

"If I were a man again and walked upon the earth, just as I did before I died on the cross, I would never disown you as so many do. For I would take your hand in public and greet you so warmly that everyone would see how dearly I loved you.

"For it is only right and proper that a wife be on homely terms with her husband. Be he ever so great a lord and she so poor a woman when they were wed, yet now they must lie together and take their rest side by side in joy and peace. It must be just like that between you and me, for I have no regard for what you have been or what you would be: I have told you many times over, I have clean forgotten you all your sins.⁶²

"Therefore I must be intimate with you and lie in bed with you. And for your part, daughter, you want to see me so very much. And so you shall: Be bold when you lie in bed, treat me just like your husband, for we are wedded. Take me as your dear darling, as your sweet son; I want to be loved as a son should be loved by his mother; and I want you to love me, daughter, as a devoted wife will love her husband. So be bold, take me in the arms of your soul and kiss my mouth, my head, and my feet as lovingly as you wish. And as often as you think of me or would do any good deed for me, you shall have the same reward in heaven as if you did the same for my own precious body in heaven. I ask nothing else from you than your heart; that you should love me as I love you; remember that my love is always waiting for you."

I gave our Lord Jesus Christ thanks and praised him for

---

⁶² Forgotten (sic) rather than forgiven gives an original insight into Christ's attitude to the repenting sinner.

the high grace and mercy which he showed me, unworthy wretch that I am.

I also experienced a variety of sounds that were signs given to reassure me. For example, there was the kind of noise a pair of bellows make that seemed to blow directly into my ear. At first this alarmed me, but then I was bidden within my soul that I should have no fear, for this was but the sound of the Holy Spirit. And then our Lord changed this sound into the cooing of a dove; and later he turned it into the song of a robin redbreast, who would often sing very merrily in my right ear. And after this particular sign, I would experience much grace. Signs such as these had been my common experience for some twenty-five years before this book came to be written.

Our Lord explained such signs, saying to me: "These are but signals that I love you. You are just like a mother, to me and to the whole world, because of the great charity that is in you. It is I that put this charity within your soul, and great will be your reward in heaven."

37

aughter, you obey my will and cling fast to me like the skin of a stockfish sticks to your hand when you have boiled it tender; I know full well you will never forsake me for any shame a man can inflict upon you.

"And even if, you tell yourself, I were to stand and confront you bodily to tell you that you should never have my love, never come to heaven, never again see my face, you declare that you would never leave me on earth, not love me any the less, nor cease to try to please me; even were you to lie in hell without end, you cannot do without my love on earth nor accept any comfort save me alone, that is myself who is your God, your only joy and bliss.

"Therefore I say to you, my beloved daughter, it is impossible that a soul such as this could be damned or separated from me, for you have such great meekness and love toward me. And so, daughter, never be afraid; all those great promises I have made to you, to all your friends and confessors, will always stand until they are fulfilled in my good time. Have no doubt about that."

On another occasion during my stay in Rome—it was shortly before Christmas—our Lord Jesus Christ told me to go to my confessor and ask him to give me permission to wear white once more. My confessor was called Wenslawe; he was the German priest who, as I have already written, had ordered me under obedience not to wear such clothes. When I told him now that it was our Lord's will, he did not dare for an instant to say no. And that is how I came to wear white from that day onward.

Our Lord also told me that over Christmas I should stay at my host's home where I had stayed before. And so I went to the poor woman whom my confessor had told me to look after to tell her that I must now leave her. Naturally, the poor creature was very sad to hear this and bemoaned the thought of my going. I told her gently that it was God's will that I leave her, and this gave her some comfort.

Later during my time in Rome, our Lord told me to give away all the money I had and make myself poor for love of him. At once, I had a burning desire to please God by giving away whatever money I had as well as any money I had borrowed from my companion of the hunched back. But when Richard found out what I had done, given away his money as well as my own, he grew more and more excited and became very angry. He spoke his mind without mincing his words. But I answered him, "Richard, Richard, by God's grace we will come home to England perfectly safe and well. And if you come and meet me in Bristol during Whit week, I will pay you back in full, by God's grace. For I firmly trust that he, who told me to give this money away for love of him, will enable me to pay it all back."

And that is what he did, as I shall presently tell.

38

When I had given all my money away in this fashion, I literally had not a penny to call my own. One day I lay at prayer in Saint Marcellus's church in Rome; I was preoccupied and obsessed with plans of how to support myself, since I had not even a single silver piece.

But our Lord answered me in my mind, saying: "Daughter, you are not yet as poor as I was when I hung naked on the cross for love of you. You still have clothes that cover your body: I had none. You have often told other people to be poor for my sake; now you must follow your own advice.

"But do not fret, daughter, money will come your way. I have promised you before that I will never let you down. I shall ask my own mother to beg for you. I remember how many times you have begged for me as well as for my mother. And so don't be afraid. I have friends in every land; I shall make sure they look after you."

When our Lord had said all these comforting words to my soul, I thanked him for his sweet strength and told him that I completely trusted him that it would all turn out as he said. Immediately afterward, I got up from prayer and, going into the street outside, I happened to meet a man whom I knew at once I could trust. And we began to talk as we walked on our way, and spoke of good and holy things. I regaled him with many good stories and holy exhortations, until God visited him so that he began to weep tears of devotion and compunction. He said he found all this a comfort and a consolation. And finally he gave me a considerable sum of money, sufficient to keep me, to my great relief, a good while.

One night, as I slept, I seemed to have a vision of our Lady. It seemed to me that she sat at table with a great company of good people and she asked them for food for me. And then I remembered our Lord's promise; this seemed to fulfill the words he had spoken to me a little while before that he would ask his mother to beg for me.

Soon after this vision, I met Dame Margaret Florentine, the worthy lady who had brought me from Assisi to Rome. Neither of us could understand the other very well, except by using signs and gestures and a few simple words. As soon as she saw me, she said: *"Margerya in poverte?"*

I understood at once what she meant and answered: *"Yea, grand poverte, madame."*

At this she bade me eat with her every Sunday; and she made me sit at her own table — and above her. Moreover, she insisted on serving me from her dishes with her very own hands. As I sat there, all I could do was to weep bitterly and thank our Lord that I was strengthened and cared for in this way, out of love of him, by people who could not even understand a word I said.

When the meal was over, that kind lady would fill a hamper for me with leftovers that served to make a good stew, which kept me going for a couple of days. She would also fill a bottle with her excellent wine. And sometimes she would also slip me eight silver coins.

There was another man living in Rome whose name was
Marcelle; and he would ask me to meals twice a week. His
wife, who was about to have a baby, very much wanted me to
be the godmother when it was born. But sadly I did not stay
there long enough.

Lastly, there was another good lady who was single and
who gave me food each Wednesday. Other than this, when I
was not provided for, I begged food from door to door.

39

ne day, I was passing a poor woman's home
when she invited me in and sat me down by a
tiny, flickering fire. She offered me wine to
drink in a stone cup. She was suckling a little boy as she sat
there; but presently he got down and ran toward me, leaving
his mother still in her chair. She looked so full of sorrows and
sadness that I burst out into tears at the very sight: It struck
me that I had seen our Lady and her son at the time of his
Passion. I was overwhelmed with so many holy thoughts that
I could never tell half of them in any detail. I began to weep
and it went on for a long time. This led the poor woman, who
could not guess the reason for my tears, to feel sorry for me
and she begged me to stop.

Everywhere I went in Rome, there was much poverty
among the people. And our Lord Jesus Christ told me, "This
is a holy place." So that I thanked God mightily that I, like
them, was poor, so that I too might share merit with them.

Now there was a well-known lady in Rome who begged me to be godmother to her baby daughter, whom she named after Saint Bridget since she had known the saint herself when she was still alive.[63] I agreed and the baptism took place. Afterward, God gave me the grace to be loved and esteemed by many people in Rome; suddenly everyone wanted to know me.

Now when the master and brothers of the hospital of Saint Thomas—where before I had been refused, as I have already narrated—heard the news that I was loved and back in favor in the city, they asked me to stay with them once more. They insisted that I would be even more welcome than ever; and they apologized in full for having turned me out of their house. I thanked them for their charity and obliged them in their wish. When I arrived, they could not have welcomed me more warmly. So I was glad I had accepted their offer.

There too I came upon my former maidservant (she who should still have been in my service) living in the hospital in great wealth and luxury; she was now their cellarer and keeper of the wine. From time to time, I would go to her in all humility and beg food and drink. The girl gave it to me quite readily, sometimes even adding a groat as well. Eventually, I made my complaint to my former maidservant and told her how sad I was that we had fallen out with each other. I reminded her of the gossip and false stories that were circulating because we were apart; but she never showed the least inclination to be with me again.

At this time, I was able to meet a lady living in Rome who had formerly been maidservant to Saint Bridget. The difficulty was that I could not understand her language; but I succeeded in finding a man who acted as interpreter. Through him I asked her to tell me what kind of a person the saint had

---

[63] Married at 13 and the mother of eight children, Bridget had left her native Sweden for Rome in 1349 at the age of 46. Having established her Brigittine Order, she made it her home for the remainder of her life. A dominant influence in the life of the Church (she aided Saint Catherine of Siena to bring the papacy back to Rome), she died there in 1373, the year Margery was born.

been; and she replied that Saint Bridget had been kind and behaved gently toward everyone. She said she always had a laughing face. A man living in the hospital also remembered her. But he declared that he never thought of her as a saint or holy woman, since she was always homely and kind with everyone who approached her.

I visited the very room where Saint Bridget died, now the church of Santa Brigida, and there I heard a German priest preach about her revelations and her way of life. I also knelt on the stone that marks the spot where our Lord appeared to Saint Bridget (five days before her death) and told her which day she was going to die. I visited Saint Bridget's house on one of her feastdays; what was her bedroom, where she died, is now her chapel.

The weather at this time was terrible. Our Lord sent a succession of storms and such violent winds that people working in the fields and indeed anyone who had ventured out were compelled to seek shelter indoors for fear of the danger of being injured. I was sure that our Lord sent these signs to show that he wanted the saint's feastday to be kept holy, and that she should be venerated more than had been their custom.

Once, on the night before I had intended to do the Stations of the Roman churches, praying from one to the next, our Lord warned me as I lay in bed that I should not leave my lodgings; there was going to be a storm the next day, with much thunder and lightning. And so it turned out. There were terrible storms with thunder and lightning, torrential rain and squalls; the old men who had lived all their lives in Rome declared they had never seen anything like it. The lightning was so continuous and dazzling that it lit up the inside of people's homes; they had a very real fear that it was about to set them on fire and burn up every stick of furniture.

In their alarm they called on me to pray for them, confident that, my being God's servant, my prayers would enable them to be helped. I acted on their pleas and prayed to our Lord for mercy. He answered me in my soul: "Daughter, never fear, no weather or storm shall harm you and so do not lose faith in me, for I shall never deceive you."

It so pleased our merciful Lord Christ Jesus that he withdrew the storms, and the people were saved from every imaginable disaster.

40

oward the end of my stay in Rome, through the mercy and providence of our Lord Christ Jesus, I encountered a priest from England whom I had never met before, nor had he ever cast eyes on me. As soon as he arrived in Rome with a party of other pilgrims, he began at once to ask after me; he told everyone that having heard about me in England, he desired at once to speak to me, if only God would grant him such a grace. And so he began to plan his long journey, putting together additional money sufficient to cover any needs I might have, once he had discovered, God willing, my whereabouts in Rome. In due course his inquiries led him to the house where I was staying. From our first meeting, he behaved with great humility and courtesy, calling me "mother" and asking of my charity if I would be good enough to receive him like my own son. I answered him that since God welcomed him as a mother, I would gladly do the same.

We fell into a long and deep conversation about holy things, and I knew at once that here was a good man. I felt

safe disclosing to him my innermost thoughts, and I was able
to tell him some of the graces that God had worked in my
soul by the power of his Holy Spirit; I also told him a little
about my poverty. He responded at once to this, saying that
he would no longer allow me to beg from door to door but
invited me instead to eat regularly with him and his companions. He accepted that other men and women might equally
from time to time ask me to a meal out of charity and for their
spiritual benefit; and he agreed that I should accept their
invitations in our Lord's name. But these apart, he insisted
that I eat at his table each day. And beyond this, he gave me
sufficient money to cover my return journey to England. This
was how our Lord's promise that he had made a little time
before was fulfilled: "Money will be forthcoming." It certainly
was, thanks be to Almighty God.

Almost as soon as we had met, some of my former companions who had journeyed with me to Jerusalem took this good
priest aside and began complaining about me, saying that I
had been going to confession to a priest who could not speak
English and therefore was quite unable to understand anything I confessed. Whereupon this good priest, who wanted
nothing more than my peace of soul, asked me whether or not
my confessor could understand in detail what I had to say to
him.

"My good son, all I ask is that you invite him to dinner,
together with your friends; then if I too may be present, you
will soon learn the truth for yourself."

And so my confessor was invited to dinner. On the night in
question, we all sat together at table, myself included, hosted
by the priest and his friends; the priest, who was a ready
talker, was soon chatting away. But my German-speaking
confessor did not know a word of English, so for most of the
evening he sat in silence, looking somewhat glum. He could
only understand what was being said when they spoke in
Latin; and this they did on purpose to test his understanding
of English.

I felt very sorry for him, for I knew he was getting bored by all this performance; so wanting to cheer him up—but also knowing that I would prove God's point—I began talking in English to him myself. I thought I would tell him a bible story I remembered hearing in a sermon back in England; I was determined to avoid small talk.

Afterward, they quizzed him in Latin to find out how much he had understood and back came the very same words in Latin that I had just spoken in English; yet it was quite clear that he could neither utter nor understand one word of English except when I spoke to him. They were simply astounded: They realized that he understood everything I had said and that I could understand him, but that if anyone else in the room spoke English, he understood not a single word. Blessed be that God who enabled a foreigner to understand me, when my own countrymen had deserted me and refused to hear my confession until such time as I would leave off my tears and pious talk.

The truth is that the only time I wept was when God sent those tears, often so abundantly that I could hardly bear it. And the more I tried to resist them or avoid weeping, the more vividly came those same holy thoughts deep in my heart that were the source of my tears. I simply could not help myself. I would sob and cry out loud, completely against my will; many men and women witnessed it and could not help but be amazed by it all.

41

ometimes when I heard a sermon preached in German or any other foreign tongue, as the priest began to teach on God's laws, I would be struck by a sudden sorrow and my heart would grow heavy and complain that, although I wished to be fed some little crumb of spiritual understanding about my most trusted and mighty sovereign Lord and Beloved, I could not understand a word. Then Christ Jesus, with a melodious voice whose sweetness is beyond compare, would sound softly in my soul: "I shall preach to you and be your teacher, because you wish it, and I find your desire acceptable."

Then my soul was fed so delightfully by this sweet conversation with our Lord, and I was like a drunken man rolling now this way and now that. I was so filled with his love that I was overwhelmed by great weeping and sobbing as the unquenchable fire of love burned fiercely in my soul.

People would be amazed at my behavior and ask what ailed me; like someone who had lost her senses because she had been love-struck, I would cry out loud: "The Passion of Christ is killing me!"

Pious women, feeling sympathy for my sorrows and taken aback by my tears and shouts, loved me even more when they witnessed this. And so, not knowing my language but wishing to comfort me after such spiritual labor, they would beg me to come home with them, even drag me there, as if they could not bear to be parted from me.

By our Lord's grace I was shown great love and favor by very many people in Rome, religious and lay folk alike. Some religious approached those among my fellow English who still befriended me and declared: "This woman has sown good seed in Rome since first she came. What we mean is that by her public example she has shown people how to love God far better than they knew before."

One day, I visited the basilica of Santa Maria Maggiore; this is where Saint Jerome lies, buried here after his body was translated by a miracle from Bethlehem. So it is a very holy place, especially since Saint Lawrence is also buried nearby. As I prayed at this spot, I had an inner vision of Saint Jerome[64] in which he spoke to my soul these words: "Daughter, you are blessed when you weep, because grieving for people's sins will lead to saving many souls. So do not fear, daughter, for this is a singular and special gift from God— your own well of tears is something no one shall ever take away."[65]

These words of the saint gave great comfort to my soul. He also gave praise and thanks to God for the grace worked in my soul, saying that if it were not for such spiritual consolations, it would have been impossible for me to suffer patiently and without complaint all the shame of the unwanted attention caused by the grace that God showed within me.

---

[64] Saint Jerome was responsible for the incredible labor of translating the bible into a standard Latin text, known as the Vulgate. This fact may not have commended the saint to Margery's attention so much as the story of his three-year stay in Rome (in 382) when he gathered around himself a group of holy women, anxious to lead holy lives. Such a story, together with the apocryphal miraculous translation, may have been regaled to pilgrims by the local guides.

[65] In Chapter 18, when she visited Julian of Norwich, Margery was told of Saint Jerome's words that "human tears torment the devil even more than the pains of hell."

42

aster, or what is sometimes called the Pasch, had come and gone and so I and my companions were making plans to return to our native England. But we were greatly alarmed to hear countless rumors of thieves along our proposed route who not only stripped pilgrims of all their valuables but were sometimes known to kill them.

I prayed to our Lord, my eyes full of tears, telling him, "Christ Jesus, I place all my trust in you, and you have often promised me over and over again that no one in my traveling party would come to any harm. And neither was I ever deceived or let down by your promises as long as I continued to put all my faith and trust in you. So hear these prayers of your unworthy servant who trusts fully in your mercy, and grant that I and all my companions—without any hindrance to our bodies or goods—over our souls, Lord, I know they hold no power—may return home again to our native land in safety just as we came—and this was for love of you—and never let any of our enemies have power over us, Lord, if it please you. As it is your will, so be it."

For reply, our Lord Jesus put these words into my mind: "Fear not, daughter, you and everyone in your party will go on your way as safely as if you were still in Saint Peter's church."

Then I thanked God with all my heart and soul that I was now brave enough to set out according to his will. And at last it was time to take leave of all my friends in Rome. In particular I had to leave my confessor, who for love of God had stood up for me and helped me with such tenderness during the wicked quarrels stirred up by my envious enemies. It was miserable leaving him, as the tears flowing down both our cheeks bore witness. I fell on my knees before him to receive a last blessing. And thus we parted, the two of us whom charity had brought together as one; in that same love we trusted that we would meet again, when our Lord willed it, in that proper native land that would be ours forever once we have passed from this wretched world's exile.

Then our party set out for England. But we had gone only a short distance from Rome, when the English priest (whom I had welcomed as my own son) became so afraid of danger on the journey ahead that he told me, "Mother, I am terrified of being killed by evil men."

But I told him, "No, my son, you will make good progress day by day and journey safely home, by God's own grace."

My words were a great comfort to him, because he had the greatest confidence in how I felt within myself. Throughout the entire journey he treated me with such warmth and love that he could have been one of my very own sons.

We came at last to the town Middelburg (in Holland), and from there our party planned to take a ship the next day, which was a Sunday. Whereupon my good priest friend asked me, "Mother, will you yourself be sailing with your friends on this fine day?"

But I answered, "No, son, it is not my Lord's will that I should be getting home so soon."

So we stayed on, the good priest and myself and a few others from the same party that had traveled from Rome, until the following Saturday, while the majority set sail on Sunday as planned. On the Friday of that week, I went out into the fields for exercise together with some of my English friends. I did my best to teach them God's ways, for they were very prone to swear great oaths and they frequently broke his commandments. I spoke out very plainly to them about this.

But as I did so, our Lord Jesus Christ told me to get home as soon as possible, for a strong and dangerous storm was brewing. And so we hurried back together; sure enough, just I had been told, no sooner had we reached our lodging than the storm broke. Many times before, while we had been on our journey and crossing exposed plains, there had been great flashes of lightning with terrible thunderclaps so that I was terrified of being struck and killed on the spot—to say nothing of the torrential rain we had to endure, which always filled me with fear and trembling.

But then our Lord Jesus Christ would say to me, "Why are you afraid, since I am with you? I am quite capable of keeping you as safe here out in the open as in the most solid church in all the world."

Because of his words, I was never quite so terrified again, because I was able to trust in his mercy: Blessed may he be, who comforts me in every distress.

Later that day, an Englishman who happened to be in my hearing swore a great oath. As I heard what he said, it cut through me so that I began to weep and mourn and was plunged into misery. I could not help my tears and grief; how could I, since my brother was quite heedless of his offense against our Lord God Almighty?

43

arly the next day, my good priest friend (who was like a son to me) came to me and announced: "Mother, I have some great news! We have a fair wind today, God be thanked."

I prayed to our Lord at once, praising him for these good tidings and asking him of his mercy that the good wind and fair weather should last until we reached home in safety. My prayers were answered; and I felt in my soul that we should all go upon our way in the name of Jesus. But when the priest realized that I was set upon going, he suddenly declared: "Mother, there is not a proper ship in port, only a tiny fishing boat."

I answered him, "Son, God is as mighty in a little boat as in the biggest ship. I will sail in this boat, God willing."

And so we set sail, but almost at once the weather began to worsen and the sky grew dark. Then all together everyone aboard began to cry out loud and call upon God to be merciful by his grace; then those same storms ceased, and we were blessed by fair weather. And so we sailed on, right through the night, and again the next day, from first light until it was time for evensong; then we sighted land. And as soon as we came ashore, I fell to my knees and kissed the ground; I thanked God from the bottom of my heart for bringing us all home in safety.

I was by this time utterly penniless. I did not even have a

halfpenny in my purse. But it so happened that we met up with another group of pilgrims; I began to tell them one or two edifying stories and in return they offered me three half-pence. I was very pleased and glad of this for now I had some money with which to make an offering in honor of the Trinity once I reached Norwich. I had done the same as I set out from England all that time ago.[66]

So it was that when I arrived in Norwich I made my offering most gladly;[67] and having done so, I went with my companions to visit Master Richard Caister, whom I was glad to find alive and well. He was very pleased to see us, and took us straight into his house to offer us hospitality.

"Margery," he told me, "I am amazed that you can be so merry when you have had so much to put up with after traveling so far."

"Sir," I answered him, "that is because I have very good reason to be merry and happy in our Lord; it is he who has helped me and cared for me all this time and brought me home again safe and sound. Blessed and worshiped may he be!"

At this, we went on to talk of our Lord for a good while; and we all had a most cheerful meal together. When we had taken leave of Master Caister, I went to visit an anchorite, a Benedictine monk who had come to Norwich from abroad and now lived in Chapel-in-the-Fields.[68] He had a very considerable reputation for great perfection; and some time before this, he had shown very great kindness toward me. But there had been a good deal of evil talk against me, so that he had turned completely against me. I was determined to meet him again; either I would be humiliated by the encounter or

[66] Margery has been away from home for fully eighteen months: it is now May 1415.

[67] This was at the cathedral itself, which was dedicated to the Trinity. To the north of the high altar, there was a wall painting depicting the Trinity. Margery would have left her offering of three halfpence, the equivalent of the widow's mite, with the priest.

[68] Chapel-in-the-Fields was a collegiate hospital that had grown quite rapidly from an original donation of land in open fields to the southwest of Norwich (around 1250). The anchorite is named by Meech and Allen as Thomas Brackley, a Benedictine, who died two years later in 1417.

possibly, I felt, I might persuade him to become my friend once more.

It turned out that when we met he welcomed me home with the briefest words. He then went straight to the point and demanded to know what I had done with my child, which, he had learned, was conceived and born while I was abroad.

My answer was as straight as his questioning: "Sir, I have brought home the only child God gave me—as God is my witness, there is nothing I did while I was abroad that would have made me pregnant!"

But nothing I could say would convince him that I spoke the truth. In spite of this, because I still trusted him, I told him simply and humbly how it was our Lord's will that I should dress only in white. At this he said "God forbid" and added that, in his opinion, everyone would simply be amazed at such a sight. I replied, "Sir, that doesn't interest me; all I care about is to please God."

At this he seemed to change, because he invited me to come and see him again and be directed under him. And he mentioned the name of another chaplain, Sir Edward Hunt.[69] I said that I would find out whether God wanted such an arrangement or not; and at that I took my leave of him. But as I walked away, our Lord spoke to me in my soul, saying, "I do not want you to be directed by him." And accordingly, I sent back word of the answer I had received from God.

---

[69] Scholars now point out that it was this priest who witnessed Brackley's will, which is still extant.

44

efore wearing white once more, I wanted to be quite certain in my mind; and so I prayed to God, saying: "Lord, since I want to be certain that it is your own true will that I should wear white, send me a sure sign—make it pour down rain with thunder and lightning—provided that it does no harm or hindrance to any living thing. Then, sinner that I am, I will be sooner able to do your will."

At this our Lord answered me, utterly unworthy as I was: "Daughter, cease your doubting, you shall have your sign within three days."

And it happened exactly to the day. On the following Friday, while I still lay in bed, I saw great lightning flashes followed by massive rumblings of thunder; then there was a great cloudburst. And almost immediately, the storm passed away and the weather was fine once more. At this I firmly made up my mind to wear nothing but white clothes; my only problem was that I had neither gold nor silver to buy any material.

But our Lord spoke to my soul, saying, "I shall look after you."

A little later I went into Norwich to visit a very good man who I knew would always welcome me. And as we sat together exchanging holy stories between ourselves, our Lord kept prompting me in my soul: "Talk to him, talk to him."

And so I confided in this good friend of mine: "I only wish

to God, dear sir, that I could find someone kind enough to lend me two nobles until I had a chance to pay them back; then I would be able to buy myself some clothes."

He answered right away, "I would be very willing to do that. What kind of clothes do you want to wear?"

I told him, "Sir, I want to wear white, God willing."

Then this kind friend of mine went off and bought ample white material; and he had made for me a generous gown together with a matching hood, an overskirt, and a cloak. On the very next day, a Saturday, he brought me all these clothes toward evening. He gave them to me out of his love of God; and he showed me a good many other kindnesses, all for our Lord's love—may Christ Jesus himself be his true reward and have mercy on his soul and on all Christians as well.

The following Trinity Sunday, I went to Communion dressed all in white. Since that day I have suffered a great deal of contempt and frequently felt ashamed in different countries and in many cities and towns—yet I thank God for all of this.[70]

Shortly after, my husband came from Lynn to meet me in Norwich. He was eager to learn how I was and how I had fared on my journey; and so we returned home together to Lynn. It was shortly after my return home that I fell very ill. The sickness was so severe that I had to be anointed, since it was felt that I was in danger of dying. But I had always wanted, provided it was God's own will, to visit Santiago[71] before I died. I was willing to undergo even more shame out of love for him—just as he had promised would happen.

Then our Lord told me within my soul that it was not yet my time to die; but I could scarcely believe this, so great was

[70] If Margery went to the cathedral (whose dedication was to the Trinity) and took Communion dressed so remarkably in white, then it is not surprising that people noticed and many took offense. A flagellant sect from the Continent who also dressed all in white had been proscribed in England some fifteen years earlier. Yet even going to her parish church, Saint Margaret's, dressed so conspicuously, Margery must inevitably have raised the hackles of parishioners.

[71] Santiago di Compostela was the most famous and frequented pilgrimage during the Middle Ages; it was here that Saint James the Great was said to be buried. Estimates put the figure of pilgrims at around two million a year.

my pain. But very soon afterward, I was once again restored to good health.

As winter began to draw in, I became so cold I did not know what to do. I was very poor, with no money at all; indeed, I was in considerable debt. At the same time, because of wearing my white clothes, I had to put up with constant embarrassment and abuse. And it was the same when I cried out loud at the memory of our Lord's Passion; I cried out very loud indeed, something my fellow townsfolk had not heard before and so they were all the more surprised. For I had first begun to cry aloud like this in Jerusalem, as I have already described.

Many people declared that not a single saint in heaven had ever cried out like me; and therefore they argued that it must be a devil within me that made me cry out so. Encouraged by this reasoning, they went about openly repeating it and adding many more cruel lies besides. But I tried to take it all patiently for love of our Lord; I knew full well that the Jews had said far worse things of our Lord during his lifetime. And so I was content to take it all in my stride.

Others declared that I suffered from epilepsy; and it was true that when I twisted and turned violently from one side to another[72] I would turn quite blue and gray, just like the color of lead. Often people spat at me in fear of what they thought to be my illness. Others poured scorn on me, declaring that I howled just like a dog; they would curse me and say that I did nothing but harm to everyone. People who had been kind to me before and given me food and drink now turned their backs on me and told me never to come to their doorstep again. This was all because of the tales and lies they had heard about me.

When at length I judged it was time to go to Santiago, I went to find my best friends in Lynn. I told them my plans to go on pilgrimage to Santiago, providing I could get to-

[72] There is a footnote here written by the Carthusian annotator in red: "and so did Prior Norton in his excess."

gether sufficient money to make the journey, bearing in mind my poverty and my continuing debts. But they asked me, "Why ever did you give all your money away? Not only that but other people's money into the bargain? How on earth are you going to get enough together now even to pay off your debts?"

I told them simply, "Our Lord God will help me perfectly well. He has never let me down, in whatever country I have been in before, so I am not going to stop trusting him now."

And then, quite out of the blue, a kind man came up to me and offered me forty pence. I spent some of it to buy a fur-lined coat. Our Lord God was always telling me, "Daughter, don't dwell on saving up money, because I am here to provide for you. Fasten your mind on loving me and remember I am always with you; I promise you firmly, I shall go with you wherever you walk—I have told you this before."

And then again, a woman came to call on me. She was one of my good and reliable friends, and immediately she offered me seven marks to pray for her once I got to Santiago.[73] And so now I said good-bye to all my friends, for I meant to set out as soon as possible.

The stories in Lynn were rife about how many thieves there would be along the way. I began to believe them and went about in fear of being robbed and losing all my gold. But our Lord comforted me, saying, "Go on your way, daughter, in the name of Jesus. No thief on earth will have any power over you."

So I set off at last and reached Bristol on the Wednesday of Whitsuntide.[74] And here I met up with the man with the hunchback who had been my traveling companion in Rome. I had not seen him for two years, when I had borrowed from

[73] The cost of pilgrimage varied as to the style of the pilgrim. Some major churches in Europe displayed recommended tariffs for the guidance of would-be pilgrims. Margery's seven marks was a modest yet adequate amount.

[74] Margery is not interested in giving exact dates; the impression of a continuing narrative is therefore misleading. Meech and Allen point out that she left for Santiago two years after her return from Rome, that is, in the spring of 1417.

him and then given all my money away to the poor at God's bidding. As I have already said, I had promised when we were in Rome that I would meet him during Whitsuntide at Bristol to pay him back—and so that was why he had come, to get his money back.

And just as our Lord had promised me he would provide, sure enough, as I made my way to Bristol I was given so much money that I could easily afford to pay this man all the money I owed him. And thus I was able to discharge my debt to him—blessed be our Lord for making it possible.

At God's bidding, I stayed on in Bristol for six weeks, waiting all the while for a ship. In fact, there was not one English ship to be had that was ready to sail to Santiago; all were requisitioned for the king.[75]

Other pilgrims who were also waiting to sail from Bristol grew impatient and, wishing to speed their departure, went off from port to port. But in spite of their best efforts, they found little success and presently returned to Bristol. Meanwhile, I stayed where I was and fared the better.

For all this time that I stayed quietly in Bristol, heeding God's inner command, our merciful Lord Christ Jesus visited me with many holy meditations and countless high contemplations and many consolations. There too I received Communion each Sunday, when I was given many tears and violent sobbings as well as loud cries and shrill shriekings. As a result, many men and women were so taken aback at my behavior that they scorned me and despised me; they went so far as to curse me, heaping slanders at me and accusing me of saying words I had never once uttered.

But all I could do was weep on account of my many sins and pray to God for his mercy and seek his forgiveness. I would say to our Lord, "Lord, just as you said upon the cross,

[75] Henry V had fought and won his famous victory at Agincourt two years previously, in the autumn after Margery's return from Rome. Now he was intent on pressing home his advantage in France with an even greater invading army. He was to spend the next five years tramping through France, dying there at the age of 35.

for those who crucified you, 'Father, forgive them, for they know not what they do,' so, I beg you, forgive these people too all their false words and scorn, their hatred; as you will, yet I have deserved far worse and I accept all that comes my way."

45

hen the feast of Corpus Christi came,[76] the priests carried the sacrament around the streets of the town in solemn procession and with many candles; a large crowd followed, paying their due respect. As I followed along with this procession, I was overcome with tears and consolation. Many holy thoughts flooded through my heart, and as I meditated upon Christ's generosity in feeding us all with his own body, I could not keep back many bitter tears and violent sobs. And then, as we went along, a woman came up to me and said outright, "God give us all the grace to follow in the same footsteps as our Lord Jesus Christ."

Her words had such an effect upon me that I could hardly remain standing; it was as if they had cut right into my very mind and heart. I staggered into a nearby house to sit down and rest. And the woman asked if I was all right, but I gasped, "I die, I die . . ." And then I roared out loudly in such a way that the little crowd of people that had gathered

[76] Possibly June 12, 1417.

around to help me were utterly astonished. They could not tell what ailed me. Yet our Lord caused some of them to treat me with love and care for me tenderly. They pressed me to stay in their home and offered me something to eat and drink. And as I began to recover and speak out loud with our Lord, they took great joy and comfort.

One of their number was a man from Newcastle[77] called Thomas Marchal. After this first encounter, he began to invite me to eat with him simply to hear more of my conversation. He declared he was attracted and utterly moved by the good words that God put in my head as I spoke of contrition for our sins and of compunction. He told me he felt like a new man as he listened to my words of consolation and devotion for our Lord. And he confessed that now he too, both by night and during the day, was visited in his heart by our Lord's grace so that sometimes, if he were outside walking in the fields, he would weep bitterly for all his sins and transgressions so much so that he could no longer bear it and would fall down on his face. He confessed to me how he had been very careless and wayward throughout his life, but that he now repented bitterly—God be thanked. He said that he blessed the day he met me, for now his mind was firm that he would try to behave like a good man.

And then one day he told me, "Mother, here I have ten marks. Please take it as your own; it will help get you to Santiago, by God's grace. And whatever alms you tell me to give to any poor man or woman of your choice, I will always offer one penny for you and a second for myself."

Then at last our Lord was pleased to send a ship from Brittany to Bristol and it was preparing to set sail to Santiago. So my friend, Thomas Marchal, went and made arrangements with the master for both of us to take passage with him. But there was a wealthy Bristol man who objected to my boarding the vessel; he declared I was an unworthy woman. I spoke up for myself and confronted this rich man: "Sir, if you put me off this ship, my Lord Jesus will throw you out of heaven. I can tell you now, sir, our Lord Jesus has no time for a rich man unless at the same time he be a good and humble man."

I went on talking to him in this way, not stinting my words and showing no respect to him for his position. And presently our Lord spoke to me in my soul: "You shall have your way. You shall sail for Santiago as you plan."

But immediately after this confrontation, I was summoned to appear before the Bishop of Worcester, who was staying at his manor three miles outside Bristol.[78] I rose early on that day and went out to where I was told to go. But, after learning that the bishop was still in bed, I chanced to meet one of his most noteworthy men in the village; and we spoke comfortably of God. When we had been conversing like this for some time, he invited me to eat with him; and when we had finished our breakfast, it was he who brought me into the bishop's hall.

As soon as I entered the room, I could not help noticing how many of the bishop's retainers were fashionably dressed, their sleeves cut and shaped into points. I lifted my hand to bless myself as I saw all this. And so they asked me, "What in the devil's name is wrong with you?"

I answered, "Whose men are you?"

"We are the bishop's men," they replied.

To which I said, "Not at all, you look more like the devil's men."

They were annoyed at this and told me off; they began to shout at me but I took it all very meekly. And presently, when I grew serious and spoke out against sin in general and how

[78] Thomas Peverel, Bishop of Worcester 1407–1419, was a Suffolk man, which explains why he knew Margery's father. He had convicted Thomas Badby, the Lollard, of heresy, and handed him over to be burned seven years before, but the movement was still threatening church order. Worcester is a tidy step from Bristol; Margery had her meeting with the bishop in his country retreat at Henbury.

badly they behaved, they fell silent. And by the time it came
for me to leave them, they had quite warmed to all I had to
say—thanks be to God.

I went into the chapel to await the bishop's arrival; and
when he appeared, I knelt down and asked if he would tell me
why he had summoned me and what he wanted. I pointed out
that it was very inconvenient since I had my plans all ready to
make pilgrimage, by God's grace, to Santiago.

He answered, "Margery, I have not summoned you, for I
know you are the daughter of John Brunham of Lynn. Please
do not be cross with me, let us be friendly with each other
and relax; I would like you to eat with me today."

"Sir," I told him, "you must excuse me, for I have
promised a good man in the village that I would eat with
him."

But he insisted: "You shall both sit down and join me."

And I stayed with him until God sent a fair wind so that
we could sail. And I was made most welcome by both the
bishop and all his household. Later I went to the bishop for
confession, and then he asked me to pray for him that he
would die in God's loving grace. He told me that he had been
warned by a holy man that he was going to die within two
years. (And so indeed it turned out to be the case.) This was
why he was sad as he was talking to me, and why he came to
ask me to pray for him so he might die in charity.

At length I took my leave of him, and he gave me gold as
well as his blessing. And he told his household to see me to
my ship, adding that on my return from Santiago, I must
come back and see him again.

That was how I made ready to board my ship. But before
doing so, I prayed to God that he would guard and preserve
us all from his vengeance, from every storm and all perils of
the sea, so we might have a safe passage out and a safe return.
I had learned that if a storm blew up, the first thing the sailors
would do was to throw me into the sea. They were convinced
that such a storm could only be because of me. They told me

to my face that the ship was all the worse for my being aboard.

Therefore I said my prayers in this manner: "Almighty God, Christ Jesus, I beg you in your mercy: If you want to chastise me, spare me until I come back to England once more. On my return, treat me as you will."

Then our Lord granted me my petition, and so we set sail in the name of Jesus, going forth with my companions. God gave us fair wind and clement weather, so that we reached Santiago on the seventh day.[79]

Now, all of a sudden, the very people who had been so unpleasant in Bristol were very nice to me. We spent two weeks in Santiago, and there I experienced very great happiness both in body and in spirit. I knew much high consolation and I endured many loud cries as I brought to mind Christ's suffering, shedding many tears of compassion.

On the homeward passage, we reached Bristol in only five days. I decided not to stay there any length of time, for I very much wanted to see the Blood of Hailes.[80] While at the shrine, I was shriven and afterward had much loud crying and violent sobbing.

There were some religious men there who took me into their company and made me very welcome. I liked them, except for the fact that they swore a good deal of the time, terrible oaths that stung my ears. And when, in accordance with the gospel, I rebuked them for their words, they seemed very surprised. But some of them took it well, even going so far as to thank me—blessed be God in his goodness.

[79] It was now early July and Margery would be away for just under a month.

[80] The ancient Cistercian foundation of Hailes (1246) was halfway between Bristol and Stratford, very much on Margery's homeward route. The abbey possessed a crystal vial containing "the Blood of Christ," duly authenticated by Urban IV who, in 1264, had instituted the feast of Corpus Christi.

46

fter this I went on to Leicester with the good man, Thomas Marchal, who had paid my passage to Santiago and traveled with me there. In Leicester I entered a church where I saw a crucifix that was pitiable and really touching to look at; and as I gazed at it, my mind was taken over by the passion of our Lord, and then I began to melt and utterly dissolve in tears of pity and compassion. Such was the fire of love that burned up in my heart that I could no longer keep it a secret to myself. Whether I liked it or not, I was forced to break out in a loud voice, an astonishing cry, and I wept and sobbed so terribly that many men and women around me wondered what was going on.

After I had been so overcome, as I left the church, a man caught me by my sleeve and asked, "Woman, why are you weeping so bitterly?"

"Sir," I answered, "it is not for me to tell you."

Then I went with my good companion, Thomas Marchal, into town to find lodgings for the night, and there we ate a meal. And when we had finished, I asked Thomas Marchal to write a letter for me and send it to my husband, asking him to come and fetch me home. While this letter was being written, the innkeeper came rushing into my room and took away my bag. He ordered me to come downstairs quickly and talk to the mayor. And so I did as I was told. The mayor immediately asked me where I came from and whose daughter I was.

"Sir," I told him, "I am from Lynn in Norfolk. And I am the daughter of a good man from the same town, who was five times mayor of that worshipful borough and also an alderman for many years; and for my husband I have another good man, who is also a burgess of the same town of Lynn."

"All very well," declared the mayor. "Saint Katherine told the truth when she was asked about her kith and kin. As for yourself, you are a false whore, a lying Lollard, a deceiver come to lead people astray. Therefore I am going to lock you up."

I answered him without hesitation, "I am ready, sir, to go to prison for the love of God—just as ready as you are to go to church."

Then the mayor went at me with many a long-winded speech. He used all manner of truly evil and horrible words; yet I managed, by the grace of Jesus, to answer his every point. But finally, in spite of this, he ordered the jailer to lead me off to prison. But this man seemed at once to take pity on me; perhaps he was influenced by my tears. He told the mayor, "Sir, I have no place to put her, unless you want me to put her in with the men."

I was moved by the kindness of this man who had taken pity on me, and I prayed for the grace of mercy for him, as if for my very own soul. But I urged the mayor, "I beg you, sir, do not put me among the men, for I would keep my chastity and my marriage vows to my husband, as I am bound to do."

And then the jailer spoke up for me: "Sir, I will undertake to keep this woman in my own safekeeping until the time comes when you want to interview her again."

There was a man from Boston [a coastal town close to Lynn] who told the wife at the inn where I had been lodging, "Believe me, in Boston this woman is known to be a holy and blessed woman."

But the jailer had to take me away into his custody, and so

we went off to his home. He showed me into a fine, comfortable room but locked the door and told his wife to keep the key safe. All the same, he allowed me to go to church whenever I wished and he invited me to eat with him at his own table. All in all, he made me most welcome, due to his love of our Lord—may God almighty be thanked.

47

hen the Steward of Leicester, who was a most handsome man, sent to the jailer's wife for me. But since her husband was not at home she would not allow me to go, not at the bidding of any man, steward or no steward. When the jailer heard about this, he came and brought me before the steward himself.

As soon as he saw me, the steward spoke Latin to me; and there were quite a number of priests standing there to hear what I would say, as well as a crowd of other people also. So I said to the steward, "Please speak to me in English, I cannot understand what you are saying."

The steward answered, "Well, the trouble is that in English you have learned to tell lies all the time."

Then I said to him, "Sir, ask me whatever question you wish in English and, by the grace of my Lord Jesus Christ, I will answer you perfectly straightforwardly."

So he began to ask me not one but many questions. And I answered all of them with perfect reason, so that he failed to find any cause against me.

Then the steward led me by the hand and took me away to a private room. And he began to talk in a dirty and lewd way, so that it seemed to me that he wanted to overpower and rape me. I was very frightened and grew miserable and asked him for mercy. Finally I told him, "Sir, out of reverence for God, spare me, for I am a married woman. I belong to another man."

Then the steward blustered, "You'll tell me honestly whether you get these words from God or from the devil. Otherwise, you'll go straight to prison."

"Sir," I answered, "I am not afraid to go to prison for the sake of our Lord's love; he suffered more for love of me than ever I can. I pray you, do your worst."

Then, angered by my boldness and sensing that I did not fear his prison, the steward began to grapple with me. He began making filthy gestures and giving me lewd looks. I was so afraid of him that I told him outright where my words came from, not from my own wit but from the Holy Spirit.[81]

Suddenly, completely taken aback by what I had said, he left off his lewdness and stupid gestures. He told me directly, as many a man had done before: "Either you are really a holy woman, or else a very wicked woman."

And he gave me back into the custody of my jailer, who led me to his home again.

Following this they took two of my pilgrim companions— my friend Thomas Marchal and another man from Wisbech —and they put them into prison on my account. I was terribly upset over their distress, and prayed to God that they would be released. And then our merciful Lord Christ Jesus said to me, "Daughter, out of my love for you, I will arrange that they will be only too glad to let them go and not hold them too long."

And on the very next day our Lord sent such storms, with

---

[81] Margery seems to have had a strict code of disclosure—as when she told the man at the church door "that is not for me to tell you." The steward has frightened her so much that she feels compelled to tell him secrets that would normally be confided only to her confessor.

thunder and lightning and a solid downpour of rain, that everyone in town was afraid because they did not know what to do. At once, the town officials were frightened that it was due to their imprisoning the two pilgrims.

So they went off in a hurry and released their two prisoners, the pilgrims who had spent a night in jail. And they led them off to the Guildhall, where they would be examined before the mayor and other important men of the town who wanted to make them swear that I was a woman of the true faith, that I believed the creed, that I was chaste and pure in body—or not!

They swore that as far as they knew, and may God help them on the Day of Judgment, I was in truth a good woman, true in faith and belief; that I was pure and chaste in everything I did, at least in their experience, both in word and deed.

So the mayor allowed them to go about freely wherever they wished. Almost at once the storm subsided and the weather turned fair once more—may the Lord be worshiped.

My pilgrim friends were so glad to be set free that they dared not stay in Leicester a moment longer. So they went about ten miles outside the town and waited there for news of what was to befall me. Afterward they told me that when they had been flung into prison, they were certain that if the mayor had his way, I would have been burned alive.

48

t was a Wednesday when I was led into the Church of All Saints in Leicester, and stood before the high altar. There was seated the Abbot of Leicester together with some of his canons and also the Dean of Leicester, another very important cleric. There were also present many friars and priests, as well as the mayor and a large crowd of laity. In fact, there were so many people crowding the church that many of them stood up on stools and benches in order to get a good look at me and satisfy their curiosity.

As for myself, I knelt down and prayed to Almighty God that I might have his grace, and the wit and wisdom to answer then and there in a way that would be pleasing to him and give him the most honor—as well as being the most beneficial to my innermost soul and giving the best example to all those people gathered there.

Then a priest came to me and, taking me by the hand, led me before the abbot and his fellow assessors who were sitting in front of the altar. They made me swear upon a book that I would answer truthfully about all matters of faith, exactly as I felt about them.

First of all, they began with the Blessed Sacrament of the altar, asking exactly what I believed about it.

So I told them: "Sirs, the Sacrament of the altar is like this: Whoever has been priested, no matter how wicked be his way of life, if he says over the bread the words that our Lord Jesus Christ himself spoke when he celebrated the Last Supper seated with his disciples, then I believe that it is his true flesh and his blood, and no longer ordinary bread. And it has been said, it cannot be unsaid."

And I went on answering their questions in this way, as many as they cared to ask me about all the Articles of the Faith; and they were very satisfied with my replies.[82]

Yet the mayor, who was dead set against me, declared, "It is quite clear that she does not mean with her heart what she says with her lips."

But the clergymen told him, "Sir, she answers us all very well."

Again the mayor continued to attack me and went on and on, repeatedly using indecent words, which are not fit to be repeated.

"Sir," I told him at length, "I take witness before my Lord Jesus Christ, whose body is here present before us in the Sacrament of the altar, that I never had any man's body in this world in any sexual act or sin, save that of my husband. I am bound only to him in matrimony and by him I have borne fourteen children. And I want you to know, sir, that there is no man in this world that I love as much as God, for him I love above all things. And, sir, I can tell you in all truth that I love all men in God and because of him."

I went on to say boldly to his very face: "Sir, you are not fit to be mayor. I shall prove what I say by holy Writ. Our Lord God himself said before he acted and took vengeance upon the cities of Sodom and Gomorrah: 'I will come down and see for myself.' Yet, at the same time, he knew all things. But this

---

[82] There is no doubt that this was a very serious business for Margery. Although her account appears to make light of the trouble she was in, clearly such a formal process being brought against her meant there was a fair body of opinion that suspected her of Lollardy, the new heresy rife among the laity. If convicted, she could well have forfeited her life in the most brutal manner, being burned at the stake. Barely two years before Margery's trial, John Claydon, a skinner by trade, had been convicted of possessing an heretical Lollard book and was burned at Smithfield, London.

was for nothing else, sir, than to show people like you that
you should not carry out punishments unless you first know
that they are just. And, sir, you yourself today have caused
me very great shame on account of something of which I am
not guilty. I pray that God may forgive you."

Once again the mayor insisted, "What I want to know is
why you wander around in white clothes. It is my belief that
your intention is to lure our wives away from us and take
them off with you."

"Sir," I answered, "you shall never hear from my mouth
why I go about in white clothing. You do not deserve to
know. But, sir, I will happily tell these priests here under the
seal of confession. Then they can make up their minds
whether or not they tell you about it."

At this the priest asked the mayor to stand aside and join
the other people below. And when the mayor withdrew, I
knelt before the abbot and the Dean of Leicester and also a
Dominican who was a good man. And I told these three
priests how our Lord in a revelation had warned me, indeed
instructed me, to wear white even before I had set out for
Jerusalem.

"And I have told my confessors as much. And accordingly,
they have told me to go about dressed like this; they themselves dare not go against my inner promptings for fear of
God. They would gladly do so, if only they could. And so,
sirs, if the mayor insists on knowing why I go around in
white, you can tell him that my confessors have ordered me to
do so. That way, you tell no lies, and he will still not know the
whole story."

At this, the priests called the mayor back again; and they
told him in confidence that it was my confessors who had
told me to wear white, and that I had agreed to obey their
ruling.

So the mayor delivered his judgment, saying, "I will not let
you leave here in spite of anything you tell me, unless you go
to my Lord Bishop of Lincoln to obtain from him a letter of

discharge. You live under his jurisdiction; and I want to be formally discharged of all responsibility for you."

I told him, "Sir, I can certainly speak with every confidence to the Bishop of Lincoln. I have already been very kindly received by him before now."

Then the others who were present asked me if I was in charity with the mayor. I told them, "Yes, and with everyone that ever God made."

I bowed to the mayor—I was now weeping freely—and asked him to be in charity with me. And I asked him to forgive me anything that I had done against him. He replied in generous terms, and I half believed him. Yet I found myself to be mistaken not long after.

So that was the conclusion: I now had the mayor's permission to go to my Lord Bishop of Lincoln. I had to procure from him a letter that would excuse the mayor from any further responsibility for me.

49

left the church and first went to Leicester Abbey and into the church there. As soon as the abbot spotted me, out of the goodness of his heart he came directly to welcome me with many of his brethren.

And when I saw them coming toward me, suddenly I visualized our Lord coming with his apostles. I was ravished at this sight, overcome with a contemplation of sweetness and devotion. I wanted to stand upright, as courtesy demands, yet

I could only lean against a pillar of the church. And I even had to hold on to this as tight as I could in case I might fall right over. I simply wanted to stand upright, but because of my overwhelming feelings of devotion I could only cry and weep most bitterly.

When I had recovered from my tears, the abbot asked his monks to take care of me. They offered me a very good wine and were hospitable to me in every way.

I then procured a letter from the abbot to my Lord Bishop of Lincoln. It detailed the controversy I had endured while I was in Leicester. The Dean of Leicester had come forward to endorse this record and be my witness. He had every confidence that our Lord loved me, and as a result he made me most welcome in his own home.

It was at this point that I parted company with my very good friend, Thomas Marchal, who had seemed like my own son. I planned to set out for Lincoln and Thomas sent a man called Patrick from Melton Mowbray, where he was waiting, to learn how I fared in Lincoln and get word back to him. Thomas was deadly afraid that I was about to be burned; and so Patrick was sent to find out how matters stood.

Thus it turned out that Patrick and I set out for Lincoln. We walked to the edge of Leicester, accompanied by many good townsfolk. They were determined to give us a good send-off; they declared that if ever I came back, they would give me an even greater welcome.

I suddenly remembered that I had left behind my walking-stick, made from a piece of Moses' rod. I had brought it back all the way from Jerusalem and wouldn't have been parted from it, not for forty shillings. So Patrick offered to go back and find it for me, together with my bag. And of course he bumped into the mayor. The whole mad thing began again. The mayor wanted to put him in prison. He got away only with the greatest difficulty. And even then he had to leave my bag behind.

So as I waited for him to return, I happened to be in the

house of a woman who was blind; I was very gloomy, dreading to learn what had happened to Patrick, and he was away for such a long time. At last he came riding by, and I called to him, "Patrick, my boy, where have you been? You've been away for such an age."

"Yes, you can say that again, mother," he told me. "I have been in such great danger on your account. I was just about to be flung into prison, all because of you. The mayor treated me really roughly, all on your account. And in the end, he took your bag away from me."

"Dear Patrick," I reassured him, "don't be all upset. I will pray for you. God will see to you for your trouble; it's all for the best."

Then Patrick set me upon his own horse and brought me safely to his house in Melton Mowbray. And there I met up again with Thomas Marchal. He was very pleased to see us again and helped me down from the horse. He was full of thanks to God to see that I hadn't been burned. And on that account, we made merry in the Lord for most of the night.

Later, we tried to find our way to meet the Bishop of Lincoln, wherever he was staying at that time. I was not entirely sure where I could find him; but I was able to meet a very respectable man, an officer of the bishop, who wore a furred hood.

He spoke to me: "Woman, don't you recognize me?"

So I said, "No, sir, I'm sorry."

"But you have been beholden to me," he insisted. "I was once very good to you."

"Sir, I am sure that what you did for me, you did for love of God. I know he will reward you. I have to ask your pardon, I take small notice of a man's good looks and so scarcely ever remember a face. That's the reason I forget him so soon."

He accepted this and told me where I would find the bishop. The required letter was forthcoming from the bishop. It addressed the Mayor of Leicester and admonished him that he should trouble me no more; neither could he hinder me from coming and going, whenever I pleased.

Again, there was a great storm. Thunder, lightning, torrential rain. People said it was to avenge me, and so they wanted me away from their part of the country. But I insisted that I would not leave until I had my bag again.

When the mayor received the bishop's letter, he sent my bag at once and agreed that I could go freely wherever I wished. I had been detained by the Mayor of Leicester for three weeks. Now I was free to leave. I hired Patrick to take me on my way; and so we came to York.

50

 hen we arrived in York, I was especially anxious to meet again an anchoress who had been my close friend before I went to Jerusalem. I was looking forward to hearing how she had fared in her own spiritual journey while I had been on my travels. I had expected—it was the eve of Our Lady's birthday—to eat with her, nothing more than bread and water. But the anchoress refused to receive me. She seemed to have heard a great deal of evil talk, so there was nothing I could do but stay with strangers. Yet they welcomed me in the love of our Lord.

Some days later, as I sat in a church in York, our Lord Jesus Christ said in my soul, "Daughter, you have many tribulations ahead to face."

I was not a little put down and dismayed at this, and so I remained just as I was, sitting still, and I did not answer. Then our blessed Lord said again, "What's the matter, daughter, are you upset at the thought of suffering for love of me? If you don't care to suffer anymore, I shall take it away from you."

But then I gave my answer: "No, Lord, let it be as you will, and make me mighty and strong to suffer everything you ever want me to suffer. And grant me meekness and your patience as well."

So from that day onward, I knew it was our Lord's will that I should suffer still more. And I received it gladly when our Lord sent any tribulation; indeed I would thank him highly and be glad and merry on any day that he sent me any distress. And as time passed, I was not as cheerful on those days when I suffered no tribulation.

Later, I was in the minster in York when a cleric came up to me and asked, "How long are you staying here, woman?"

"Sir," I answered, "I plan to stay for fourteen days."

And that is what I did. And during that time, several good men and women invited me to eat with them, and they were glad to spend their time with me in long conversations; they all said they found it unusual to have talk that was so spiritually creative.

But I also had many enemies who spoke ill of me, despising and scorning me. One priest even came up to me in the minster and grabbed me by my collar: "You wolf," he snarled, "what kind of cloth is this you wear?"

I stood quite still, but I would not answer him or justify myself. And then some schoolboys of the minster who were filing by told the priest, "I know, sir, it is plain wool, sir!"

The priest was furious with me because I would not answer his question, and he began to swear great oaths. Then I spoke up for God's cause; I was quite unafraid of him. I told him, "Sir, you should keep God's commandments. You have no right to swear as lightly as you do."

The priest then asked me who I thought ever kept the commandments.

"Them, sir, that do," I told him.

Then he asked me, "Do you yourself?"

I replied, "Sir, it is my will to do so, since I am bound to it, and so are you and everyone who will be saved on the last day."

And he went on with this wrangling for a long time, and then suddenly he slipped away without my seeing exactly where he had gone.

51

n another occasion, an important cleric came up to me and asked me what I understood by the words of Genesis, *crescite and multiplicamini*.[83]

I gave him my answer: "Sir, these words are not to be understood as being only about having children in the physical sense, but also about gaining virtue. That means spiritual growth, such as listening to the words of God, giving a good example, having meekness and patience, charity and chastity, and the like—because patience is much better than working miracles."

I was able to give this answer—which greatly pleased the priest—solely by the grace of God. Our Lord in his mercy always made some people come to love me and support me. And it turned out in the same way in this city of York.

---

[83] God's first words to all creation, "Grow and multiply" (Gen. 1:22), were frequently used by some to justify free love.

Master John Aclom,[84] a doctor of divinity who was a canon
of York Minster, and Sir John Kendale and another good
priest who sang in the bishop's chantry were, all three, my
good friends among the priests of the minster.[85]

So I stayed on in York for fourteen more days, as I have
described, and a little longer. On Sundays I would go to the
minster and receive Communion with much weeping and sobbing and loud cries, so that people wondered what ailed me.
And after mass one day, a cleric came up to me and said,
"Woman, when you first came here you declared you would
stay only fourteen days."

"Yes, sir, begging your pardon, I did say that I would stay
fourteen days. I did not say that I would stay either more or
less time, but now, sir, I can tell you that I am in fact not
leaving yet for a while."

But then he named a particular day when I must appear
before him in the chapter house. I told him I would willingly
comply with his request.

But I went at once to Master John Aclom, the doctor of
divinity I referred to before, and begged him to be at my side
on that day. And he was there, and he was able to carry much
support among them all. There was another master of divinity
who had promised to stand by me, but then he turned reluctant until he could see which way things would go, for me or
against me.

There was a large crowd of people in the chapter house on
the appointed day who were eager to hear what would be said
and done to me. I was waiting in the minster, ready to speak
up and answer for myself. My friends, who had come to give
their support, told me to be cheerful; and I thanked them,
saying I would be all right.

---

[84] Margery rarely chooses to name names. She has already admitted that she found difficulty in remembering faces and names. There is no historic trace of Dr. Aclom, a canon of York
Minster.

[85] The "good priest who sang" refers to a chantry priest paid to say masses regularly at the
tombs of the deceased. Chantries may be not only elaborate tombs but also little rooms containing an altar for this sole purpose.

A priest came up to me and his manner was very courteous; without delay he took me by the arm to lead me through
the crowds of people. He brought me before the worthy doctor who had required me to come before him on this day in
the chapter house in York Minster. Seated with the doctor
were a great number of other very reverend and worthy clerics, and among them were some of my close friends.

The worthy doctor began by asking me directly: "Woman,
what are you doing here in this part of the country?"

"Sir, I have come on pilgrimage to make my offering here
at Saint William's shrine."[86]

Then he asked, "Do you have a husband?"

"Yes," I told him.

"Do you have a letter giving his permission for your absence?"

"Sir," I told him, "he gave me permission with his own
mouth. Why do you go on at me this way, more so than with
all the other pilgrims who are also here? They have no letters
either, any more than I have. You allow them to come and go
in peace and quiet, completely undisturbed. And yet I am not
left to myself when I come among you. And, sir, if there is any
cleric present who can prove that I have said things I should
not have said, then I am very willing to put the matter right. I
will never hold to any error or heresy, for it is always my
intention to believe only what is held by Holy Church, so as
to please God in full."

Then the clerks examined me on the Articles of the Faith
and they went on to include many other details as well. I
answered all their questions fully and correctly; so they had
no reason to take action against me for anything I said—
thanks be to God.

But then the doctor who sat before me as my judge ordered
me to appear before the Archbishop of York. He named the

---

[86] Saint William of York (d. 1154) had been canonized 100 years after his death after
miracles were reported at his tomb. His cult was still vigorous in Margery's day.

day and the place, a town called Cawood, where the archbishop had his palace. And, finally, he ordered that I be kept
in prison until the day of my hearing.

At this, the lay people in the crowd spoke up for me. They
called out that it would be shameful if I went to prison. They
would stand guarantee for me and bring me themselves before the archbishop. And so the priests had nothing more to
say to me at that time. They stood up and went off about their
business, and I was free to go wherever I pleased—thanks be
to Jesus!

A little later, one of the clerics—who had sat there against
me—came up to me and said, "Woman, I beg you not to be
cross with me, although I sat beside the doctor against you. In
truth, he kept on bullying me continually, so that finally I had
no choice to do otherwise."

"Sir, I am not annoyed at you for that," I told him.

"I beg you to pray for me," he answered.

"Sir," I said, "I will pray for you most gladly."

52

A monk who was about to preach in York
had heard all the slanders and wild talk
against me. And when he came to preach
there was a large congregation who had come to hear him,
and I was among them. When he began to preach, he re-
counted many matters so openly that the people listening
knew quite well that it was myself he was criticizing. When

my friends heard him speak out like this, they were very sorry for me and grew gloomy; but I was perfectly happy because I had been sent something to test my patience and my charity. And because of it, I hoped to please our Lord Christ Jesus.

When the sermon was over, a doctor of divinity who loved me very much, as well as many others, came over to me and asked, "Margery, how have you done today?"

"Sir," I said, "very well indeed, may God be blessed. I have good reason to be very happy and glad in my soul that I may suffer any small thing for love of him, for truly he suffered much more for me."

A few days later a man who had also become a devoted friend, together with his wife and some other people, came and found me, and they escorted me seven miles from York to the palace of the Archbishop of York. And I was shown into a fine room where we were met by a cleric. He said to my friend who had accompanied me, "Sir, why have you and your wife come with this woman? She will only give you the slip when she gets the chance, and then you will both end up looking very silly."

The good man answered firmly, "I have no doubt at all that she will stand her ground and answer her case very willingly."

It was not until the following day that I was brought into the archbishop's chapel. As we waited, many of his household came in to take a look at me; and then they started mocking me, calling out "Lollard" and "heretic" and swearing many horrible oaths that I should be burned. But in the power that came from Jesus I answered them, "Sirs, I fear it is yourselves who will burn in hell without end, for you do not keep God's commandments. At least, I could not swear on your keeping them for all the money in this wide world."

Hearing this, they drifted away as if they were ashamed of themselves. Then, to prepare myself for my ordeal, I prayed inwardly and asked for the grace to conduct myself throughout that day in a way that would bring most pleasure to God, as well as profit to my soul, and be a good example to my fellow Christians. Our Lord answered me that all would go well.

At last, Archbishop Bowet came into the chapel with his retinue of clerics. He began at once and quite abruptly: "Why do you wear white all the time? Are you a virgin?"

I had been told to kneel before him and from there I gave my reply: "No, sir, I am not a virgin; I am a married woman."

He ordered a servant to bring two chains; I must be shackled at once, he insisted, since I was nothing but a lying heretic.

But I told him, "I am not a heretic, nor will you be able to prove me one."

The archbishop then went away. I was left, now standing upright, all on my own. For a long time, all I could do was to say my prayers to Almighty God and ask him to help me against all my enemies, both of the spirit and the body. I was trembling all over and incredibly shaky. I was relieved to put my hands under my mantle so that my trembling would be less obvious.

At last the archbishop returned to the chapel with even more clerics. Among them, I recognized the same doctor who had been in charge of my examination in York, as well as the Benedictine monk who had preached against me there. Then people began muttering, asking whether I was a Christian woman after all; perhaps I was a Jew! Some insisted I was a good person, some said otherwise.

Then, with much ceremony, the archbishop took his seat and his clerics sat down around him, each one in his own place according to rank and position. And there were also many other people present. All the time the people were coming together and the archbishop was taking his seat, I stood simply in the background. I was still praying all the while for help and strength against my enemies and I was deeply consoled, so that suddenly I was overcome and melted in tears of devotion. At length, I cried out loudly; and the archbishop, his clerics, and all the people present were startled—they had never heard the like of it, such a shrill cry.

When I had recovered from my crying fit, I came before the archbishop and knelt down. He was very rough with me, saying, "Why did you cry like that, woman?"

I replied, "Sir, you will wish one day that you had cried as bitterly as I have."

Then the archbishop had me answer the Articles of Faith; God gave me his grace to answer them truly and easily, without any hesitation. I did not even pause to think, so that there was nothing the archbishop could criticize.

He said as much to his clerics: "She knows her faith well enough. What shall we do with her?"

The clerics then said: "We knew all along that she knows her Articles of Faith, but we don't want her to keep living here. People like to hear her talking, and she could very easily lead some of them astray."

Then the archbishop said to me: "I am told some very bad things about you. I hear you are a very wicked woman."

And I answered him, "Sir, I have also heard about you, that you are a wicked man. If you are as wicked as people say, then you will never get to heaven unless you repent and change your way of life while you are still alive."[87]

"Why, you wretched . . . ! What do people say about me?"

"Others can tell you easily enough."

Then an important-looking cleric with a furred hood came forward and said to me: "Peace! You speak about yourself, and let him alone!"

Eventually the archbishop declared: "Put your hand upon the book, and swear on it that you will leave my diocese as soon as you can."

[87] Henry Bowet was zealous in pursuing the Lollards. He was also a warring bishop, having fought against the Scots. His reputation among the people was that of a thoroughly worldly, fat-living prelate. Margery shows great courage in talking to him so directly.

"No, sir," I replied. "I pray you, give me permission to return to York and take leave of my friends."

He gave permission for me to have one or two days in York. But I thought this too short a time and told him, "Sir, I cannot leave this diocese in such a hurry. I must stay on and speak with various good men before I leave. After that I must, with your permission, sir, go to Bridlington and talk with my confessor. He is a good and holy man, confessor to Prior John of Bridlington who is now canonized."[88]

Then the archbishop tried to make me promise: "You swear that you will not teach people or stir them up in my diocese?"

"No, sir, I will not swear any such thing," I told him, "for I shall continue to speak of God and always rebuke anyone who swears great oaths. This I will do until the Pope and Holy Church decree that no one shall be so bold as to speak of God; surely God himself, sir, does not forbid us to speak of him. Have you not read in the gospel that after a woman had heard our Lord speak she came to him and said openly, "Blessed is the womb that bore you, and the breasts where you suckled." And our Lord answered her, saying, "Truly, I tell you, rather blessed are those that hear the word of God and keep it." For this reason, sir, I believe the gospel gives me permission to talk of God."

"Oh now, sir, here for sure we know she has a devil," the clerics accused, "for she speaks freely of the gospel."[89]

The important cleric then suddenly produced a book and quoted Saint Paul against me, where he declares that no woman should preach. But I answered him, "I do not preach, sir. I have never gone up into a pulpit. I only speak privately, using good words. And I will continue to do so as long as I live."

[88] Saint John of Bridlington had died in 1379 and was canonized in 1401. An Augustinian, he had led a humble monastic life—cellarer, precentor, finally prior. Miracles were reported at his grave. His confessor, to whom Margery also went, was William Sleightholme who was also reputed to be a holy man.

[89] Margery's familiarity with scripture and her readiness to quote it in her defense suggests to her accusers that she is one of the Lollards who had illicitly translated the gospel into English.

The York doctor—my first accuser—stood up and declared: "Sir, under examination she told me the worst story
about a priest that I think I have ever heard."

So the archbishop insisted on hearing this tale from me.

"Sir, by your Grace's leave, I spoke about a priest and gave
him as an example," I said. "The story was just as I had heard
it told:

"A certain priest was on a journey and he got lost in a
wood—this was a trial sent him by God for the good of his
soul. Night fell and there was no other shelter but a dry place
beneath a tree in a kind of clearing. And so he rested there for
the night. And in the middle of the clearing was a beautiful
pear tree covered in blossoms. He could not take his eyes
from it all night long. But presently, a great wild bear came
up to the tree and shook it so that all the blossoms fell to
the ground, and then the bear hungrily ate them all. And
when he had eaten his fill, turning his tail toward the priest,
he emptied himself of all the flowers he had so greedily
devoured.

"The priest was revolted by this disgusting sight and the
smell; at the same time he was disturbed, wanting to know
what it meant. And the next day, when he went on his way,
he was distracted and downcast. He chanced to meet an elderly man, handsome and dressed like a pilgrim. This man
asked the priest at once why he was looking so thoughtful
and sad. The priest told his story, just as it had happened, and
as he did so he felt once more a great sadness and fear because the beast had ruined all the beautiful blossoms from the
pear tree by eating them and then passing them so horribly
from his rear end before the priest's very eyes. He simply
could not understand what this might mean.

"Then the pilgrim spoke out and revealed himself to be a
messenger from God: 'Priest, you yourself are the pear tree.
You appear to flourish and flower most beautifully as you say
your masses and give the Sacraments, but you do so with
scant devotion. For in truth you pay very little attention when

you say matins and when you offer mass—you are only intent on babbling away until you finish. There is little sorrow for your sins as you say mass with so little devotion. You take Communion, the fruit of everlasting life, with an empty head. And after this start to the day, you spend the rest of your time badly; you are obsessed with buying and selling, you barter this and exchange that, just like any other worldly man. You sit long over your beer, you give your body over to gluttony and excess, you allow your body its lusts through lechery and impurity. You break God's every command. You swear, you lie, you gossip and speak spitefully and readily practice many other sins.

'Your behavior is just like that of the foul bear: You eat and destroy the flowers and blossoms of good living. You make for your own damnation, you stand in the way of others; you have great need of the grace of repentance and change.' "[90]

The archbishop was silent for a moment. Then he declared that he admired the story greatly, it was a good tale. And then the doctor, my prosecutor, was heard to say, "Indeed, sir, this story strikes right to my very heart."

But I told him: "Good and worthy doctor, sir, in my hometown lives a worthy cleric who is good at preaching. He is fond of speaking out against people's misbehavior. He will flatter no one. He says over and over again from his pulpit: 'If anyone doesn't like my sermons, take a good look at him; he gives himself away as guilty.' And I am reminded of you, sir, how you have treated me. May God forgive you for it."

The doctor was covered with confusion when I said this, and he had nothing more to say. But later, he came to find me and asked me to forgive him for all that he had brought against me. And he earnestly begged me to pray for him.

To conclude, the archbishop asked, "Where may I find a man who might escort this woman for me?"

[90] This tale is clearly genuine, and through it Margery affords us a rare, detailed insight into the imagery and mentality of the common people of her day.

There were many young men who immediately signaled their willingness. They all said, "My lord, I will go with her." The archbishop told them, "You are all too young; I will not appoint you."

Then a good and reliable man from the archbishop's household asked what his lord would offer if he were to escort me, and he was told five shillings. The man asked for a noble, but was told by the archbishop that he was unwilling to spend so much on my bodyguard.

But I said to the man, "Come sir, remember that our Lord will reward you right well."

Finally the archbishop said: "Here are the five shillings; get this woman out of my diocese, double quick!"

So I knelt for his blessing, which he gave me. And he asked me to pray for him, and then he let me go free.

When I returned to York, I was met by a great crowd of people and there were many good clerics among them. And they were all glad in our Lord that he had given me—uneducated as I was—the wit and wisdom to answer so many clever and learned men without any shame or blame. May God be thanked.

53

fterward, the good man who had become my escort brought me away from York and on to Bridlington to my confessor, a priest named William Sleightholme. We spoke with him and many other good men who in the past had all offered me their encouragement and support. But I did not wish to stay long among them, and asked their forgiveness to set out on foot upon my journey. Hearing this, my confessor asked me if I dared stay no longer on account of the Archbishop of York. But I told him, "Truly, that is not my reason."

And the good priest gave me silver and asked me to pray for him. And so we went on our way to Hull. During our stay there we joined in a religious procession, and a lady of some importance took the occasion to make fun of me and treat me with utter contempt. But I answered her not one word. Many other people threatened me and declared that I should be put in prison. In the face of all this hostility, a good man came forward and invited me to his table and offered me his hospitality. But the same hostile people came crowding to his door, saying that he should offer me no such kindness as they knew full well that I was not a good woman. Early the next morning, my host escorted me for my own safety to the edge of town. He was truly frightened that I should stay any longer with him.

And so I came as far as Hessle, on the river Humber,

which I was intending to cross. But it so happened that I chanced to meet up with two Dominican preaching friars and two yeomen of the Duke of Bedford.[91] The friars told the yeomen who I was, and they arrested me just as I was stepping into my boat; they also arrested the archbishop's man who was traveling with me.

"Our lord, the Duke of Bedford, has sent for you," they told me. "You are reckoned to be the greatest Lollard in all this part of the country, and even in London itself. We have been searching for you in many places; we shall have one hundred pounds for bringing you in to face our lord."

I replied, "Good sirs, I will willingly go with you wherever you will lead me."

When they brought me into Hessle, the men called out "Lollard!" and their women came running out of their houses —some still clutching their distaffs—and the crowd screamed, "Burn her, she is a false heretic!"[92]

As we made our way toward Beverley—quite a procession we were, the two yeomen, the two friars, and ourselves as prisoners—several times men came alongside us and urged me: "Woman, give up your way of life. Go and spin, card wool, just like other women. Why put up with such shame and make your life a misery? We wouldn't put up with the half of it, not for any money on earth."

But I told them: "I can never suffer as much sorrow as I would like for our Lord's love. I only have to put up with sharp words, yet our merciful Lord Christ Jesus—may his name be adored—had to suffer hard blows, bitter scourges, and at the end a painful death. He suffered thus for me and for all mankind, blessed may he be. In comparison to what he endured, my discomfort is truly nothing."

And as we went along the roads with these men, I told

---

[91] The Duke of Bedford, the king's younger brother, was appointed Lord Lieutenant of England while King Henry V was away on his military campaign in France.

[92] This spontaneous demonstration by housewives carrying the symbol of their office, the distaff, seems to indicate how Margery's singular way of life upset the majority of women.

them some of my stories. And one of the Duke's men, the one who had formally arrested me, said presently, "I am beginning to regret having met up with you, for it seems to me that you talk good sense."

He even said, "If ever you're a saint one day in heaven, my lady, pray for me."

But I told him, "I hope, sir, you yourself will be a saint, as is everyone that comes to heaven."

We went on our way in this fashion until we came to Beverley, where lived the wife of the man who had arrested me. They marched me straight to her home, and they took away my purse and my ring. But they put me in a decent room with a comfortable bed and everything I needed. Then, locking the door on me, they went off with the key.

The archbishop's man who had been my guide was put into prison. And soon afterward, word came that the archbishop himself was on his way to the town. When he arrived and was told that his servant had been put into prison, he ordered his release. As soon as he was free, he came to me and said angrily, "I wish I had never met you! I have been to prison all because of you . . ."

I tried to pacify him by telling him, "Calm down and have patience. Your reward in heaven shall be great."

So he went away and left me locked up in the house. I went to the window and soon a small crowd gathered, as I told edifying stories to anyone who would listen. Soon some of the women began to weep bitterly. They began to murmur sadly, "How terrible it all is; why ever should you be burned?"

I was very thirsty, so I asked the wife of the house for a drink. But she explained that she could not get in to me, since her husband had taken away the key. But presently she brought a ladder and, setting it against the window, she was able to offer me a pint pot of wine with a cup. She pleaded with me to hide both pot and cup in case her husband might notice them on his return.

54

n the middle of the following night, I suddenly heard a loud voice sounding in my ears: "Margery." As soon as I heard this voice I woke up, very frightened. So I lay utterly still and said my prayers as best I could. And soon our merciful Lord, who is present everywhere, was comforting me, saying, "Daughter, it is more pleasing to me that you should put up with scorn and humiliation, with shame and abuse, wrongs and upsets than if your head were to be chopped off three times every day for seven years! And so, my daughter, do not worry or fear what any man can say to you. Because of my goodness and by reason of the sorrows that you have had to put up with, you have much to rejoice in. When you come to heaven, every sorrow shall turn into joy for you."

The following day I was brought into the chapter house of Beverley Minster and there, once again, was the Archbishop of York and many important clerics at his side, priests, canons, and lay men as well.

Then the archbishop accused me, "What's this, woman, have you come again so soon? I would rather see the back of you!"

And then a priest brought me up close before him, and the archbishop said out loud, so that all present could hear: "Sirs, I have had this woman before me previously at Cawood. And there my clerks and I examined her in matters of faith, and we found no fault in her. Moreover, sirs, since then I have spoken with good men who assure me that she is a perfectly good woman. And yet in spite of all this, I gave a man of mine five shillings to lead her out of my diocese, so that the people would not be disturbed. But as they were making their way upon this journey, they were taken and arrested. My own servant was put in prison on her account; also her gold and her silver was taken, together with some beads and her ring. And now she is brought before me a second time. Is there any man present who has anything to say against her?"

Some men at the back spoke up: "There is a friar here who knows plenty to bring against her."

The friar stepped forward and began by saying that I talked down all the men of Holy Church; he went on to mutter a great jumble of evil rumor all about me. He declared that I would have been burned at Lynn long ago if it were not for his order (he belonged to the Order of Preachers). "And, sir, she says that she can weep when she will and this brings her perfect forgiveness of all her sins."

They called the two men who had arrested me. They said that I was Cobham's daughter[93] and was sent by him to carry letters around the country. They insisted that I could never have traveled to Jerusalem nor the Holy Land nor on any other pilgrimage (as I had, in fact).[94] They denied anything that was true about me, and instead maintained a complete fabrication of lies about me as many had done before. They went on like this for a long while. And then, finally, they held their peace.

When they were done, the archbishop asked me, "Woman, what have you to say to all of this?"

[93] This was serious, if erroneous, evidence. Sir John Oldcastle (called Lord Cobham because his wife was Lady Cobham), a notorious Lollard and traitor against the king, had already been condemned by Arundel, Archbishop of Canterbury, and handed over for execution to the civil authorities. He had escaped from the Tower of London, incited the Scots to invade England, and was still at large when Margery was being questioned. He was finally taken again and hung, drawn, and burned in 1417 in the presence of the Duke of Bedford.

[94] Lollards refused pilgrimage as a pious sham that bore no relevance to the Christian life.

I told him, "My lord, except for your reverence, every word spoken here is a lie."

Then the archbishop said to the friar, "Friar, these words are not heretical: yet they are full of slander and error."

"My lord," said the friar, "she may know her faith well enough. But my Lord of Bedford is angry with her, and he is determined to have her."

"Well, friar," the archbishop said, "you had better escort her to him yourself."

"No way, my lord. It is not a friar's task to take a woman about with him."

"I will not tolerate," the archbishop exclaimed, "that the Duke of Bedford should be angry with me because of her."

He turned to his men: "Watch over this friar until I need to see him again." And he ordered someone else to guard me, until he had time to see me again. But I begged his lordship not to let me be put in custody with men, as I was a married woman. And he said, "No, of course, not; you shall come to no harm here."

Then my guard took me by the hand and led me back to his own home. He invited me to sit at his table and eat with him, and altogether he made me most comfortable. While I was at his house, many priests and other lay folk came in to visit me and talk. They all said how sorry they were that I had been so badly treated.

In no time at all, the archbishop sent for me once more. I was led right into his bedchamber, to his very bedside. And I began by bowing to him and I thanked him for his gracious favor and the kindness he had shown me before.

"Yes, yes, that's all very well," he said, "but now I have heard even worse things against you than before."

I answered, "My lord, if you would take the time to examine me, I will swear to tell the truth. And if I am found guilty, I will abide by your sentence."

Then a Dominican stepped forward who was a suffragan to the archbishop. And the archbishop said to him, "Now, sir,

I want you to repeat in her presence everything you told me before she came in."

"Shall I do so?" asked the suffragan; and the archbishop told him to go ahead.

"Woman," he began, "you were a guest of my Lady West-morland."[95]

"Sir, when was that?" I asked.

"At Easter," said the suffragan.

I did not give him a direct answer but said, "What of it, sir?"

Then he launched into his charge: "My lady was very pleased to meet you, and she admired your conversation. But you advised Lady Greystoke that she should leave her husband; she is married to a baron and is the daughter of my Lady Westmorland. That matter is quite sufficient to have you burned."

He continued to press his case, using many vicious words in front of the archbishop, words that would be unseemly to repeat.

At last I was able to reply to the archbishop: "My lord, if it be your will, I have not seen my Lady Westmorland for over two years. Sir, she sent for me before I went on pilgrimage to Jerusalem. If you will allow, sir, I can go to her again and obtain her witness that I have given no such advice to her daughter."

"No," people around me began to suggest, "let her be detained in prison while we send a letter to the noble lady. And if it is true, what she has said, then let her go free without any more fuss."

I said that I would be quite content with this.

Then an important priest who stood to one side of the archbishop suggested, "Put her in prison for forty days, and then she will love God even better for the rest of her life."

[95] A lady of the first rank, Joan de Beaufort, Countess of Westmorland, was the daughter of John of Gaunt (fourth son of Edward III) and the sister of Cardinal Beaufort, Chancellor of Henry V, who was made cardinal by the pope because of his reforming zeal.

The archbishop asked me exactly what story it was that I had told Lady Westmorland when we met.

I answered, "I told her a good and edifying story about a lady who was damned because she failed to love her enemies; about a bailiff who was saved because he loved his enemies by forgiving their debts against him, and yet he was judged an evil man."

The archbishop agreed that this was a harmless tale, and a good one. Then his steward spoke out, and was joined by many another who shouted out loud: "My lord, we pray you, let her go this last time, and if she ever comes back we will burn her ourselves."

Then the archbishop declared, "I believe there has never been a woman in the whole of England that has been treated as she has been."

Then turning to me, he said simply, "I don't know what to do with you."

"My lord," I told him, seizing my chance, "I pray you, let me have a letter from you, with your seal upon it, as a record that I have answered plainly all my accusers and cleared my name of all error and heresy that was put against me, thanks to our Lord. And let me have your man John to see me safely over the water."

The archbishop agreed to all that I had asked him—our Lord give him his just reward. He handed me back my purse, as well as my ring and beads, which the Duke of Bedford's men had taken from me. The archbishop was very curious to learn how I obtained my money to travel so freely about the country. And I told him that good men gave me alms in return for my prayers offered for them.

At last, I knelt down before him and received his blessing before taking my leave of him. With a very happy heart, I left his bedchamber. The archbishop's household asked me to pray for them. But his steward was angry when he saw me laughing now that I was so cheerful at my release. "Saints shouldn't laugh," was all he said to me.

But I told him, "Sir, I have every reason to laugh, because the more scorn and shame I have to bear for our Lord Jesus Christ, the merrier I am in him."

When I came downstairs into the hall below, I saw standing there the Dominican who had been the cause of all my unhappiness. But I passed on with the archbishop's man, who carried the archbishop's letter of record. And he brought me to the river Humber where he left me in order to return to his lordship. And he took the letter off with him. I was now alone once more, surrounded by strangers.

This great troublesome incident happened on a Friday. May God be thanked that everything fell out so well.

55

I had no sooner crossed the river Humber than I was arrested again on suspicion of being a Lollard. I would have been led away into prison there and then but, fortunately, someone who had been present at my hearing before the archbishop spoke up for me to the bailiff. He obtained leave for me to pass unhindered on my way, declaring that I was no Lollard. And so I made my escape in the name of Jesus.

On the journey, I fell in with a man from London who was accompanied by his wife. And I traveled with them until we came to Lincoln, where once more I suffered much mockery and many abusive words. I answered this, standing up for God's cause, without difficulty. My replies were wise and discreet, so that people could not help but be amazed at my knowledge.

Some lawyers asked me, "We have studied for many years and yet we do not possess sufficient knowledge to give answers like yours. From whom do you get such knowledge?"

I could only tell them, "From the Holy Spirit."

Then they demanded, "Do you have the Holy Spirit?"

"Why yes, sirs," I answered, "no one can say a single good word without the gift of the Holy Spirit. Our Lord Jesus Christ told his disciples, 'Do not worry about what you are to say, for it will not be you who will be speaking but the Spirit of your Father will be speaking in you.'"

It was our Lord who gave me the grace to answer them like this, worshiped may he be.

Another time, some men who belonged to a great lord came up to me. They were swearing coarse oaths all the while as they demanded, "We've been told you are the one who can say whether we shall be saved or damned."

I told them, "Yes, that is true, I certainly can. As long as you continue swearing in such a vile way, breaking God's commandments deliberately and refusing to stop your sinning, then I expect you will be damned. But if you confess and receive absolution for your sin, willingly do penance and determine not to go back on your sin, then I expect you to be saved."

"What! Is that all you can tell us?"

"Isn't that enough for you?"

After that, they left me alone.

I continued my journey home and came at last to West Lynn, with only the river Ouse between me and my home. But I did not continue; instead, I sent word over to Bishop's Lynn—to my husband, to my confessor Master Robert, and to Master Aleyn—asking them to come to me. At this time I told them little of my troubles; and when they came to me, I explained that I could not cross to Bishop's Lynn until I had been to the Archbishop of Canterbury and obtained a letter from him with his seal.

"When I was brought before the Archbishop of York," I explained, "he would not believe what I said because I did not have such a letter with his seal. So I promised him that I would not return to Bishop's Lynn until I had my Lord of Canterbury's letter signed and sealed."

Having explained my plan, I took leave of these good clerics, receiving their blessing, and continued on my way with my husband to London.[96] When we arrived, I was very quickly able to obtain my letter from the Archbishop of Canterbury.[97]

We stayed in the city of London a long while; and there I was very well received by a great number of worthy men.

On our journey home together to Lynn, my husband and I had almost reached Ely when suddenly a man came riding after us at great speed. He arrested us, declaring that he was going to take us off to prison. He chastised us with many cruel words, haranguing us for some time until my husband, at my suggestion, showed him my Lord of Canterbury's letter. The man read it through, and then his manner changed. Now he only spoke handsomely and considerately to us, saying, "Why did I not see your letter before?"

So we left him and went on to Ely. At last we came home to Lynn. And here I suffered much humiliation, many reproofs, much scorn, many slanders, and many curses.

One time a silly man, who was quite indifferent to his reputation, purposefully poured a bowl of slops down upon

---

[96] It is typical of Margery's spare narrative that she offers us few personal details. This is the first time she has seen her husband for something like three years. We suppose that the letter she intended to send him shortly before her first arrest was never written. Now, suddenly, he is back at her side. Her book is no autobiography in the modern sense.

[97] Henry Chichele had been elected to Canterbury on the death of Arundel in 1414. He was to remain in charge of the English church for the next thirty years. His major concern as leader of the church would continue to be that of his predecessor—how to cope with the rising tide of Lollardy. His main thrust was to be by improving his priests' education: He founded two Oxford colleges, Saint John's (named at first Saint Bernard's) and All Souls'.

my head as I was walking along the street below him. I was not upset in the least but said to him, "God make you a good and holy man." And I went on my way, thanking God for the accident; such was my way of accepting many similar things that happened to me all the time.

56

A fter this, I was punished by God with a succession of many different illnesses. For a long time I suffered dysentery, until I became so weak that I was anointed for fear that I was going to die. But our Lord Jesus Christ spoke in my soul, telling me that it was not yet time for me to die. And after this, I recovered, but only for a short while.

Very soon I was afflicted by another sickness, first in my head and then in my back; it was so grievous that I thought I was going mad. But once more I managed to recover, only to fall sick again almost at once. This time it was a pain that lodged in my right side and lasted for the following eight years, less eight weeks.[98]

The pain would come and go; sometimes it would last for thirty hours, sometimes for twenty, ten, eight, or only a couple of hours. But it hit me so hard that I must sometimes evacuate the entire contents of my stomach. The pain felt as

---

[98] Possibly inverticulitis, inflammation of the small intestine, a psychosomatic disorder brought on by nervous stress.

bitter as gall; I was unable to eat or drink anything until it subsided, and I would lie groaning until it had gone.

I would pray to our Lord: "Ah, blissful Lord, why did you become a man and suffer so much pain for my sins and the sins of all mankind that shall be saved, when we are so ungrateful, Lord, in return? Miserable me, I am so unwilling to suffer this small pain. Lord, seeing your great pain, have mercy on my little pain; with the merits of the great pain you suffered, do not send me as much pain as I deserve, for I cannot endure as much as I truly deserve. But if you wish that I should bear it, Lord, send me patience also, for otherwise I may not endure.

"Dear blissful Lord, I would rather put up with all the sharp and hurtful words that people say about me and all the clerics preach against me for love of you—only provided no man's soul is put at risk—than have to endure this pain of mine. Suffering harsh words for love of you hardly hurts me one bit; for the world can take nothing from me save my name and my possessions. And I give nothing for the world's opinion of me.

"Deny me, Lord, I pray you, all worldly honors and goods, every kind of earthly love, especially love and attachment to those things that lessen my love for you or decrease my reward in heaven. But every kind of love and all those things that you know in your wisdom would quicken my love for you, I pray you Lord, grant me in your mercy for your neverending honor and glory."

On occasion, in spite of the pains of my physical illness, the passion of our merciful Lord Christ Jesus was so vividly at work in my soul that I would then be oblivious to my own illness; but, recalling our Lord's sufferings, I would weep and sob just as if I were witnessing the pain of his passion with my very own eyes.

At length, after eight years had elapsed, my sickness passed so that it was no longer the weekly occurrence I had come to expect. Yet now my weeping and crying out loud grew to such a degree that the priest decided against giving me Communion publicly in church, preferring to house me privately in the prior's chapel in Lynn where I was away from public earshot.

It was in this chapel that I had much lofty contemplation and many soliloquies with our Lord. I felt during Communion there as if my soul was being torn from my very body; two men had to support me in their arms until I had stopped crying. I was overwhelmed by the insupportable abundance of love that I felt when receiving the precious sacrament, for I firmly believed it was truly God and very man in the form of the bread.

Yet our blessed Lord told me, "Daughter, I will not have my grace that I have given you hidden from human eyes. The more people try to hide and prevent it, the more I shall spread it far and wide so that the whole world shall know."

57

ne year at Removing Time[99] a visiting Benedictine monk came to stay at Lynn; he had no time for me, and he refused me entry to the chapel where it had been my practice until then to receive Communion.

I heard this from the prior himself, Dom Thomas

[99] Tenants—especially tenant farmers—would move on Lady Day, March 25. Not less than one year's notice had to be served by the landlord.

Hevingham, who had asked to see me one day together with my confessor, Master Robert Spryngolde. He begged to be excused, but said: "A fellow monk of mine has come and he refuses to come to chapel so long as you are there. I fear you will have to find an alternative place to receive Communion."

Master Robert replied, "Then, sir, we are bound to give her Communion in church. For we have no option in the matter: She has at hand my Lord of Canterbury's letter, which binds us in virtue of holy obedience to hear her confession and give her the sacrament as often as she asks it of us."

From now on, I received Communion at the high altar of Saint Margaret's church. And whenever I received Communion our Lord visited me with such great grace that I would cry out so loud it could be heard throughout the church and even outside. It was almost as if I were dying at that moment; and sometimes the priest was unable to give me the Sacrament but had to turn to the altar again and wait until I stopped my crying out. And then he would turn back and give me Communion in the normal way. It happened in this manner very many times; but sometimes I would weep only very gently and in silence as I received the precious Sacrament without any convulsions at all; it depended on how our Lord would visit me with his grace.

One Good Friday, I watched as the priests were kneeling with other good men and holding lighted candles before the Easter Sepulchre. This, according to the Liturgy of Holy Church,[100] was to remind us of the terrible death and sorrowful burial of our Lord Jesus Christ. I was suddenly in mind of our Lady's sorrows, how much she suffered as she watched beneath the cross to see his precious body hanging there; and

[100] On Maundy Thursday, after celebrating mass on the commemoration of the Last Supper, the consecrated bread is taken aside from the altar (which is stripped) and kept safe in a side chapel. The faithful keep vigil, "with lighted candles." No mass is celebrated on Good Friday but Communion is distributed. The Easter Sepulchre was an architectural feature in many medieval churches that represented Christ's tomb. Only one such remains, in Saint Andrew's Northwold (Norfolk), described by Pevsner as having "seated soldiers in agitated attitudes and little trees separating them."

then as she saw him buried before her own eyes—my heart was filled with these memories.

My whole mind was totally drawn into the passion of our Lord Jesus Christ; I saw him with my spiritual eye, as truly as if I had seen his own precious body being beaten, scourged, and crucified with my physical eyes. This sight and spiritual beholding worked its grace so fervently in my mind that I felt wounded with pity and compassion; I sobbed and I roared; I spread my own arms out wide and cried loudly, "I die, I die!" And many people about me were perplexed to know what ailed me. And the more I tried to contain myself and prevent my cries, the louder they grew. It was not within my control but as God would have it. Then a priest took me up in his arms and carried me into the prior's cloister[101] so that I could breathe fresh air; he judged that I was in such affliction I would not otherwise have lasted. And indeed I was sweating profusely and had turned as blue as lead.

This manner of crying out loud lasted for about ten years. As each Good Friday came around during this time, I would weep and sob uncontrollably for five to six hours at a time, and was unable to prevent myself from crying out loud again and again until I was utterly weakened by the effort. Sometimes on a Good Friday, I would weep for a whole hour for other people's sins; I had more sadness at these sins—which remained unconfessed—than at my own, which I knew our Lord had forgiven me before I set out for Jerusalem.

Notwithstanding, I would weep for my own sins most mightily when our Lord was pleased to visit me with his grace. Sometimes I would weep for as much as an hour for all the souls in Purgatory; then another hour for all those who might be in trouble or in dire poverty or some other calamity; another hour I might spend for the Jews, for the Muslims, or for all those led astray by false heresies—I would ask God in

---

[101] The priory was adjacent to Saint Margaret's church and linked to it by means of this cloister.

his goodness that he should take away their blindness, so that they might, by his grace, turn to the faith of Holy Church and become children of salvation.

Often when I was at prayer, our Lord would ask me, "Daughter, tell me what you want and you shall have it."

I would answer, "For myself, Lord, I ask for nothing, save what you may give me, which is mercy, and that too I ask for everyone else's sins. Over the year you often tell me that you have forgiven my sins. And so now I ask mercy for the sins of other people, just as I would for my own sins. Because you, Lord, are full of love; it was your love that brought you into this world, which is so full of pain, and that same love caused you to suffer the hardest pains for our sins. So why should I not share your love for people and beg forgiveness for their sins?

"Blessed Lord, I know that you have shown great love toward me, and I am an unworthy sinner. You are as loving with your grace toward me as if I were a pure maid, the purest anywhere in the world. You treat me as if I had never sinned.

"And so, Lord, I wish I had a well of tears with which I might persuade you not to take final vengeance upon man's soul, nor to separate him from you without end. For it is the hardest thing to imagine that any man on earth would ever willingly sin and thus might never see your glorious face.

"If it were up to me, Lord, to give your people contrition and tears as powerful as those you gave to me, on account of my many sins and the sins of the world—as simply as taking a penny piece from my purse—then I would fill men's hearts with sorrow so that they would repent and leave off their sinning. I am continually amazed, Lord, that I should feel such fierce love for my fellow Christian souls, for I must be the most unworthy and sinful of all creatures that you ever showed your mercy to in all this world. I sometimes think that even if they were to condemn me to the most shameful death man or woman might imagine, I would still be able to forgive them out of your own love, Lord, and beg that their souls be saved from hell everlasting.

"Therefore, my Lord, as I weep, I shall never stop weeping for them, whatever happens to me. And if ever you wish my tears to cease, I beg you, Lord, take me from this world. For what could I do here, if I could no longer do any good? And even if the whole world were to be saved through these tears of mine, that would never be thanks to me. But all praise, all honor, all worship is yours, oh Lord. As for me, if it spelled out my love for you and made known your name, Lord, I would willingly be chopped up into little pieces like meat for a stew."

58

nce when I was at prayer, I felt a great hunger for the word of God and I said, "Alas my Lord, you have so many priests in this world, and yet you will not send a single one who could fill my soul with your word by reading your Holy Scripture. I sometimes think that my soul will always be hungry; no matter how many sermons I hear, they shall not satisfy me. If only I had the money, I would gladly give a noble every day to hear a sermon, for your word is worth more to me than any money in the world. Blessed Lord, take pity on me; you have sent away from me the anchorite who was my only solace and comfort. It was he who so often refreshed my spirit with your holy word."

Then our Lord answered me in my soul, saying, "Someone is coming from far away, and he will answer your purpose."

And so it was, a good time later, that a priest came to Lynn who had never met me before. But as soon as he saw me walking one day in the street, he asked about me. He felt compelled to speak to me, and so he asked in several quarters what kind of a woman I was. They all said that they trusted in God that I was, in truth, a very good woman.

So the priest followed this up by inviting me to come and talk with him and also with his mother. He had hired rooms for himself and his mother, and I came to where they boarded together. I was curious to know what he wanted, and so I began conversing with his mother and himself, both of whom received me with great kindness.

Presently, the priest reached for a book. And there he read how our Lord had wept over the city of Jerusalem, how he had foreseen her misfortunes and the sorrows to come, while she did not know when her visitation would be. And as soon as I heard these words telling how our Lord had wept, I too wept bitterly and began to sob out loud and with great cries. Neither the priest nor his mother could guess the reason for my tears. But when all my crying out and weeping came to an end, they were very glad and merry in our Lord. After a while, I took my leave of them for that day.

When I was gone, the priest commented to his mother, "I am astonished at the way this woman cries out and weeps so much. Even so, I am sure she is a good woman, and I would like very much to see more of her."

His mother was more than content with this and told him that he should certainly do so. From then on, this priest became a close and trusted friend of mine. He blessed the day we met, for he declared that he derived great spiritual comfort in knowing me. I was the reason he came to unearth so many good passages in scripture; he would also not have looked up the words of so many learned writers and doctors had it not been for me.

He began to read regularly and widely to me. There were books on prayer and contemplation and many others besides: Saint Bridget's *Revelations,* Hilton's book,[102] *Stimulis Amoris* by Bonaventure, Richard Rolle's *Incendium Amoris,* and many similar works. I then knew that the answer I had received when I complained about my lack of reading—"Someone is coming from far away, and he will answer your purpose"—in fact foretold a spirit that would be sent from God. I came to see from my own experience that this was indeed a spirit that I could trust.

And this priest went on to read to me in this way for the better part of seven or eight years. In doing so he greatly improved both his learning as well as his merit; but at the same time, he had to put up with many an evil word due to his friendship and love of me, as he read to me regularly and defended my fits of weeping and shouting.

Later on, he took up a benefice that involved him in looking after a large number of souls; and he said how glad he was that he had done so much reading in preparation for his new work.

---

[102] Walter Hilton, renowned English mystic. Little is known of his life, save that he was an Augustinian canon. His most famous work is *Ladder of Perfection.*

59

t was by hearing holy books read aloud and also listening to sermons that I was continually fed in my
contemplation and meditation of holy matters. I
would find it impossible to write an account of all the holy
thoughts, the sacred conversations, and the high revelations
that our Lord sent me; many of these were personal to me,
others concerned many different souls; some who were to be
saved, others lost forever.

This latter knowledge was a great punishment and a cruel
pain for me to bear. I was only too glad and full of joy to learn
who would be saved, because I longed as much as I dared for
everyone to be saved. But when our Lord revealed to me
some who would be damned, this was a grievous pain. I did
not want to listen, nor could I believe that it was God who
showed me such terrible things; and I tried to rid my mind of
them as much as I could. Our Lord reproached me for this
and told me to believe that it was indeed part of his secret
mercy and goodness to reveal his hidden counsels in this way.
He told me in my heart, "Daughter, you must hear tell of the
damned as well as all those who shall be saved."

But I could not listen to such advice from God; I preferred
to believe that these words were from some evil spirit intent
on deceiving me. Then, because of my boldness and my lack
of belief, our Lord took away from me every good thought
and all my memories of the holy sermons, pious conversa-

tions, and high contemplation that I had known before. Instead, he allowed me to have evil thoughts in place of the
good thoughts I had previously entertained. And this trial
went on for twelve days all told; whereas before I had been
accustomed to having four hours of holy speeches and conversations with our Lord each morning, now I had to endure
as much time suffering foul thoughts, filthy memories of lechery and dirtiness. It was as though I had prostituted myself
with a whole crowd of different people.

Thus did the devil lead me in a dance, plying me with these
accursed thoughts, whereas before it had been our Lord who
entertained me with good and holy thoughts. And whereas
before I had enjoyed so many glorious visions and experienced such high contemplation of the manhood of our blessed
Lord, about our Lady and many great saints, so now I had
horrible and truly loathsome visions—and there was nothing
I could do to help myself. I kept seeing men's genitals and
many other abominations.

I had the sight—I mean it really felt as if I were looking
with my very own eyes—of different religious men, priests
and the like, both heathen and Christian. They would come
parading before my eyes so that I had no chance of avoiding
them or turning my head away: and they all showed me their
naked genitals.

And as they did, the devil would whisper to me that I must
choose which one I would have first of all, but that I must
eventually sleep with every one of them. And he suggested
that I liked one of them better than any of the rest. I believed
he spoke the truth: I could not say no, I knew I had to do as
he said. Yet for all the world, I would not have done what he
bade me do. All the same, I thought it would happen: I
thought that all these horrible acts would in fact be delicious
to commit against my will. And wherever I went and whatever I was doing, these accursed thoughts stayed perpetually
with me. When I looked at the Blessed Sacrament, when I
was saying my prayers, as I tried to do some good deed—

these accursed thoughts would keep coming into my mind. I
went to confession, I did all I could think of, but nothing
made any difference. I found no respite; I was nearly in despair. I cannot write or tell what pain I felt, the sorrow of it
all.

At last I said: "Alas, my Lord, you have always told me
that you would never desert me. What truth is there now in
your promises?"

And as soon as I said this, my good angel came to me,
saying, "Daughter, God has not left you alone, he will never
do so. He has given his word. But since you refuse to believe
that it is the spirit of God who speaks to your soul and shows
you his secret counsels, how some shall be saved and others
damned, then God punishes you in this way. And it will continue like this for twelve days until you accept that it is God
who speaks to you and not some devil."

I answered my angel: "Oh, I beg you, pray for me to our
Lord Jesus Christ, that he will grant me the favor of taking
away from me these accursed thoughts, that he will speak to
me as he did before! I now make a solemn promise to God
that I shall believe it is he who spoke to me before this all
started. I cannot put up with this pain any longer."

My angel told me once more, "Daughter, my Lord Jesus
will not take it away until you have suffered for twelve whole
days. In this way, he wants you to learn whether it is better
for God to speak to you, or the devil. My Lord Christ Jesus
is not angry with you, even though he permits you to suffer
this pain."

So I suffered the pain of it until the twelve days were over.
And afterward, I had as many holy thoughts, holy illumina-
tions, holy aspirations, holy conversations and talks with our
Lord as ever I had before. Our Lord said, "Now will you
believe for yourself that I am no devil talking?"

I was full of joy when I heard our Lord talking to me just
as he always had. So I said, "I shall take every good thought
as words from God. Blessed may you be, Lord, that you have

agreed to comfort me once more. I would not, for all the world, go through the pain of these past twelve days again. I thought I was in hell. Blessed thanks to you that it's all over. And now, Lord, I shall lie still and be obedient to your word. Lord, I beg you speak in me whatever is most pleasing to you."

60

My good friend the priest, who kindly read aloud to me, fell gravely sick, and I was determined to nurse him. If there was ever anything I thought he needed that I myself could not provide, I would go and find some generous man or woman who was willing to help us out. He became so ill that people began to think he would not survive, especially after his sickness had lasted for so long.

One day, when I was at church hearing mass, I prayed for him; and our Lord reassured me that the priest was going to recover from his illness and go on to prosper very well. Then I felt moved to go to Norwich and Saint Stephen's Church, where is buried Richard Caister, the holy vicar who had died not long before[103] and for whose sake God had already shown great and merciful signs to many of his people. I wanted to offer thanks for the safe recovery of my priest and friend.

[103] Richard Caister, with whom Margaret had had a memorable first encounter (see Chap. 17), died March 29, 1420: almost at once, miracles were reported at his tomb.

I took leave of my confessor and made my way to Norwich. As soon as I came into the churchyard at Saint Stephen's, I began to cry out and bellow loudly; I wept, then fell down flat upon the ground, so on fire I was with the love burning away in my heart.

After a while, I got to my feet and made my way, still weeping, into the church and up to the high altar. And here, once more, I fell flat, weighed down by my violent sobbings. I began to cry out loudly at being beside the grave of my good vicar. I was utterly ravished by a spiritual comfort from our Lord's goodness; it was the good vicar who had worked so much grace for his servant, and who had been my confessor so many times for all those years, and had given me the Sacrament from this same altar. I was all the more moved to know that our Lord had worked such special graces in someone I myself had known.

I was overcome with so many blissful memories and sacred thoughts that I could no longer contain my weepings nor my cries of joy. And presently, this drew a crowd of people who were amazed at my behavior. They came up to me, supposing that perhaps I was a blood relation or special friend of the vicar's. "Are you all right, woman?" they asked. "What is the matter with you? We were his friends as well, you know."

But some priests were also present who were used to the way I behaved. And they were kind enough to bring me to a tavern and offer me a drink. And they were very kind and hospitable toward me.

On another day, a lady very much wanted me to eat with her. And so, out of courtesy, I went across to the church where she normally heard mass. There I saw a *Pietá*, a statue of our Lady bearing her dead son across her lap. And as I gazed at this *Pietá*, I was flooded with thoughts of the passion of our Lord Jesus Christ. I felt at one with our Lady, Saint Mary, and her sufferings; I knew how bitterly she would have wept, how loudly she must have cried, so loudly that she might have died.

Then the priest of the lady I was to meet came to me and said, "Woman, Jesus died a very long time ago."

It took me some time to compose myself. And then I answered, "Sir, his dying is as present to me now as if it were this very morning that he died. And I think it should feel the same to you, and to anyone who calls himself a Christian. We ought to remember his kindness every new day, and always be in mind of his doleful death and how it was that he died for us."

Then the good lady who had invited me, hearing what had been said, declared, "Sir, this serves me as a good example, as it should to others also, telling of the grace that works within her soul."

That was how the good lady answered on my behalf. And so she took me home to eat at her table; she showed me great affection and kindness for as long as I was willing to stay. Then it was time to return to Lynn and see how my priest friend—on whose behalf I had undertaken my special journey of thanksgiving to Norwich—was faring. My priest friend, my reader for seven years, was now up and about, able to go wherever he would—thanks be to Almighty God for his great goodness.

61

hen there came into my life a friar who had a
great reputation both for holiness and preaching.[104] Indeed his fame was linked to his gift for
preaching. People I knew would come up to me and say,
"Margery, now you will have a feast of sermons. For here is
the most gifted preacher in all England, come to live with our
own friars in Lynn."

I was happy and glad; I heartily thanked God that such a
good man had come to live in our community. Soon after his
arrival, he was to preach at Saint James, our chapel of ease in
Lynn; and a good crowd of people had come to hear his very
first sermon. Just before he preached, the parish priest took
him aside and warned him thus: "Sir, I hope you will not be
annoyed, but a woman will be in the congregation who frequently, when she hears the story of the passion of our Lord,
or indeed any profound devotional words, weeps and sobs
and cries out loud. But it's soon over. So don't be put off if
she should demonstrate like this as you preach. Take no notice and don't mind her."

The good friar duly took the pulpit and began to preach his
sermon. He spoke well and said many holy and devout words;
and then, as he began to tell of our Lord's passion, I could no
longer bear it. I tried as long as I could to keep myself from

---

[104] A note in the margin names "Melton": the Franciscan preacher William Melton.

crying out, but then at last I burst out with a loud shriek, a cry that frightened me greatly. The good friar took my outburst patiently and said not one word about it at the time.

Soon after this he was to preach again at the same place, and I came once more. As I saw how many people came hurrying to hear his sermon, I was overjoyed; I thought to myself and prayed, "Dear Lord Jesus, I truly believe that if you yourself were here to preach in person, everyone would be overjoyed to hear you. I pray you, Lord, may your holy word settle in their souls as I wish it will also come down to me; and may as many people be persuaded by his voice as if you yourself were to preach here today."

It was with such thoughts and holy reflections that I asked grace for the people who were gathering together at that time. When the sermon was over, it was such a holy sermon and, moreover, my own thoughts and a grace of devotion had been working in me; and all this worked so intensely within me that I succumbed to violent weepings.

At this the good friar declared, "I want this woman out of church. She is annoying the people so."

But some friends of mine spoke up for me: "Sir, please excuse her. She simply cannot help herself."

But many turned against me, encouraged that the friar had spoken out so plainly. Some men began to spread the rumor that I had a devil in me; they had said as much often enough before, yet now they grew bolder. They thought that public opinion was running for them on account of the good friar. And he decided that I could no longer attend his sermons unless I would stop my sobbing and crying out.

Now my priest friend, who read scripture to me, knew well enough what was at the root of my loud crying. He had words with another priest, someone who had known me for a good many years and who told my priest friend that he was thinking of going to see the friar and try to touch his heart in all humility.

My priest friend said he would willingly come with him to help persuade the friar, if only he could be of use. So they went together and pleaded with the friar that he allow me to go to his sermons, as quietly as I could, but that if I were to call out he should try to bear this with patience, as many other good preachers had done likewise.

His answer was short and to the point: If I came into any church where he was due to preach and made any of my noises, he would speak straight out against me. He simply would no longer tolerate any calling out on my part.

Following this meeting, there was a worthy doctor of divinity, a Carmelite, who tried to intervene on my behalf. He was an extremely sober priest, an elderly scholar with a solid reputation who had known me for a good number of years and had formed his own conviction that God's grace worked within me. He, together with another worthy man—a bachelor of law, well versed in scripture, who was my confessor— also went to visit this friar[105] just as the two good priests had done before. They sent out for wine so as to soften his mood before pleading with him that he have the charity to look kindly on the workings of our Lord concerning me; and they begged him once more to behave in a more kindly and supportive way should I happen to cry out loud or sob while he was in the middle of his sermon. These two worthy clerics assured him that it was a gift of God; and they told him that I could experience such a manifestation only when God chose to give it to me. And that, however hard I tried, I could not resist such a thing when God so chose; moreover, God would withdraw it when he pleased. I had been told as much in a revelation—which the friar otherwise had no means of knowing.

But the friar would not listen to what the doctor or the bachelor had to say; he preferred to side with public opinion.

[105] Margery must mean Dr. Aleyn and Master Robert Spryngolde, whom she had summoned to West Lynn together with her husband before she went to the Archbishop of Canterbury.

He said he would not condone my crying out loud in church, not for any consideration, and he flatly denied that it was a gift from God. He told them that if I could not suppress such a cry when it arose, then it must result from a heart condition or perhaps some other ailment. If I was prepared to admit as much, then he would have pity on me and ask people to pray for me. Only on such a condition was he prepared to be patient and permit me to cry in moderation.

For my part, I knew full well through revelation and experience that this was no mere illness. And accordingly I was not willing, not for the world, to say anything other than how I felt. And so there was no agreement to be had. As a result, the worthy doctor and my confessor both advised me against attending any more of the friar's sermons. And that caused me great pain.

Even after this attempt, one of the town worthies (a few years before he became the Mayor of Lynn) approached the friar and asked the same favor as the good clerics had asked in my behalf. And he received a similar reply.

Then I was formally told by my confessor that I should not attend any church where this friar would be preaching. If he was to preach in one church, I should go to another. I felt so sad, I hardly knew what to do. Here I was, excluded from hearing sermons, which were to me the highest comfort on this earth, if I could but hear them. Equally, not to do so was the hardest pain on earth. And yet, when I was all alone in one church while he was busy preaching to everybody in another church, I still had shrieks as loud and surprising as when I had been in public, with everyone around.

For years on end I was forbidden to attend his sermons; all because it pleased our Lord to bring to my mind such a real beholding of his own bitter passion that I could not keep myself from crying out loud. Not that I was prevented from hearing other sermons—only those preached by the good friar, as I have explained. Meanwhile, many sermons were preached by numerous worthy doctors and clerics that I was able to attend, and where, on many occasions, I cried out very loudly and sobbed violently. Yet these preachers put up with me very patiently, and my friends, who had talked to me privately and understood my way of life, asked people to excuse me whenever they heard them murmuring or grumbling about me.

62

n the feast of Saint James, the good friar preached outside in the churchyard of Saint James's chapel. Although at this time he was not a doctor nor even a bachelor of divinity, he had a great reputation for holiness and was an extremely popular figure. Once they had heard that he was to preach, people would come from miles around and took great pleasure in what he had to say; may God be blessed, this friar's sermons were extraordinary for their holy burden and devout effect.

But on this particular occasion, he chose to devote a great deal of his sermon to speaking against me. Not that he mentioned me by name, but to everyone who heard what he had to say, it was clear who he was referring to. This caused a lot of ill feeling among the crowd, for many of them held me in great affection. People were sad and regretful that he had spoken out against me so forcibly; they said they wished they hadn't turned up to hear him on that feastday.

When he realized there were murmurings and grumblings among his congregation—and felt perhaps that he would be opposed by my friends on another day—he thumped the side of the pulpit and cried: "If I hear any more of this, I shall hit the nail on the head so hard that it will put to shame every single one of her supporters."

After this threat, quite a few who said they were on my side fell silent out of an empty fear about what he had said; and they dared to speak well of me no more. Among this group was the same priest who later on agreed to write this book for me; but at that time, he made up his mind never again to trust and believe in my inner feelings.

And yet our Lord drew him back on my side in no time at all—blessed may he be! From then on, he loved me all the more and trusted in the sincerity of my weeping and shouting more than ever before.

It so chanced that he read about a woman called Mary of Oignies;[106] and there he learned about her manner of life and the wonderful consolation she enjoyed on hearing the word of God; of the notable compassion she had for his passion, of the copious tears she wept. And how all this weakened and enfeebled her so that she found it hard to look upon the cross or hear a narrative of our Lord's suffering without dissolving into tears of pity and compassion.

About her gift of abundant tears, this book goes into great detail. In Chapter 18, which begins *Bonus est, domine, sperantibus in te,* and again in the next chapter, the book tells how— at the request of a priest that he should not be disturbed by her weeping and sobbing as he said mass—she went outside the church door and continued to cry out in a loud voice because she was unable to restrain herself.

Then our Lord chose to visit the priest of Lynn with such

---

[106] Mary—who had lived in Brabant and died in 1213—had been married against her will at fourteen, yet soon persuaded her husband to live celibately together. They began to nurse lepers while Mary developed a mystic inner life remarkably similar to Margery's. She would cry out at any mention of the passion of Christ, swoon at Communion, and the like. She later became an anchorite.

A collection of her life together with the lives of several other holy women survives in the Bodleian Library, Oxford. Margery's amanuensis could well have come across a similar volume.

grace and devotion when he read the holy gospel at mass that
the priest also wept, to such a degree that his vestments and
even the altar vessels became wet. He found himself unable to
control his tears or his sobbing, nor could he even stand
steady at the altar.

This convinced him that in my case too the tears were
impossible to hold back; so whereas before he had had little
sympathy for me, now he realized how my weeping, my sobbing, my loud cries were well nigh uncontrollable, especially
since he judged that I had a more abundant gift of grace than
his. Then he came to recognize that God gave his grace to
whomsoever he pleased.

Thus the priest who later came to write my book (at the
persuasion of a worthy cleric who was also a doctor of divinity) had already found and read an account of a case similar
to my own. He did not give as much detail in my book as was
contained in the original one, because by the time he came to
write this account he no longer had a very clear memory of it.

Having at first avoided me after the friar's sermon, he now
approached me more comfortably because he was firmly on
my side. He went on to read the spiritual treatise entitled *The
Prick of Love*, especially the second chapter where Bonaventure writes of himself: "Ah Lord, what shall I say and call
out to you now? You hang back and do not come to me.
While I grow weary and am so weighed down by my desire
that I begin to lose my mind, for it is love not reason that
rules me. I run swiftly wherever you beckon to surrender to
you, my Lord. Those who stand by are irritated by me or take
pity on me, seeing me drunk with love of you. 'Lord,' they
exclaim, 'look at that madman shrieking along the street.' But
little do they know of the desire that eats my heart."

He also read something very similar by Richard of
Hampole, the hermit,[107] called *The Prick of Love*, which gave

---

[107] Richard Rolle of Hampole (near Doncaster in the north of England, 1295–1349) was
one of the first mystics to write in English as well as Latin. His lyrical style was used to great
effect, nowhere more so than in his *Meditation on the Passion*. The reference to his work is

him further evidence in my support. It was also written of Elizabeth of Hungary in her book that she was given to crying out with a loud voice.

And many other people, who had at first been critical of me because of the friar's preaching, began to change their minds and think well of me as time passed. But the friar himself remained firmly set in his opinions. In each sermon he preached there would be a passing reference to me, whether or not I was present; and this had the continuing effect of making many people think ill of me for many a long day.

Some were sure I had a devil in me; some would even tell me to my face that the friar should have driven these devils out of me. In this way I was slandered daily, eaten and gnawed by people's wagging tongues. And all this was because I could not choose otherwise nor contain my weeping, sobbing, and crying out bitterly whenever the grace of God worked in me to bring about so much contrition, devotion, and compassion. If only it were within my own power.

---

confusing: *The Prick of Conscience* was originally attributed to Rolle (yet is now doubtful) whereas *Stimulus Amoris* is by pseudo-Bonaventure.

63

As things got worse, some of my friends came to me and advised that I would be better off moving away from town and living somewhere outside, since so many people were against me. But I told them that I preferred to stay where I was as long as God wanted.

"My sins were committed here, in this town," I explained to them. "It is only right and fitting that I suffer here because of them. And yet I do not have as much shame and distress as I truly deserve, for I have offended against God. I am thankful to Almighty God for whatever he sends me, and I pray to him that all sorts of wickedness that anyone can think of saying against me may stand toward remission of my sins. And likewise any good that anyone has to say of the grace that God works in me may turn to God's worship and praise. And may it magnify his holy name without end, for all honor and glory are his, but every shame and rebuke must be mine. I have deserved it well enough."

One day I was in the chapel of our Lady called the Gesine[108] when my confessor came to me, saying, "Margery, what are you going to do now? Apart from the moon and the

---

[108] Old French for a crib. This was a special shrine in a side chapel at Saint Margaret's dedicated to the birth of Christ, before which the townsfolk of Lynn paid for a lamp to burn constantly. Once a year, the crib was taken in procession around the streets by the Guild of the Holy Trinity, which was based in the church. When Margery describes the great fire at Lynn, she tells us that the Guild's hall was the first to suffer in the flames.

seven bright shiners in the sky, there is no one left to turn against you. There's hardly anyone left on your side, except me."

I answered him, "Cheer up, sir, everything will turn out right in the end. I'll tell you the truth, my Lord Jesus gives me great comfort of soul, for otherwise I would be in despair. My blissful Lord Christ Jesus will not allow me to despair, whatever reputation for holiness the good friar may have. My Lord tells me that he is very displeased with this friar; he says it would be better if he had not been born if he goes on like this, despising God's workings in me."

Our Lord told me, "Daughter, if he, a priest who knows well enough the reasons behind your tears and cries, derides you, then he is doomed."

Then one day, when I was hiding myself in the prior's cloister not daring to go into church for fear of disturbing the people with my loud cries, I was heavy-hearted but our Lord said, "Daughter, I tell you now, go over into the church because I will take away your crying so that you will no longer shout out so loud. It will not be as it was before, even if you wanted to do so."

I did as our Lord told me, and I let my confessor know what had happened and exactly how I felt. And in fact, matters turned out just as I had been told they would. After this time, I no longer cried out loud; I behaved quite unlike I had before. But later I did continue to sob as extremely and weep as bitterly as ever; sometimes it was loudly, at other times silently within myself, just as God himself ordained it.

When this became public knowledge people would say that I dared not cry out any more because of the way the good friar had preached against me and stood up to me. They said what a holy man he really was, and what a false masquerading woman I was. Just as they all spoke against me when I did cry out, so now they spoke against me when I didn't. So I was surrounded by slander and bodily pain from all sides; but it was all to my spiritual good.

Our Lord spoke again to me, his own unworthy servant: "Daughter, I will tell you comforting news: Now you can see your road to heaven. I myself walked along this same path, and all my disciples did the same. Now you can realize much more clearly what sorrow and shame I had to bear for your love. Now you will have even greater compassion when you dwell upon my Passion. Daughter, I have told you many times that this friar has no right to speak evil of you. But I am warning you now that you are not to tell him anything about our inner conversations and the things I say in private to you. I do not want him to hear any of this from you. And I assure you that he will be punished most severely. As high as his reputation stands at present, so it will be muddied, but your name will be held high. And I shall cause as many to love you out of my love as have despised you for my love. Daughter, you will find yourself inside the church while he will be outside. It was in this church that you have suffered so much humiliation and hurtful words on account of the gifts I have given you and because of the grace and goodness I have worked in you. And therefore in this church and in this special place I will be worshiped for my presence in you. Many will say, 'It is plain that God loves her dearly.' I tell you, daughter, I will work such grace in you that all the world shall come to wonder and marvel at my goodness."

Then I made my reply to our Lord with great reverence: "I am not worthy that you should show such grace to me. Lord, I shall be content if you save my soul from endless damnation, in your great mercy."

"What I do, daughter, is to my own honor, so I want you to have no other will than what is mine. The less you think of yourself, the more highly I think of you and the more I love you, my daughter. Make sure you do not grieve about worldly trappings. I have tested you in poverty, I have corrected you as I wanted, both inwardly and outwardly through people's harsh words. Listen to me, daughter, I give you your heart's wish, you will have no other Purgatory apart from this present world.

Daughter, you often tell me in your thoughts that rich men have every reason to love me. And what you say is true, since I have given them so much with which they can love and serve me. But, daughter, all I ask of you is that you love me with all your heart, and then I will give you everything you can ever want to love me with. Heaven and earth will sooner fail, than I fail you. And if people let you down, you will never falter. Even if all your friends desert you, I will never leave you. A long time ago you made me steward of your household and your executor to carry out all your good works. I will be your true steward, your trusty servant in carrying out your will and all your deepest desires. I shall provide for you, daughter, as I would for my own mother and my very own wife."

64

hen I said to my lord Christ Jesus, "Ah, blissful Lord, I wish I knew how best I might love and please you. If only my love for you were as sweet to you as your love feels to me."

Then our sweet Lord gave me his answer: "Daughter, if only you knew how sweet your love is to me, you would never do anything other than simply love me with all your heart. Therefore, daughter, be certain, my love for you is never so sweet as your love for me. Daughter, you cannot tell how much I love you for it may never be counted sufficiently in this world, nor may it be felt as it truly is, for you would faint and burst and never be able to suffer it, for all the joy you would experience. And so I ration it in the measure that I know you can withstand, for your greater ease and comfort.

"But daughter, you shall know in another world how much I loved you on this earth; and there you will have every reason to thank me. For there you will see clearly forever all the good days you passed on earth—all your contemplation, your devotions, and all the love you were given toward your fellow Christians. Such will be your reward when you come home into heaven.

"There is not a single scholar in all this world, daughter, who can teach you better than I can. If you will listen to my words, I will listen to yours. What better sign of love than to weep for your Lord's love? You know very well, daughter, that in the devil there is no such thing as love. He is angry with you and he might sometimes do you harm, but he can never injure you, except perhaps a little. From time to time, while you are in this world, he will frighten you. Then you must pray all the more mightily for my grace and put all your love in my direction. There is no scholar who can gainsay the life I will show you; if he tries to do so, he is the devil's scholar! I tell you the truth when I say that if there is anyone in this world who would be willing to suffer as much humiliation for love of me as you have done—and would cling as faithfully to me, not ready to let go no matter what is said or done—I shall honor him in justice and afford him great grace, both in this world and in the next."

Then I made bold to say, "Ah, my beloved Lord, you should show this kind of life to religious folk and your priests."

But our Lord answered me, "No, no, daughter, for the things I best love, they avoid: that is, humiliation, contempt, confusion, and the world's harsh words. And so they may not have my grace. For, daughter, I tell you this, anyone who shrinks from the world's derision may not perfectly love God. For, daughter, under the trade of holiness much wickedness is hidden. Daughter, if only you knew the wickedness that goes on in the world, you would wonder that I never take my vengeance. But, daughter, I hold back for love of you. You shed tears every day for mercy, and I must grant it; and still people refuse to believe the good I work in you on their behalf.

"Even so, daughter, a time will come when they will be only too glad to believe the grace I have given you for them. And I shall say to them when they have passed from this world, 'Now do you see, I caused her to weep for her sins and you despised her, but her love for you never dried up.' And so, daughter, the just shall have reason to thank me greatly for the grace and goodness I have given you; and the wicked will complain at the great pain they have to suffer when they see what graces I have given you. Therefore I will punish them just as if their sneers had been aimed at me."

But I pleaded, "No, my beloved Lord Jesus, do not punish anyone on my behalf. You know well that I seek no vengeance. Rather I ask mercy and grace for all men, if it be your will to grant it. But punish us as you wish, Lord, rather than have us separated from you forever. I know in my soul, Lord, that you are full of love, for you have said that you do not want the death of the sinful man. And you also tell us that you want all men saved. Then, Lord, since you want all men to be saved, I must want the same thing, since you tell me to love all my fellow Christians as I do myself. And so, Lord, you know how much I have wept and sorrowed all these many years so that I might be saved. And I must do the same for my fellow Christians."

65

ur Lord Jesus Christ told me, "Daughter, you shall see once you are in heaven that no man is ever damned unless he well and truly deserves to be; and then you yourself will be more than satisfied by all my works. And so, daughter, be grateful to me for bringing so much love into your heart as it is myself, Almighty God, who makes you weep each day for your sins; for the great tenderness you have toward my bitter passion; for all the sorrows my mother suffered on earth, the anguish that she underwent and all the tears she also wept; as well, my daughter, for the holy martyrs in heaven—for I know that when you hear of the martyrs you give thanks to me, crying and weeping for the grace that I have manifested in them; and again, whenever you see lepers you have great sympathy with them, and are thankful to me that I have treated you more kindly than them; and also, daughter, for the great compassion you have for this world, that you might help everyone here as much as you want to help yourself, in body and spirit; and also for the sorrow you have for the souls in Purgatory, wishing them to be free from their pains so that they might be with me, praising God without end.

"All of this I have given you from my goodness, and because of it all you feel a great bond of gratitude toward me. Even so, I thank you for the great love you have for me, as well as for that great will and desire you have for every man and woman to love me dearly. It is only right for everyone—both holy and unholy alike—to seek to fulfill their temporal needs and find money sufficient to live on, but few are as concerned to love me as they are to win the goods of this world.

"Also, daughter, I thank you for seeking to regain my presence when you feel apart from me. And I thank you especially, daughter, that you try to stop people from breaking my commandments. And when they swear by taking my name, this is a great pain to you and so you are always ready to correct their swearing for love of me. As a consequence, often you have had to suffer many sharp words and rebuffs, and because of that you will have many joys in heaven.

"Daughter, I once sent Saint Paul to strengthen you and bring you comfort,[109] and thus you could speak out boldly about me from that time onward. Saint Paul told you that you had suffered a great deal of trouble on account of his writing. And he promised that because of this, you would have as much grace for loving him as you had pain and humiliation. He also told you of the great joys of heaven and of the very great love that I have toward you.

"And, daughter, remember that there is no saint in heaven who will not be ready, if you just speak to them, to comfort you and speak with you in my name. My angels, too, are ready to bring you holy thoughts and carry your prayers to me together with the tears that fall from your eyes, for your tears are drink to the angels, tasting better to them than mulled wine with spice and honey.

"Therefore, my own dear daughter, never tire on earth of sitting alone and thinking of me and my love; I am never weary of you but my eye of mercy is always gazing at you. Daughter, you may say quite openly to me *Jesus est amor meus*, meaning "Jesus is all my love." And so, daughter, let me really be all your love, the only joy in your heart.

[109] Nowhere in the text does Margery give any other details of this vision.

"Daughter, if you think carefully about it, you have every reason to love me more than anything because of the great graces I have given you up till now. And yet there is one more reason, since now you have your wish and are chaste, just as if you were a widow, although your husband is still alive and in good health.

"I have taken the love that your heart once had for men and turned it solely toward me. There was a time, daughter, when you believed it was impossible for that to happen. And then you were suffering great heartache because of your worldly loves. You remember, you would cry out to me, 'Lord, by all the painful wounds you suffered, turn the love of my heart and fix it on you alone.'

"Daughter, for all these reasons and many others as well as the graces I have given you, both in England and abroad, you have much cause to love me."

66

 ow, daughter, you must listen to me. I want you to eat meat again as you once did. In this way, you can be docile and obedient to my will, and you should tell your confessors to allow you to act in conformity with my will. You will have no less grace, but even more; you will have the same reward in heaven as if you were still fasting as you yourself prefer. It was my will first to tell you to give up meat at your meals, and you have followed my will for many years. And now I bid you to take up eating meat again."

But I answered this with fear and reverence: "Ah, blessed Lord, people who have known me to abstain from meat over many years and then see me starting to eat it again will be shocked—and, I suppose almost certainly, will begin to despise and mock me because of it."

"You should take no notice," our Lord answered, "but let them have their say."

Then I went as bidden to my confessors and told them what our Lord had said. And recognizing the will of God, they bade me by virtue of obedience to eat meat as I had done many years before. So I was subjected to yet more mockery now because I was seen to be eating meat once again.

I had also taken a vow in honor of our Lady to fast once a week for as long as I lived; and this I kept for many years. Our Lady came to me in my soul and said that I should go to my confessor and say that she wanted to dispense me of my vow. In that way I would be strong enough in body to perform my spiritual duties, for without a strong body these would wear me down. My confessor agreed that this was only prudent, and he told me to eat in moderation, just as others did, when God wanted me to eat. And this resulted in more grace rather than less, because, if it had been God's will, I would rather have fasted.

And our Lady told me, "Daughter, you are already weakened by your tears and crying out loud, both of these sap your strength. And so I must thank you more for eating meat for love of me than for carrying on your fasting. In this way, you will be able to continue your practice of weeping."

67

ne January day [in 1421], a great fire swept
through Bishop's Lynn. One of the first
buildings that was burned down was the hall
of the Guild of the Trinity. And the flames came so near to
our parish church of Saint Margaret, a noble and richly decorated building, that it was a miracle it was spared. Indeed the
whole town was threatened by these terrible flames.

I myself saw it all happening and realized the danger the
town was in. All through that day I was in church praying. I
cried out loudly and wept copiously, praying for grace and
mercy for all the townspeople. Unlike any other time, when
people would not tolerate my crying and weeping that was
the work of God's grace, now they believed it would help
them in their danger. So they let me cry out as much as I
would, and no one protested. Rather, they urged me to persevere, believing that through my crying and weeping our Lord
would bring them his mercy.

My confessor came and asked me if it would help to carry
the precious Sacrament toward the heart of the flames.

I told him, "Yes, sir, do that at once! Jesus Christ our Lord
has told me that will help."

So my confessor, who was parish priest of Saint Margaret's Church, took the precious Sacrament and walked out as
devoutly as he could toward the flames. But very soon he was
back and as he came into the church I saw sparks flying

through the doorway. I wanted to accompany the precious Sacrament so I made my way to the church door. But as soon as I saw how close the terrible flames had come, I cried out at once in a loud voice and with many tears: "Good Lord, make everything well again!"

These words lingered in my mind. For our Lord had said to me before that he would make all things well and so I began to cry out again, "Good Lord, make all things well. Send down your rainstorms and in your mercy quench this fire and bring peace to my heart again."

Having prayed thus, I moved back into the church. And then I saw that sparks were showering down through the wooden lantern tower. Now my heart was full of fresh sorrow; I cried out yet again for grace, very loud and with many tears. And soon after, three good men came into the church, their clothing all covered with snow. "See, Margery, God has shown us great grace and sent down a good snowfall to quench the flames. Take heart and thank God for us."

I praised God and with a great cry thanked him for his mercy. He had said that all would be well, even when it appeared almost impossible save by a miracle and very special grace. And now that everything was well once more, I had very great cause to thank our Lord.

My confessor came back and declared that he believed it had been due to my prayers that God had delivered us from that great danger. For without the power of prayer, he insisted, it was impossible that a bright clear sky should suddenly be changed and huge dark clouds begin to send down great flakes of snow. Thus was the terrible fire prevented from carrying through its natural course—blessed may our Lord be.

Yet in spite of the grace that God had showed for me, once the danger was over some people still complained when I cried out. "Why do you insist on crying out loud?" they asked me, adding that even our Lady had never cried out like this. I told them I could not stop myself or do otherwise.

And after this, I got away from the people by going into the prior's cloister so they would have no further cause to complain. Yet as soon as I was there, I had such intense recall of the passion of our Lord Jesus Christ, of his precious wounds and how dearly he had bought me, that I cried out with an amazing great roar that could be heard a long way off. I simply could not prevent myself from doing so.

But I went on to marvel how our Lady had survived and endured the sight of his precious body being scourged and then hung up on the cross. I remembered people telling me that our Lady, Christ's very own mother, did not cry out as I did, and this made me say as I wept, "Lord, I am not your mother. Take this pain from me, for I cannot bear it any more. Your passion will finish me."

And there was a devout priest who came by at that moment, and he said to me, "I would gladly hand over twenty pounds if I could experience such sorrow as yours for our Lord's passion."

And this same doctor invited me to come to him and speak with him in his study; I gladly went to his rooms and I was still weeping. This kind and admirable man then made me a drink and went out of his way to make me welcome and at ease. Then he led me before an altar and wanted to know exactly why I cried and wept so bitterly. I told him in general that there were many very good reasons that I wept as I did, yet I did not disclose to him any particular revelation. And he agreed that I had ample motive to love our Lord so, since he had offered me so many signs of his own love toward me.

On one occasion, a preacher came to give a course of sermons, mornings and afternoons. He had a degree and preached devoutly, touching upon many holy matters. As I listened to him, at length I burst out with a loud cry. And people at once began to grumble, for this was around the time that the good friar was preaching against me and before this compulsion to yell aloud had been cured and taken from me. (I should perhaps have told this story earlier, but here it is now.)

Well, the priest stopped in the middle of his sermon. And he paused for a moment; then he said to the people, "Friends, be at peace, do not complain about this woman. For any one of you could sin mortally because of her. Yet she is not the true cause, but your own judgment is. Her way of behaving could seem either good or bad; but you yourselves ought to decide what is best for your peace of mind. For myself, I have no doubt at all that it is an excellent thing. I go further—it is a very great gift of God's grace. Blessed may he be."

The people murmured their approval of these good words and were convinced that he was a holy man in both word and deed. And when the sermon was at an end, one of my close friends happened to meet the friar who had preached against me so critically, and he asked this friar again what he thought about me. But he was adamant: "She has a devil." There was no shift from his opinion; he stood firm in his error.

68

oon afterward, the Order of Preachers held their general chapter at Lynn. Many good priests of the order arrived and one was to preach at the parish church.

One of these Dominicans attending their general chapter was a good doctor called Master Constance who had known me for a good number of years. When I heard he had arrived, I therefore went to visit him. I wanted to consult him about my habit of weeping and crying out to see if he could find anything amiss.

This doctor then told me, "I have read of one holy woman to whom God had given a remarkable grace of tears and loud crying, just like yourself. And at the church she attended there was a priest who had a very poor opinion of her behavior. And at one time, he insisted that she leave the church. As she stood in the churchyard, she prayed to God that he would give this priest some inkling of what this gift was like for her. For she was certain that it was not her choice to weep or cry out except when God so willed. And sure enough, God suddenly sent him such devotion in the middle of the mass that he could not hide it. And ever after, he no longer wanted to criticize her but rather chose to comfort her."

Therefore, the doctor confirmed that my crying out and weeping was a recognizable grace and gift from God, and told me I should thank him greatly for it.

This same doctor accordingly went to another doctor who was engaged to preach at the parish church and warned him that if I cried out as he was speaking, he should take it calmly and not be upset or complain. The day came and this worthy doctor was duly led into the pulpit. He began to preach a devout and holy sermon on the Assumption of our Lady. In the middle of his words, I was taken up by a high consolation and sweet devotion, so that I burst out weeping very loudly and bitterly. At this, the good priest stood perfectly still and waited patiently until I had subsided. Then he continued preaching until he had concluded all he had to say.

That same afternoon, he invited me to his lodgings and made me most welcome. I was able to thank him for his humility and kindness in suffering my weeping and calling out that morning during his sermon. The good man simply said, "Margery, I wasn't going to criticize you, not even if you had wept through till evening. And if you ever come to Norwich, you will be most welcome and I will be glad to offer you such hospitality as I can afford."

In such a way, God sent me an excellent patron in the person of this eminent doctor. He was able to offer me encouragement in the face of all my critics, thanks be to God.

When Lent came around, an Augustinian priest preached in his own priory and there was a very large audience attending his sermon; I was among the throng. The preacher was inspired, by God's goodness, to describe in detail the passion. He did so very devoutly and with such tender sensitivity that I could not bear it. I fell down in church weeping and crying so demonstrably that people were extremely angry at my interruption. They imagined I could have stopped my crying at once on hearing their protests, for they knew the friar had already warned me in his own sermons. But this good priest stopped his sermon and said, "Friends, please be quiet—you can hardly know what she is going through."

People listened to him and were quiet again. And we all heard the remainder of his sermon at peace in both body and spirit.

69

nd then one Good Friday at Saint Margaret's Church, Prior Thomas Hevingham himself was due to preach. He took as his title, "Jesus Is Dead." I was deeply moved and felt full of pity and compassion. I cried out and wept as if I could see our Lord's dead body with my own eyes. The good prior, a doctor of divinity, took all this with perfect patience and never even referred to it afterward.

On another occasion, Bishop Wakering of Norwich came to preach at Saint Margaret's Church in Lynn. And once again I was moved to cry out and weep very loudly during his sermon; but he took it quietly and with patience. And so did many another priest, both secular and regular; indeed no single priest ever objected publicly about my behavior except the Franciscan friar whom I have mentioned above.

But in his mercy, and exactly as he had promised, our Lord provided for me. He disposed two more good priests in my favor. They had both known me for the space of several years. In the course of our many conversations, they had come to know how much I longed for perfection and were therefore willing to speak out on my behalf and make excuses for me. They did so both publicly and in private, and would bring the scripture to add weight to their argument. These priests were, first, Master Aleyn of Lynn, the Carmelite, who was a doctor of divinity; and second, my confessor, Master Robert Spryngolde, a bachelor of canon law and a man much versed in the study of scripture.

But some people who were envious of me complained to the Provincial of the Carmelites[110] that Master Aleyn was seeing too much of me. They specified that he also supported me in my weeping and would answer any question on scripture that I cared to put to him. The outcome was that he was admonished and, under holy obedience, no longer permitted to speak to me, or enlighten me further on the scriptures. He found this sentence very painful. He told his friends that he would rather have given away one hundred pounds—supposing for one moment that he had such a sum—than give up talking with me, for he vowed it was so spiritual and nourishing to him.

When my confessor heard that Master Aleyn was under obedience not to speak with me, he obliged me solemnly not

110 Thomas Netter (d. 1430) was inquisitor of England and took the lead in putting Wycliffe out of his Oxford teaching post, persecuted the Lollards, attended the Council of Constance, and witnessed the burning of Jan Hus. He was confessor to Henry V (who died in his arms), also to Henry VI, and he instituted the Carmelite nuns in England and was patron of women anchorites, yet wished them not to seek publicity. Note that the charges against Margery's confessor mention knowledge of the scriptures, deemed the hallmark of Lollardy and particularly unacceptable with regard to women.

to go to the friars anymore, nor speak to the doctor nor ask him any more of my questions. At this, I was very gloomy and felt shut off from all spiritual comfort. I would have given anything to talk with him, for I felt that he had greatly helped my spiritual progress.

Much later, I happened to be walking along the street when I saw Doctor Aleyn. Neither of us spoke, yet I let out a great cry and went straight past him, shedding many tears. Later that day, as I came to pray, I complained to our Lord Jesus Christ, "Alas, my Lord, why can't I seek comfort from this good priest who has known me all these years and often given me new strength to love you? Let me count: You took away my anchorite—very well, I trust your mercy—but he was the most special friend and comfort I had upon this earth. And he only ever loved me out of love for you. He would never have left me as long as he lived, no matter what anyone said or did. Now Master Aleyn is cut out of my life. He may not see me, I may not see him. Then there was Sir Thomas Andrew, Sir John Amy—they have both gone away to benefices out of town. So now I have no one, man or boy, to comfort me."

Our merciful Lord Christ Jesus answered my complaint in my mind, saying, "Daughter, I can offer your soul more than your anchorite and any of the others you name. I myself shall comfort you, and I would speak to you more often than you allow. That apart, you can be sure that you will speak to Master Aleyn again, just as you did in the past."

Then our Lord sent another priest, at the dispensation of the Prior of Lynn, to be keeper of the chapel of our Lady, the Gesine shrine. And he heard my confession many times, whenever my own confessor was not available. To him I confided my whole life, as near as I was able to recall, from my girlhood onward; I told him my sins, my travails, my trials, my contemplations as well as those graces that God had worked in me through his mercy. And this priest was able to confirm that God was indeed working great grace in me.

70

here came a time when God visited Master Aleyn with a grave illness. No one could say if he would last. And when I heard about his state, I was saddened for him. I thought of my revelation that I would indeed one day speak again with him; yet if he were to die, this would show that I had untruly discerned my spirit.

I was very upset and ran at once into the choir of Saint Margaret's Church, and there, kneeling before the Sacrament, I prayed these words: "Lord, I pray you, with all the kindness you have shown me, and for the sake of your love, let this priest not die until I have spoken with him. For you yourself promised me as much. And you, Queen of Mercy, remember the words he spoke of you in his sermons; he would say that anyone who had you for a friend was blessed indeed. When you prayed, he told us, all the company in heaven prayed with you. So now, for the blissful love you have for your son, let him live until he is able to speak with me and I may talk to him. But for now we are separated by obedience."

Then I had an answer in my soul that he would not die before I had leave to speak with him and he with me, just as we had before. And according to our Lord's will, a little while later this good priest recovered his strength and went outdoors hale and hearty; and presently he had leave to speak with me once more. And I also received my confessor's word that I might meet with Master Aleyn once more.

It turned out that the doctor was to dine in town with a good woman who had taken the mantle and the ring,[111] and he sent for me to come and talk with him. I was not prepared for this, but having received permission, I went and found him. When I arrived at his house, I could not speak for weeping and for the joy I had in our Lord. For I now knew that my feelings had not been false, as now I had full permission to speak with him and he with me.

The good doctor said as he greeted me, "Margery, you are most welcome. I have been kept away from you for so long a time, and now our Lord has brought you here so that I can speak with you, blessed may he be."

We had dinner together with great joy and gladness, far more in spirit than in body, for our conversation had the sauce and flavoring of many stories from Holy Scripture. And when we were done, he gave me a pair of knives—in token, he declared, of his promise that he would always stand by me in God's good cause, just as he had done in the past.

[111] That is, she had become an anchoress; Thomas Netter encouraged holy women of this kind, providing they did not seek attention. Possibly it was judged that Margery had now proved herself in some degree and it was thus thought appropriate for Master Aleyn to attend to her once more.

71

ne day, a priest called on me and assured me that he had every confidence in my inner feelings as well as my revelations; yet he would like to put them to the test in various ways. He began by asking me to pray to our Lord and see whether I might have some knowledge about the prior of Lynn, whether or not he would stay in his present office or be replaced by another. I was to give this priest a simple account of how I felt. I prayed about the matter and had my answer. I told the priest, who had his own reason for wanting to know since the prior was a good patron to him, that he would soon be called home to Norwich and another of his brethren would replace him. And so indeed it turned out. Yet the new prior who came to Lynn stayed only a short while. And the former prior of Lynn returned once more and stayed on again for some four years before he died.

But meanwhile I had the continuing feeling that the priest from Norwich, who had stayed only a short while before being called home to Norwich, would again become prior at Lynn. But I could scarcely take this seriously, since he had been recalled after so short a time.

But one day, as I walked up and down in the Carmelite church at Lynn, I smelled a most wonderful and sweet scent as if from heaven itself. I thought that it alone could have sustained me, with no more need of food or drink, if only it might have lasted. And at that moment our Lord told me, "Daughter, by this sweet smell you should know that in a little while there will be a new prior in Lynn. And he will be the priest who was recently moved from here."

And soon after this, the prior died; and then as I lay one day in bed, our Lord said, "Daughter, reluctant as you seem to believe my promptings, you will see the man I spoke of become Prior of Lynn before this week is over."

And our Lord repeated his message to me each day for a week, until I recognized that it was indeed true and I was very glad and overjoyed that my feelings were not false.

The new prior was a very good man, well respected and a doctor of divinity. Not long after he was installed, he was appointed to join an envoy together with many other of the most distinguished clerics in the land to meet with the king in France. And a priest, who was an officer of the prior, came and asked me to be mindful, when I was in prayer with God, to discover whether or not the prior should cross the sea on this business. And so I prayed about the matter and was answered that the prior would not go. But for his part, he still expected to make the crossing, and indeed all his plans were made. He had taken leave of all his friends, and with some grief, since—being a sick man—he expected never to return. But while he was making his preparations, the king died, and so the prior stayed at home.[112] Thus my feelings were shown to be true and without deception.

There was also a rumor at this time that the Bishop of Winchester[113] had died, yet I had a feeling that he was alive —and it turned out that this was the truth. I had similar feelings about many other matters that cannot be written down; God in his mercy had revealed them to me, although I was unworthy to know such things through any merit of mine.

[112] Henry V died of a fever at Vincennes, August 31, 1422.
[113] Henry Beaufort, the brother of the Countess of Westmorland whom Margery had visited. He had been Henry V's chancellor.

72

As time passed, my mind and my every thought were so fixed upon God that I never forgot him; he was constantly in my mind, and I would see him in all his creatures. And the greater my love and devotion increased, so I became more aware of my sorrow, contrition, poverty of spirit, meekness, and my simple dread of our Lord. I was also keenly aware of my own frailty; when I saw someone being punished or rebuked, I would know that I myself should have been chastised in their stead, since I had behaved so unkindly toward God. Then I would cry and weep and sob on account of my own sin and out of compassion for the person I saw being punished or chastised.

When I witnessed a prince, a bishop, or some other man of importance in rank or office being honored by his fellow men who would abase themselves in his presence, this always gave me fresh cheer in our Lord. Seeing how mere mortal men on earth enjoy such great honors, I would think about the joy and bliss in heaven among all his saints as they give him his due honor and reverence. But most of all, when I saw the precious Sacrament carried in procession through the town with tapers and due ceremony, and people falling to their knees, then I would have so many holy thoughts and meditations that I would often cry out with a great roar, thinking I might burst my lungs, because of the faith and trust I knew in the reality of the precious Sacrament.

More and more people sent for me to be with them on their deathbeds. They wished me to pray for them; and, although they themselves had had little time for it during their lifetimes, they expected me to weep and cry out loud for them as they lay dying. And I would help them in that way. As I saw them being anointed with the holy oils, I had so many holy thoughts. My meditation, as they lay dying, would center on our Lord's own dying; or another time I might be with our Lady as she lay dying; this was all according to how God chose to illumine my spiritual sight and give me understanding. Seeing our Lord or our Lady dying, I would weep and cry out amazingly loud. As I witnessed people die who would far rather have lived, I would think, "My Lord, I would very gladly come to you, yet you do not seem to want me." Thoughts such as these only increased my weeping and my sobbing.

One day I was talking to a lady who had sent for me to meet with her. As our conversation developed, I became more and more aware that she was affording me a special kind of respect and could not help herself from praising every word I uttered. It was very painful for me to have such attention; yet I offered it up to our Lord—my only real desire was that he should be praised, not me—and I gave a great cry with many devout tears.

I have found that neither praise nor honor, and neither the love of people nor their wounding detractions, would take me away from God's love. As Saint Paul writes; "For those who love him, God makes all things turn to their good." And such was my experience. No matter what I saw or heard, my love and spiritual affection for our Lord grew stronger—blessed may he be, who worked such grace in me for men's benefit.

One day, I was sent for by another highborn lady who was surrounded by her retainers; and they showed me nothing but the highest reverence. And when I had to endure this kind of treatment, I started to weep and cry out in abject sorrow. A priest who was present and saw how I cried out and wept proved incapable of discerning the spiritual values of my behavior. All he could ask was, "What the devil's got into you? Why ever are you weeping? May God bring you every misery!"

I sat quietly and said not a word. Then my lady took me to one side and led me out into her garden. There she inquired why I was so grievously upset. I thought it only proper and polite to tell her, at least in part, my reasons. The lady listened and was at once displeased with what the priest had said; but her love for me knew no limits and she insisted that I remain there with her. Yet I decided to excuse myself, explaining that I did not approve of the manner of dress or the behavior that I had witnessed in her household.

73

ne Maundy Thursday, I was taking part in the procession with everyone else; and I saw in my soul our Lady, Saint Mary Magdalene, and the twelve apostles. And in my spiritual eye I witnessed the manner in which our Lady took her farewells of her blessed son, Jesus. I saw, too, how tenderly he kissed her and every one of his apostles, as well as his dearly beloved Mary Magdalene. I knew it then as a sorrowful parting but a joyful one. As I beheld this sight in my soul, I fell down upon my face in the field in front of all those people.

Then I cried out loud and roared and I wept fit to burst. I was not in the least able to control or master my feelings, but I went on crying out loud and roaring to the astonishment of the crowds that were there—that I had any perception of them, for my mind was totally absorbed with our Lord.

At that moment I experienced many a holy thought that I would be unable to speak of later. All earthly matters were set aside, and I could contemplate only spiritual things. I thought that all possible joy had left me, for I saw my Lord ascend into heaven; yet I could not live without him on this earth. So I desired only to go with him, for he was all my joy, he was all my bliss. I knew well that I would never have true bliss until I came to him. Such were the holy thoughts and sacred desires that made me weep so hard, yet the people could not guess what ailed me.

In another vision, I beheld our Lady dying. She was surrounded by the apostles, who knelt before her asking for grace. Then indeed I cried out and wept bitterly. The apostles turned toward me as they begged me to stop my noise and be still. But I answered the apostles, "Would you really want me to witness the death of our Lady and yet not weep? That cannot be: I am so full of sorrow that I cannot bear it. All I can do is cry out and weep."

Then in my soul I said to our Lady, "My blessed Lady, pray for me to your son. Beg him that I may come to you and no longer be held back from you. Lady, this is too great a sorrow for me, to be both at your son's death and your own death. For I may not die along with you, but am left behind here where there is no more joy or comfort."

Then our Lady, answering me in my soul, promised to pray for me to her son. And she said, "Daughter, all these sorrows that you have borne for my son shall turn for you into great joy and bliss in heaven without end. And never doubt, my daughter, that you shall come to us and you shall be most welcome when you come. You may not come for a while, yet in very good time you will come. Daughter, be sure that I will be your own true mother to you. I shall help you, strengthen you, just as a good mother should her own daughter. I shall bring you grace and virtue. For that same pardon granted you

before on Saint Nicholas's Day[114] is given not just to you but
to all those who believe, and shall believe until the world's
ending, that God loves you, and who thank God for your life.
Also if they turn from their sins, truly intending to sin no
more, if they grieve for what they have done and do penance,
then they shall have pardon, the same pardon granted to you.
This is all the grace of pardon that is in Jerusalem, as was
given you at Ramleh."

74

ne day, as I was hearing mass, I was thinking
hard about when I would come to die. I
sighed and sorrowed so much because I felt
that blessed day would never come. And so I prayed, "My
lord, how much longer must I wait, weeping and mourning
for love of you and my desire to be with you, in your presence
at last?"

Our Lord answered me in my soul, "All of fifteen years."

"Then, Lord, I shall count that many a thousand years."

"My daughter, you must recall my own blessed mother,
who lived after me on earth for fifteen years. Also, Saint John
the Evangelist and Mary Magdalene, who were both very
dear in my love."

"My blissful Lord, I wish I were as worthy of your love as
was Mary Magdalene."

[114] In Chapter 30 Margery reports how she had a vision of our Lord who gave her a "full
pardon" or plenary indulgence when she was returning from Jerusalem.

"In all truth, my daughter, I love you just as well; the same peace I gave her, I give to you. Daughter, no saint of mine in heaven is upset when I love a creature on earth as much as I love them. And so they never want anything other than my own true will."

In this way, our Lord Christ Jesus wished to draw me to love him by recalling his passion, so that I could scarcely bear to see a leper, nor even look at any man who was sick, especially if he bore any open wounds. For then I would cry and weep just as if I had seen our Lord himself with his very own gaping wounds. For then, seeing that sick person, my mind could only behold the person of our Lord Jesus Christ.

Then would I feel great mourning within my soul, sorrow that I might not kiss these lepers, for love of Jesus, whenever I saw them or met them in the street. Yet now I came to love what before I had hated most. Then, when I had been rich and prosperous, there had been nothing more loathsome than the sight of a leper. Now, through our Lord's mercy, I would gladly have taken them into my home, kissed and embraced them, had I but the means and the place.

But when I told my confessor of my wish to kiss lepers, he warned me off trying to kiss men. If I wished to kiss anyone, I should kiss women. Acting upon this permission to embrace sick women, I made my way to a house where I knew women lived who were very ill indeed. I went down on my knees in front of them and begged to kiss them on the mouth for love of Jesus. And I embraced two of them, with many holy thoughts and tears; and when I had kissed them, I spoke with them at length on many holy subjects. I encouraged them not to resent their illness but to accept their sufferings with humility and patience, thanking God for the bliss they would enjoy in heaven through the mercy of our Lord Jesus Christ.

One woman I met there told me that she had so many temptations she did not know which way to turn. Her spiritual enemy so dominated her that she dared not even bless herself nor offer any prayer to God, in case the devil killed her. She was tormented by many foul and horrible thoughts, too many to count; yet she assured me that she was neverthe-less still a virgin. I went back to visit her regularly, praying with her and offering her what comfort I might, asking God to fortify her against the enemy. And I have every reason to suppose that he did so, blessed may he be.

75

was at my prayers in Saint Margaret's Church one day, when a man came and knelt down just behind me. I was aware that he was very agitated, since he kept on wringing his hands, so I asked him the cause of his distress. He told me that things were very difficult for him at home; his wife had just had a baby and had gone out of her mind.

"And what is more," he told me, "she no longer even rec-ognizes me or any of our neighbors. She shouts loudly and cries all day long, which frightens everyone in sight. At times she gets so violent, hitting out and biting, that she has to be manacled to restrain her."

So I asked him if he would like me to go and visit her and he replied, "Yes, lady, for the love of God, come quickly." So I went at once with him to see his wife.

As soon as I entered their home, the poor woman who had been deranged spoke to me with a measured voice and said I was most welcome. She added that she was glad I had come and my visit was a very great comfort. "You are a very good woman," she declared. "I can see that you are surrounded by angels. I beg you not to go away, because you are such a comfort to me."

But when anybody else came near her, she cried out and opened her mouth as if making to eat them. She told them she could see only devils all around them, so she would not let them near her but roared and shouted abuse practically night and day. This so annoyed her neighbors that they no longer wanted her living nearby. So a room was found for her on the edge of town where she was out of earshot. And they had to bind her hand and foot in case she struck out at anyone.

I visited her daily, at least once or twice each day. And whenever I was with her, she was perfectly calm. She was able to talk to me perfectly normally; there was no sign of her roaring and shouting. I prayed for her each day, asking God, if it were his will, to restore her wits. And our Lord answered me in my soul and promised that she would recover. Encouraged, I redoubled my prayers every day with tears and weeping until God did indeed bring her to her proper senses. And presently she was brought to church and purified, just like any other mother with a newborn child. May God be blessed for it.

This whole episode was thought to be a very considerable miracle by all those who knew the facts. And certainly the scribe who is writing this book had never in his life seen either man or woman so far out of their mind nor so difficult to restrain as this woman had been. Yet afterward, he witnessed her return to being a normal and reasonable person. May God be thanked and praised without end for his great goodness and mercy, God who always helps us in the hour of need.

76

hen one day, my husband had a fall. He was over sixty at the time and was coming down from his bedroom in his bare feet and still in his nightshirt when he skidded and missed his footing. He fell the full length of the stairs; his neck was wrenched and he was badly cut and bruised. He had to have five linen plugs to staunch the bleeding, and he was confined to bed for several days while his head healed.

Some neighbors, God permitting, guessed what had happened as soon as they heard the commotion; and they came in and found him lying all crumpled at the foot of the stairs. Finding him in this terrible state, all covered in blood, they judged him more dead than alive. And, although they sent for the priest, they guessed he would never be able to say a word, unless there were some kind of miracle.

I was called and came around at once. He was put to bed in his room and his head patched up, and there he stayed for many a day; and many feared the worst. And people began to whisper that if he were to die, it would be his wife's fault. They argued that I, who should have been caring for him, had neglected him as an old man. We had not been living together, it was true, but neither had we been sleeping together; we had both agreed to that. And to be on the safe side, having both freely vowed to live chastely, we had lived separately. In that way, there could be no doubt about our chastity. In truth, we had lived together at first; but then people told lies about us and put it about that we still slept together in spite of our vow. Even when we went on pilgrimage together, or even when we visited someone together on purely spiritual matters, it was the same—tongues wagged. People who spread such evil talk only hurt themselves; when they made up their stories that we crept away together to the woods in order to enjoy the lust of our bodies, they showed neither love nor fear of our Lord Jesus Christ.

In truth we knew full well how ready people were to believe the worst of us, so in order to avoid all cause for gossip, we separated and went to live in different houses. This was the chief reason I no longer lived with my husband; and it also meant that I was more free to say my prayers and attend my devotions. But people still went about saying that if he ever died from this fall of his, I was to blame and should have to answer for it. My only recourse was to pray to our Lord, begging him, if it be his will, that my husband might live for at least a year in order to clear my name.

Our Lord told me in my mind, "Daughter, your request will be granted, he will live. I have already wrought a great miracle for you in that he is not dead already. Now take him home with you and look after him for love of me."

"No, good Lord," was my reply, "because then I will not be able to spend my time attending to you."

"Yes, you must, daughter, for you shall have as much reward looking after him and caring for his needs at home as if you were on your knees in church. How often have you said you wanted to look after me; so care for him now for love of me. Remember how he has at one time and another done what we both wanted. He let you go free, so that you could serve me and live a pure and chaste life; so I want you to make yourself available for him now that he needs you. Do this in my name."

"Lord, in your mercy, always give me the grace to obey your will, and never let my spiritual enemies have the power to stop me from fulfilling what you ask."

After this, I took my husband back to my home and looked

after him for several more years, right up to his death. It was a very great labor, especially toward the end when he became quite childish and lost all memory. He was also either unable or unwilling to use the lavatory, but he would empty his bowels just as he sat, at table or beside the fire; he didn't seem to care where he was. This made my work all the harder, washing his clothes and drying them every single day. And I had the extra cost of keeping a fire going. It all kept me away from my prayers. And I had a great distaste for all these chores; but I remembered how, when I was younger, I had entertained many sensual thoughts, given in to physical lust, and pampered my body in every way. So that now I was glad to punish my body in this manner; it helped me put up with my life as I tried to care and look after him just as I would have cared for Christ himself.

77

hen I first started my crying out loud, I was praying and conversing one day with my sovereign Lord Christ Jesus. "Lord," I said to him, "why do you choose to give me these great cries, so that people wonder what is happening to me? It is said that my very soul is in danger, since I provoke so many people to such anger. But you know, Lord, that I would rather be plunged into the deepest prison than give anyone an occasion of sin. I would spend every minute there weeping for my own sins and for the sins of all men, rather than be the cause of anybody deliberately sinning on my account.

"Lord, the world won't let me do your will and follow your promptings, and so, I pray you, if it is your will, take away these cries of mine during sermons. Let me not shout out when the priest preaches, but give these cries to me when I am alone. Then I will not be stopped from hearing your holy sermons and your own holy words. I can't think of any worse pain than to be prevented from hearing your holy words. If I were in prison, this would be my sharpest pain, not to listen to your sermons and your holy words. So, good Lord, if I must cry out, let me do so in my own room; let it be as loud as you like there, but not in public where everyone can hear. Please, Lord."

Our Lord Christ Jesus gave me his merciful answer in my mind: "Daughter, you should not pray for this. I will not give you your own way, even though my mother and all the saints in heaven pray for you. I want you to be obedient to my will; you shall cry out when I will it, now loud, now quiet. I have told you, daughter, you are mine and I am yours, and so shall it be without end.

"Daughter, consider how the planets obey my will; see how sometimes great thunderclaps come and they make everyone afraid. At times, you may see great lightning flashes that burn down houses and even churches. At other times I send great gales that bring down steeples and batter houses, or they rip trees out of the ground. Yet in spite of all this damage everywhere, you cannot see the wind; you may only feel it.

"This is just the manner in which I choose to exercise the power of my Godhead. No man's eye may see me, yet a simple soul like you may feel me as I work my grace within you. Just as the lightning comes suddenly from heaven, with equal swiftness I may light up your soul with the light of grace and understanding. I may set it all on fire with my love, and make that fire burn within to purge it free from all earthly grime. And sometimes, daughter, I make earthquakes to frighten people and remind them that they should fear me.

"This is the way I have dealt with you, daughter, and with

others I have chosen to save like yourself. I turn over the earth in their hearts; I make them afraid, so that they fear my vengeance will come upon them on account of their sins. That was how it was with you, when first you turned toward me. All young beginners are the same; yet now, daughter, you have good reason to love me, and the perfect charity that I bring you casts aside all your fear. Other people may think little of you, yet I know your true worth. As you are always sure that the sun is going to shine, likewise be sure that God's love is the same at all times.

"Again, daughter, you are familiar with the weather, how sometimes I may send rainstorms and heavy showers, or sometimes only a gentle drizzle. That is how I treat you, my daughter: When I wish to speak to your soul, I will sometimes give you great shouts and roars that make people fear the grace I show in you, a sign that the sorrows my mother had to endure may be recognized through you. Then men and women may come to have more compassion for all her sorrows that she suffered for me.

"And a third sign, daughter, is this: Whoever will grieve for my passion as much as you have and then give up their sins, they shall have bliss in heaven without end.

"And a fourth sign: Every creature on earth, however grievously they have sinned, need never despair if they follow your example and take up your way of life insofar as they are able.

"And, daughter, I will give you a fifth sign: I want you to know, by the pain you have when you cry out loud for my love, that once you leave this world you will have no more pain. Also that you shall suffer less in your dying moments; because you have shown this compassion for the pains I suffered in my flesh, I would spare you such pain in your own flesh.

"And so, daughter, let people say what they like about your loud cries, for these are no cause for them to sin. People sinned over me, daughter, yet I was not the cause of their sins."

And so I answered him: "My good Lord, blessed may you be, for I think you do everything that you ask me to do. In Holy Scripture you tell me to love my enemies. And I know well enough that I never had an enemy in all the wide world as great as the enemy I have been to you. Therefore, Lord, if I were to be killed a hundred times in a day for love of you, supposing that were possible, I still could never pay you back for the goodness you have shown me."

Then our Lord answered me: "All I ask, daughter, is that you should never give me anything other than your love. Nothing will please me more than for you to have me always in your love; nor can any penance you do please me as much as your very own love. Daughter, if you want to be close to me in heaven, keep me always close to you now, insofar as you can. Do not forget me, even at your meals, but always imagine that I sit forever in your heart. And there I know your every thought and every blinking of your eye."

I answered again, "Now, in truth, my Lord, I wish that I could love you as much as you are able to make me love you. If only it were possible, I want to love you as much as all the saints in heaven and as well as all creatures on earth love you. And, my Lord, I would that I might be laid naked upon a hurdle for all men to stare at me to show my love for you—so long as it did no harm to their immortal souls. I would that they might throw mud and muck all over me, that I might be drawn from one side of town to the other every single day of my life, if this would please you and not harm any man's soul. But your will, not mine, be done."

78

ach year, as Palm Sunday came around and Holy Week began, I would join the outdoor procession around the churchyard and attend the ceremonies with all the priests and the people. As we knelt before the sacrament it seemed to me in my spiritual sight that I was back in our Lord's days in Jerusalem; it was as if I could see our Lord, truly a man, being welcomed by the people as he went about upon the earth.

It was at these times that I found myself overcome with so much sweetness and devotion that I could scarcely bear it, but cried out and wept and sobbed; there was no holding back my emotions. I had many holy inspirations about our Lord's passion, and felt I saw him in my spiritual sight as clearly as if I had truly been physically present at our Lord's passion. Therefore I could not hold back my weeping and sobbing or my loud cries when I saw my Savior suffering such great pains for love of me.

Then I would pray for all people living upon the earth, that they might give our Lord his due honor and reverence then and at all times; and that they might be worthy to hear and understand his holy words and the laws of God, humbly obeying them and truly fulfilling them as far as they were able.

It was always the custom in Lynn to have a special sermon on Palm Sunday. And on one occasion, a well-known doctor of divinity was in the pulpit giving the sermon; the words he kept repeating were: "Our Lord is pining for our love." These words kept working around in my mind; and whenever I heard it said how perfectly our Lord had loved mankind, how dearly we were bought by his passion, and heard the way he shed his blood for us in his bitter passion, pouring out his heart's blood for our redemption — the shameful death that wrought our salvation — then I could no longer keep the fire of love contained within my breast; but I must let it forth, whether I chose or not, for what was within would come out.

Whereupon I cried out very loudly and wept and sobbed most bitterly. It was as though I could have burst for the pity and feeling I had for our Lord's passion. And sometimes my crying out would be so violent that I would sweat all over; and it was so loud that people were upset and cursed me openly, imagining that it was only a pretense.

Yet early on, our Lord had told me, "Daughter, this is most pleasing to me. Because the more shame and contempt you put up with on my account, the more shall you have with me in heaven. That is as it should be."

There were other times when I heard great sounds and melodies with my own ears. It made me think how happy it was in heaven and I felt a very great longing to be there. I was reduced to silence at such moments.

Frequently, our Lord Jesus Christ would tell me, "Daughter, just now there are many healthy people busy about their lives, yet within the twelvemonth, they shall all be dead." And he told me, in advance, when the plague would break out. And then I saw it happen, just as I had known it would; and this all strengthened me in the love of God.

Our Lord would also say, "Daughter, those who do not credit the goodness and the grace I give you while they live, I will make them recognize the truth of it once they are dead, when they have finally gone from this world. You show great charity and zeal, daughter, in wanting all men saved, and so do I. And most men say as much for themselves. Yet see how this cannot really be true: Look how they sometimes hear the word of God, yet do not act upon it; neither will they sorrow for their sins, nor will they even allow others to do penance on their behalf.

"Notwithstanding, daughter, I have decided that you must be a mirror before them. You are to know great sorrow, to set them an example so they may have some small sorrow in their hearts for their sins. Then they will be saved, although now they have so little desire to hear a word about sorrow or contrition. Yet, good daughter, you must do your duty. Pray for them while you are in this world and you shall be rewarded in heaven, just as if you were to save the entire world by your goodwill and prayers. Because, daughter, I have told you that thousands shall be saved through your prayers. Some who even now lie at death's door shall know grace through your merits and prayers. Your tears and your prayers are very sweet and acceptable to me."

Then I would tell our Lord Jesus Christ, "My good Jesus, blessed may you be without end. I have so much to thank you for, to love you with my whole heart. It seems to me that you are all love; you constantly pour yourself out to help and heal man's soul. Lord, I cannot help thinking that it would have to be a very wicked man that could be parted from you without end. He would have to want no good, do no good, nor ever know good. And so, Lord, I thank you for all the goodness you have shown me. I am your most unworthy daughter."

On Palm Sunday after the procession, the priest takes the pole of the processional cross and knocks at the church door. Then the door is opened and he goes through, carrying the sacrament, as all the people follow him through into the church. Then I thought how God had spoken to the devil and opened the gates of hell. How he had confounded him and all his army—what grace, what goodness he has shown these people, to deliver their souls from that everlasting prison! Defeating the devil and all who were on his side!

Many were the thoughts that teemed in my head. I could

never number or tell them, nor could I tell all my holy desires
—tongue may not tell the plenteous grace that I knew,
blessed be our Lord for all these his gifts.

And, again, when we would come into the church, I saw
the priests all kneeling before the crucifix; and as they sang,
the celebrant slowly unveiled the cross. Three times he stood,
raising it higher and higher, so that all present should see the
crucifix upon which Jesus hung.[115] At such a moment, my
mind would be taken utterly from earthly things and fastened
on spiritual truths. I would pray to have sight of him at last in
heaven, who is both God and man in one Person.

During the mass that followed,[116] I would weep and sob
aplenty and sometimes, too, in the middle of it all, I would cry
out loud most fervently. For I thought I saw our Lord himself, as truly in my soul with my spiritual eye, as before I had
seen the crucifix unveiled before my own eyes.

[115] Margery refers to the unveiling of the crucifix on Good Friday. Immediately prior to the
Creeping to the Cross—when everyone would come and kiss the feet of Christ—the crucifix is
carried the length of the church, and its Lenten purple cover is removed in three stages as the
celebrant chants "Behold, the cross upon which he hung for us." The people reply, "Come let us
adore him."

[116] Margery's imagination is racing: there is no mass on Good Friday, merely distribution of
Communion.

79

As I meditated upon the passion of our blissful Lord Christ Jesus,[117] I saw him coming to face his sufferings. But before he went up to Jerusalem, he knelt down to receive his mother's blessing. Then I saw his mother fall down in a swoon before her son, saying, "Alas, my own dear son, how will I really suffer this sorrow, and lose the only joy I have on earth? My dear son, if you must die, let me at least die before you. Never let me suffer such a day of sorrow, for how may I ever bear this pain that I shall know at your death? Rather, son, I want to die in your place, so that you may not die, provided man's soul might be saved in such a way. Son, if you have no pity for yourself, at least have pity on me, your mother; for you know that no one may comfort me in this world except you alone."

Then our Lord lifted his mother up, and bearing her in his arms he kissed her most tenderly and said, "Blessed mother, be of good heart, how often have I told you that I must suffer death, or else no man will be saved or ever come to bliss. For, mother, it is my Father's will; therefore I pray you, let it be your will also. For my death shall become a great honor for me, and a great joy and benefit for you and for all mankind.

---

[117] The substance of this typically medieval meditation on the passion would have been familiar to most of Margery's contemporaries. Following the popularity of Saint Bonaventure's *Lignum Vitae*, where in his preface he echoed Saint Paul: "With Christ, I am nailed to the cross," such a narrative recollection of the passion of Christ provided frequent material for preachers.

For everyone who trusts in my passion and lives his life accordingly.

"Therefore, dear mother, you must remain here after I have gone, for in you rests the faith of Holy Church; by your faith, its own faith shall grow. And so I beg you, my beloved mother, cease your sorrowing, I will not leave you without comfort. I shall leave you John, my cousin, to comfort you in my place; and I shall send my holy angels to comfort you on earth. And I myself shall comfort you in your soul, for, Mother, you know full well that I have promised you the bliss of heaven. Be sure of that.

"Beloved mother, what better could you wish than that where I am king, you shall be my queen; and there all the angels and saints shall obey your will. And whatever grace you ask of me, I shall not deny you. I will give you power over devils, so that they shall be afraid of you, yet you shall not fear them. And also, my blessed mother, I have told you before, I myself shall come for you as you pass out of this world. I shall come with all my angels and saints of heaven and bring you to my Father; then there shall be music and melody and joy. There I shall crown you queen of heaven, lady of the whole world, empress of hell.

"Therefore, my beloved mother, I pray you, bless me and let me do my Father's will; for this I came into this world, for this cause I took flesh and blood from you."

When I contemplated this glorious sight within my soul, and saw how he blessed his mother and how his mother also blessed him, I then saw that his blessed mother could speak no more to him, but fell down again upon the ground. And so they parted from one another, his mother lying still, as though she were dead. Then I imagined that I myself clung to our Lord's clothes and fell down at his feet. I prayed for him to bless me, and then cried out loud and wept bitter tears, saying in my mind, "Dear Lord, what shall become of me? I would far rather you slay me than let me stay in this world without you, for without you, Lord, I cannot abide to stay here."

Then our Lord answered, "Be still, daughter, and rest here with my mother. Comfort yourself in her, for she is my own mother yet she must suffer this same sorrow. But I shall come again, daughter, to my mother, and comfort both her and you. Then shall all your sorrow be turned to joy."

Then, seeing our Lord go upon his way, I went to our Lady and said, "Blessed Lady, rise up; let us follow your blessed son as long as we can keep him in our sight, so that we may see him as long as possible before he dies. Dear Lady, how can your heart withstand it, to see your blissful son in all this woe? For, Lady, I may not endure it, yet I am not his mother."

Then our Lady answered, "Daughter, you have heard him say that it may not be otherwise; therefore I must simply bear it for love of my son."

Then I imagined that we followed the steps of our Lord, and saw how he prayed to his Father on the Mount of Olives. And we heard the beautiful response that came from his Father, and our Lord's own answer to his Father.

Then we saw how our Lord went across to his disciples and told them to wake up. His enemies were drawing near. Then came a great rabble, many of them bearing lanterns. And others had staves and swords and poleaxes, for they sought our Lord Jesus Christ. Then our merciful meek Lord, like a lamb, asked them, "Whom do you seek?"

They answered him rudely, "Jesus of Nazareth."

Our Lord told them only, *"Ego sum."*

Then I saw all his enemies fall to the ground—they could not keep on their feet for fear—but they got up again and continued their hunt. Our Lord asked once more, "Whom do you seek?"

"Jesus of Nazareth," they repeated.

"I am he," he repeated.

And I watched as Judas came and kissed our Lord; then at once they arrested him most roughly. And our Lady was full of pain and sorrow to see the Lamb of Innocence manhandled so despicably and dragged away by his own people, to whom he had been specially sent. Soon after this, I saw with my spiritual eye how those brutal men blindfolded our Lord before they beat him and buffeted him about the head. They struck his sweet mouth and shouted at him so cruelly, "Tell us now, who was it hit you then?"

They did not spare him but spat into his face in the most shameful way they knew. And then our Lady and I, her most unworthy maidservant at that time, wept and sighed so bitterly because of the way our Lord was so unfairly treated and with such anger. They did not stop short, but pulled his ears and tugged his beard most spitefully.

And after all this, I saw them pull off his clothes and strip him quite naked as if he had been the world's worst criminal. But he stood meekly before them, as naked as on the day he was born. Then he walked silently toward a stone pillar where they bound him as tightly as they could. And they took rods to his fair white body, and beat it with whips and scourges.

Then I thought how our Lady wept with such incredible sorrow that I too must weep and cry. As I witnessed these terrible spiritual sights, as plain as if they were before my very eyes, I thought that our Lady and I would always stay together to witness our Lord's pains.

These were the kinds of spiritual sights I would always have every Palm Sunday and Good Friday; I witnessed them in many different ways over a long period of years. This was the true reason why I felt frequently compelled to cry out loud, for which I suffered much contempt and chastisement in many places.

But our Lord would speak to my soul, saying, "Daughter, these sorrows and many more besides I suffered for love of you, together with many other pains, more than any man on earth may count. Therefore, daughter, you have every reason to love me well, for I have bought your love most dearly."

80

At another time, I saw in contemplation our Lord Jesus Christ bound to a pillar, his hands tied above his head.[118] I then saw sixteen men with sixteen scourges. Each scourge had eight tips of lead, and each tip was full of sharp spikes, just like the rowel of a spur. And these men with their scourges promised that each would give our Lord forty strokes.

On seeing this piteous sight, I wept and cried out loud as if I would burst for the sorrow and the pain. When they had beaten him severely and had scourged him, they untied him from the pillar and gave him his cross to carry on his shoulder. Then I thought our Lady and I should go by another way to meet him. And when we came to meet him, we saw that the cross was so heavy that it caused him great pain; in truth it was so heavy and so huge that he could barely support it.

Then our Lady spoke: "My sweet son, let me help you carry your heavy cross."

But she was not strong enough and fell down and swooned. She lay there like a dead woman. Then I saw our Lord fall down too beside his mother. And he comforted her

---

[118] In Margery's day, the warring Bishop of Norwich, Henry Despenser, successfully put down the peasant's revolt as it threatened to overwhelm the city. Having shriven the ringleaders, he handed them over for execution. He celebrated his success by commissioning a "retable" or altar painting of Christ's passion. In one tableau of the scourging, Christ's hands are tied to a pillar above his head. Having been lost since the Reformation, it was discovered as the underside of a table; and now, restored, is to be seen in the cathedral today.

with many sweet words. When I heard his words and saw the compassion his mother had for her son, and the son for his mother, I wept—I sobbed and cried as if fit to die. The pity and compassion I felt at that piteous sight, the holy thoughts I had at that moment, were all so subtle and so heaven-sent that I could never afterward tell of them, certainly not in any way as vividly as I had felt them.

After this, I went on in my contemplations, through the mercy of our Lord Jesus Christ, to the place where he was nailed to the cross. Then I witnessed the soldiers tear away from our Lord's precious body a silk cloth. It had stuck fast to his body, so firmly and so tightly that as it came away all the skin came too and opened up his precious wounds, making the blood run freely on all sides. His precious body seemed to me so raw, like some creature newly flailed out of its skin, that it was most piteous to see. So I had a fresh sorrow; and now I wept and cried out very bitterly all over again.

Next, I saw how the cruel Jews[119] laid his precious body on the cross. Then they took a long nail, all rough and jagged; and placing it on one of his hands, they drove it through brutally and with great violence. His blessed mother—and I at her side—seeing this, and seeing how his blessed body went into spasms and cringed in all its veins and sinews as he felt that pain, sorrowed and mourned and sighed so grievously.

Then I witnessed, in my spiritual eye, how the Jews bound a rope around his other hand. His arm had so contracted, the veins and sinews being so warped with pain, that it would not reach as far as the hole they had prepared.[120] So they

[119] It is quite apparent how deliberately the blame for Christ's death was firmly projected upon the Jews who had failed to believe in him. This prejudice was callously perpetuated, and as a result the Jews suffered periodic outrages against them. Just outside Norwich was a small chapel dedicated to Saint William, a small boy who had been murdered in 1146. He was abducted by a pervert, shaved, crowned with thorns, and crucified. The Jews were blamed by popular myth and the chapel became a place of pilgrimage.

[120] The English tradition for realistic meditation upon Christ's passion had begun with Saint Aelred and continued in the writings of Saint Edmund of Abingdon. But their most popular thrust came in the Mystery Plays performed annually in many cathedral cities to tell the story of

stretched it out to make it reach their hole. As I watched, my pain and sorrow grew. Then, at last, they pulled his blessed feet out straight in the same way.

At that moment, I thought I heard our Lady speak to the Jews: "Alas, you cruel Jews, why do you treat my poor son in this way? He never did you any harm. You have filled my heart with sorrow."

I heard the Jews' reply shouted back, yet they seemed to move away from her son.

And I thought that I also spoke out against the Jews: "You accursed Jews, Why are you killing my Lord Jesus Christ? Kill me instead! Let him go free!"

Then I wept my bitterest and cried out so uncontrollably that people in church were very disturbed. But then I saw the crowd take the cross with our Lord's body hanging there, and they made a great noise and cried out as they lifted it up above the ground and then let it drop down into its socket. At this, our Lord's body shook and shuddered, and all the joints of his blissful body burst and split apart; his precious wounds became rivers of blood that flowed down on every side. Never had I more reason for weeping and grieving.

Then I heard our Lord, hanging there upon the cross, say these words to his mother: "Woman, behold your son, Saint John the Evangelist."

Then I thought our Lady fell down and fainted, and Saint John took her in his arms and comforted her with sweet words, as best he could. I said to our Lord, or so it seemed to me, "Alas, Lord, you are leaving your mother here full of woe. What are we to do, how shall we bear this great sorrow which we have for love of you?"

Then I heard what the two thieves said to our Lord, and our Lord replied to one of them, "This day, you shall be with me in Paradise."

---

salvation. Margery's image here appears to be based on a quotation from the York Mystery play: "It fails a foot and more, the sinews are gone so thin."

I was glad when I heard this answer. And I prayed to our Lord that, of his mercy, he would be as gracious to my soul when I would come to die and pass on from this world as he was to the thief. Yet I thought I was far worse than any thief.

Then I thought that our Lord commended his spirit into his Father's hands. And with that he died. I thought I saw our Lady faint and fall down and lie still upon the ground. For myself, I thought I ran around like a madwoman, crying and roaring. Presently, when I came to our Lady, I fell down on my knees in front of her and said, "I beg you, Lady, stop your grieving, for your son is dead and has finished with pain. I think you have grieved long enough. But, Lady, I will grieve for you: Your sorrow is my sorrow."

Then I imagined Joseph of Arimathea taking down our Lord's body from the cross, and laying it before our Lady upon the marble slab.[121] Our Lady had some kind of relief as her dear son was taken down from the cross and laid upon the slab in front of her. Then our Lady bent forward to her son's body and kissed him on the mouth. She wept so copiously over his blessed face that she washed away all the blood from his face with her tears.

Then I believed I heard Mary Magdalene tell our Lady, "I beg you, Lady, give me leave to touch his feet and kiss them. For this would win me grace."

Our Lady at once gave leave to her and to all present there to give that precious body what honor and reverence they wished. And Mary Magdalene attended to our Lord's feet, and our Lady's sisters held his hands. One sister held his right hand, the other his left, and they both wept most bitterly, kissing his hands and blessed feet. And I felt like a madwoman, rushing to and fro. I would have liked to have had his precious body to myself alone, for I believed I would

---

[121] Margery had been shown such a marble slab in Jerusalem, in the Church of the Holy Sepulchre.

have died with weeping and mourning for his death, with all the love I felt for him.

It was time then for Saint John the Evangelist, Joseph of Arimathea, and other friends of our Lord to come and bury our Lord's body. And so they asked our Lady's leave to bury that precious body. Our Lady, full of sorrow, said to them, "Sirs, would you take away from me my own son's body? While he lived, I could never see enough of him. I beg you, let me have him now that he is dead; do not part me from my son. But if you must bury him, bury me too, since I cannot live without him."

I heard them again ask our Lady very gently, so that at last she let them bury her dear son with great honor and full reverence, as was meet and fitting.

81

As our Lord was being buried, our Lady fainted as she tried to leave the tomb; so Saint John took her in his arms, and Mary Magdalene went to help her, both of them supporting her and offering what comfort they might. I wished to stay beside the tomb, mourning and weeping and crying out loud with the tenderness and compassion I had for our Lord's death. God put many mournful wishes in my heart at that moment. Because of all this, people were alarmed and wanted to know what was the matter with me. They could not understand the way I behaved. I thought I could never leave that place, but wanted to die there and be buried with our Lord. Later on, I saw our Lady going home, and as she went upon her way many good women approached her, saying, "Lady, we are very sad that your son is dead, and that our people have done him so much shame."

But our Lady thanked them only by her looks and the expression on her face; she could no longer speak for all her grieving heart. Then I imagined I saw our Lady reach her home and lie down. And I made our Lady a good hot dish of gruel and some spiced wine. I brought this to her to make her feel better, but our Lady told me, "Take it away, daughter, how could you bring me food when all I want is my own child."

All I could say was, "Blessed Lady, you must comfort yourself and give up this grieving."

"But, daughter, where may I go, how can I exist without sorrow? I can tell you, never a woman lived who bore a better baby, nor a child more biddable than my son was to me."

I thought I heard our Lady call out in a heart-rending voice, "John, what have they done with my son, Jesus Christ?"

Saint John replied, "Dear Lady, you must know that he is dead."

"Oh, John, that is terrible news for me."

I heard her reply quite clearly. It sounded just like someone having a conversation, albeit in my soul's understanding. Soon after, I heard Saint Peter knocking at the door, and Saint John called out to know who it was. Peter replied, "It is me, sinful Peter. The man who deserted my lord Jesus Christ." Saint John wanted him to come in, but Peter would not until our Lady invited him inside. But he called out to her, "Lady, I am not worthy to come into your home," and he stayed where he was, outside.

So Saint John went to our Lady and told him that Peter was so ashamed that he was standing outside and did not dare to come in. But our Lady told John to go at once to Peter and make him come inside. Then I saw Peter, in my spiritual sight, come to our Lady and fall down to his knees with great weeping and sobbing and tell her, "Lady, I beg your forgiveness. I abandoned your beloved son who was my sweet master and who loved me so well. And so, Lady, I will never be worthy to see him again, or you either, except by your great mercy."

"Dear Peter," our Lady told him, "never fear, for although you denied my dear son, he never denied you, Peter. And he shall come again to bring us all true comfort. This was his promise to me, Peter; he told me he would come again on the third day and comfort me. It seems to me," our Lady continued, "it will be a very long time before that day comes when I shall see his blessed face once more."

Then our Lady, lying still upon her bed, listened as the friends of Jesus lamented at the sorrow they all felt, while our Lady lay motionless, mourning and weeping with the saddest look upon her face. At last, Mary Magdalene and our Lady's sisters took their leave of our Lady so as to go out and buy ointment with which to anoint our Lord's body.

Now I was all alone with our Lady; and I thought it would seem like a thousand years before that third day dawned. But on that day, I was with our Lady in a chapel when our Lord Jesus Christ appeared to her and spoke the words: *"Salve, sancta parens."* [Hail, my holy mother.]

I thought I heard in my soul our Lady say, "Are you truly my sweet son, Jesus?"

And he replied, "Yes, my blessed mother, I am your son, Jesus."

Then he took his mother into his arms and kissed her with the utmost tenderness. I saw how our Lady began to feel all over our Lord's body, as if she were searching to see if there were any soreness still or if any pain remained. And I heard him tell her, "Dear mother, all my pain is over and I shall live forevermore. And, mother, your own pain will be transformed into the greatest joy. Mother, you have only to ask me anything you wish to know, and I will tell you."

After he had let her ask and he had answered all her questions, he told her, "Mother, with your permission I must go and speak with Mary Magdalene."

Our Lady told him, "That is well, for, my son, she is very sad at your absence. But I beg you, come back soon to me."

These spiritual insights and this fresh understanding of our Lord's passion and resurrection made me weep and sob and call out very loud; often on Easter Sunday and any other holy days when our Lord would visit me with his grace, I was unable to restrain myself and lost control—blessed and honored may he be.

After a short while, I went—in my meditations—to join Mary Magdalene, who was mourning our Lord and looking for him at his tomb. I heard and saw our Lord come to her, in the guise of a gardener, and say, "Woman, why are you weeping so?"

Mary did not recognize him but was all on fire with love. She replied, "Sir, if it was you that took my Lord away, tell me where you have put him and I shall take him back again."

Then our merciful Lord took pity and compassion on her, and spoke: "Mary!"

At this one word, she knew it was our Lord and fell at his feet. She wanted to kiss them. "Master!" she exclaimed.

But he told her, "Touch me not."

And I thought I heard Mary Magdalene tell him, "Dear Lord, I can see that you do not wish me to be as familiar with you as I once was." And she looked very miserable when she said this.

"Yes, but Mary, I will never leave you now, I will be with you always."

Then our Lord told her, "Go, tell my brethren and Peter that I have risen."

Then I imagined how Mary went off with great joy, which surprised me greatly. For I thought to myself that if our Lord had spoken to me like that, I could never have been happy. That is to say, when she had wanted to kiss his feet and he had told her, "Touch me not." These words always caused me great grief and sorrow, so that whenever I heard them in any sermon, as I did time and again, I would weep and become full of sorrow and cry out loud as if I were dying for my love of our Lord and my desire to be with him.

82

n Candlemas, the Feast of our Lady's Purifi-cation, when I saw all the people with their lighted candles in the church, I was taken out of myself. I saw our Lady offering her blessed baby son, our Savior, to the priest Simeon in the Temple. It seemed to me I saw her too in my spiritual understanding as truly as if she were physically present to me. I was greatly comforted by this contemplation in my soul, by which I beheld our Lord Jesus Christ, his blessed mother, Simeon the priest, Joseph, and other people who were present when our Lady was purified. I thought I could hear heavenly canticles as our blissful Lord was offered by Simeon. I was so moved that I could hardly hold my candle and carry it up to the priest as we were all meant to do; but I went lurching from one side to another as if I were some drunken woman. And I wept and sobbed so much that I could hardly stand upright, because of all the fervent love and devotion God had placed in my soul by means of this high contemplation. It often happened like this;

I found I simply could no longer stand upright but fell down in the midst of everyone, calling out loudly. And this made a lot of people wonder at me, for they were curious to know what was the matter with me. The fervor of my spirit was so intense that my body could no longer withstand the stress but collapsed under it.

I always had such holy thoughts and meditations whenever I was present at the churching when a mother received purification after the birth of her child. Then I would imagine I saw our Lady herself being purified. And I would have a contemplation as I saw their women companions coming forward to make offerings on behalf of these new mothers. My mind was lost to worldly thoughts and anything physically visible. I had eyes only for spiritual sights, which were so inviting and so holy that at such times of fervor I could not keep myself from weeping and sobbing and crying out. On account of this I had to suffer much public curiosity, many an insult, and much contempt.

And whenever I attended a wedding, a man and woman joining together according to the law of Holy Church, I would immediately think how Mary was joined to Joseph, and of the joining of man's soul to Jesus Christ. Then I would pray to our Lord that my love and affection might be joined to him only, without end; that I might be given grace to obey him, love and dread him, worship and praise him, and love nothing save what he loved. Neither did I want anything save what he wanted, for I was ever ready to do his will, night and day, without resentment or sadness but with alacrity of spirit. I had so many more holy thoughts, more than I could ever repeat. And they did not come from any studies of my own, nor from my own wit; but they were all his gift, whose wisdom is unfathomable to all creatures save those whom he chooses to enlighten, either more or less, just as he himself decides. For his will is never subject to any restraint; he is free to do as he pleases.

I entertained all these thoughts and desires with abject

tears, sighs, and sobs, sometimes too with great cries out loud, just as God would send me. Yet sometimes these tears were discreet and came to me softly and in secret. I could weep neither quietly nor out loud, save as God would send such tears to me. And sometimes I was devoid of tears for a whole day, or part of the day; then I would experience such pain as I sought them that I felt I would give the world for even a few tears, or be glad to suffer some severe pain in my body if only to have them back once more.

When I was dry like this, I could find no joy or comfort in anything—for instance, food or drink, or a nice conversation. I would stay with my gloomy looks and mood until such time as God sent tears to me again. Only then would I be happy once more. And even though our Lord sometimes took away his gift of abundant tears, he did not withdraw for years on end my holy thoughts and desires, for my mind and aspirations were continually fixed upon our Lord. But I would think there was no taste or sweetness except when I might weep, for only then did I feel that I could pray properly.

83

here were two priests who trusted that my habit of crying and weeping was real; yet they too sometimes had their doubts, and would wonder whether or not I was being misled. Because they had only seen me cry out and weep in public, they had an idea to test me without my being aware of it. They wanted to see whether or not I cried out only so that people would notice me. So one day these two priests came and asked me if I would accompany them on a short pilgrimage, just about two miles from where I lived. They named a church that was out in the country, a good way from any dwelling; it was dedicated to God and Saint Michael the Archangel. And of course I accepted their invitation very gladly.

They took one or two children with them to this church. And once they had prayed aloud for a while, I was overcome with so much sweet consolation and devotion that I could no longer keep it within myself. I burst out in a fit of violent weeping and sobbing; I cried as loud as ever I did when I was with my parish congregation at home. For I could not contain myself, no matter that there were only two priests present and one or two children who had also come along.

As we came home after this walk, we met some women who were carrying their babies in their arms. And so I asked them if there was a boy baby there, but the women said no. At that moment my mind was swept up into the childhood of Christ, I so wanted to see him as a baby boy that I could not bear it. I fell down to the ground and wept and cried so intensely that those who heard it marveled. Then the priests had even more faith that all was indeed well with me; they had heard me cry out loud in backwoods places as well as in public, and in the fields as we were coming home as well as in the streets.

A group of nuns also wished to meet me; they thought that getting to know me would help them make spiritual progress. So I went to their church at midnight to hear their matins. And our Lord sent me such high devotion in their church, and such great spiritual comforts, that I was all on fire with love. This increased to such a degree that I fell down and with a loud voice began to cry out. And our Lord's name was magnified among his servants; those good, simple, meek souls had fresh belief in the goodness of our Lord Jesus Christ, who gives his grace to those he will. My crying out also benefited others, especially those who had no doubts but trusted in the efficacy of prayers, for it led them to grow in merit and virtue. But whether or not people believed in my crying, my own grace was never weakened but continued to grow. Our Lord would visit me with equal kindness by night as by day— whenever he wanted, any way he wanted, and wherever he wanted to visit me. Indeed, no grace was withheld from me, except when I doubted or mistrusted God's goodness: that is, if I began to fear it was all the work of my spiritual enemy tricking me and trying to lead me astray.

And it is true that many times I was tempted to abandon my way of life and grow slack by giving way to such thoughts, whether they came from someone else or from some evil spirit in my own mind; but then the mighty hand of God stood me firm against that great malice. It was at those times that I lacked all grace and devotion, and all my good thoughts and recollections failed me, until in God's mercy I was forced to believe firmly, without wavering, that it was indeed God who spoke in me. It was his will to be magnified in me for the sake of his own goodness, and for my merit and the merit of many others besides.

But as soon as I believed that it was truly God and no evil spirit that gave me so much grace of devotion, contrition, and holy contemplation, then I enjoyed many holy thoughts and held many holy conversations within my soul. I was taught how to love God, how to honor him and serve him; so numerous were these teachings that I could only ever rehearse a few. Indeed, for the most part, they were so high that I was loath to tell them to anyone else. They were all so far removed from human understanding that I could never really express them in ordinary words so as to explain the experience. I simply understood them better in my soul than ever I could say.

If one of my confessors had come to me directly after I had left my contemplation or meditation, I might perhaps have told him many of the things that our Lord had spelled out to my soul. Yet within a very short time I had forgotten the most part of it; almost all had slipped away.

84

he Abbess of Denny, who ruled a house of Franciscan nuns near Cambridge, had often invited me to come and speak with her and her sisters. But there came a time when I wished to put off my visit until the new year, such were the difficulties in making the journey. But when I was at meditation one day, and having great consolation and devotion, our Lord told me that I must go to Denny and comfort the ladies who had asked to talk with me. He said in my soul, "Daughter, set off for the convent of Denny in the name of Jesus. I want you to comfort them."

But I was still reluctant to travel; there was a good deal of plague around in the countryside and I thought no good purpose would be served by dying there. But our Lord spoke again in my mind, saying, "Daughter, you shall go there and come home again in perfect safety."

I went to a friend of mine, a merchant's wife whose husband was very ill, to tell her of my plan to set off for Denny. She was set against my making the journey: "I would sooner lose forty shillings than have my husband die while you were away."

But I told her, "If you offered to pay me one hundred pounds not to go, I still would not stay at home."

I knew that when I was told something in my soul like this, I must always do it and not resist. I was sure I had to go, whatever happened. It was the same when I was told to stay at home; then I stayed and would not go out-of-doors for any reason.

But then our Lord assured me that the merchant would not die. So I went back to his wife and told her to be content, her husband was going to live: He would make steady progress and soon get well again. The good woman was overjoyed and told me, "May what you tell me be the gospel truth."

So now all I wanted was to make my journey as quickly as I could. But when I came to the river ferry, all the boats for Cambridge had already left before I arrived. And I was very upset at the risk of not fulfilling our Lord's bidding. But at once I was reassured in my soul that I should not be anxious or downhearted, because everything would fall into place. I would get there and return safely enough; and it turned out exactly so.

After this our Lord showed his thanks to me that in my contemplations and meditation I had been maidservant to his mother and had helped look after him as a child as well as later on, indeed right up until the time of his death. He thanked me in this way: "Daughter, you shall have a great reward in heaven for all your kind labors. All the good deeds that you have achieved in your mind and meditations are just as valid as if you had done them externally in your own body. But also, daughter, whenever you look after anyone, make your husband's meal, bring him a drink; when you look after anybody's needs, your own, your confessor's or anyone else that you welcome in my name—your reward will be the same as if you did it for me or for my blessed mother. And I myself shall thank you for all this service.

"Daughter, you agree that it is right that I should be called All Good; you shall come to know how I am all good to you. And again, you tell me that I am called All Love, but you shall come to find how truly I am all your love, for I know every secret of your heart. I know, for instance, how you have dreamt that if you had lots of churches full of money, you would have given it all away in my name. And also how you have often thought that, if you had enough money, you would like to found many abbeys out of love for me, so that monks and nuns could live in them; then you wanted to be able to give them a hundred pounds each year so that they might live their whole lives in my service. And you have also imagined having lots of priests in Lynn, who would all sing and read my holy word night and day in my service, praising me and thanking me for all the good I have shown you on this earth.

"And therefore, daughter, I promise you the same reward in heaven for your goodwill and all these good intentions as if you had performed them in reality. Daughter, I also know many other kind thoughts you have in your heart for all manner of men and women, for all the lepers, for prisoners—I take for real whatever sum of money you would like to be able to give them so that they might come to be my servants. And, daughter, I thank you for the love you show toward all men and women who live lecherous lives; you pray for them and weep for their sins, wanting them to be delivered. You ask me to be as forgiving toward them as I was to Mary Magdalene; and you ask that they be given as great a love as she had for me. And with this intention in mind, you would like them all to have twenty pounds a year so that they might love and praise me.

"Daughter, the love you show in your prayers pleases me much. Also I thank you, daughter, for the charity you show when you pray for all the Jews and the Saracens and all unbelieving people. You pray that they may find the Christian faith, so that my name may be proclaimed in them; I thank you for the holy tears you shed for them, praying and wishing that if any prayer or grace might bring them to believe as Christians it should be your prayer for them, if only it were my will.

"Also, daughter, I thank you for the universal charity you show toward everyone living in the world, and all that are to come until its end. Your wish is to be chopped up like meat for the stewing pot for love of them all, if by your death you could save them from damnation, yet only if it were my will. You often say in your mind that there are enough souls in hell, and you only wish that no more would ever deserve to go there.

"Therefore, my daughter, for all these many good wishes and longings of yours, you shall have a high reward in heaven. You can count on this, never doubt me. For all these graces come from me, I work them in you myself, so that your reward in heaven will be greater. I tell you, daughter, every good thought and every good desire that you have in your soul is God speaking; and this is true even when you do not hear me speak to you directly, as I sometimes do.

"It is true, my daughter, sometimes I am a hidden God in your soul. I withdraw your tears and take away your devotion from you. Because then you realize you have no goodness of your own, but all good comes from me. At those times, you can see clearly what pain it is to be without me and how sweet to feel me; then you grow busy to seek me out again. That also shows you, daughter, how others feel in similar pain, when they would like to feel my presence but may not. There are many men living who, if they could have for only one day in their lives what you enjoy many days, would love me so much better and thank me always just because of that single day. While you yourself, daughter, cannot do without me for a single day without feeling great pain, and because of this, daughter, you have every reason to love me mightily. It is not through anger that I sometimes take away your feelings of grace and devotion, but to make certain that you do not become vain from any of your weeping, or crying out, or the sweetness and devotion you feel at the memory of my passion, or for any of the special gifts I send you. They do not come from the devil, these gifts are all from me: special graces that I offer my chosen souls, whom I knew before the beginning of time would come to know my grace and one day dwell with me forever.

"In performing all these actions, you could easily grow

vain should you so choose; in all the understanding you enjoy when you say your rosary, in frequent fasting and performing public penance, you could do all this so that people would notice you; and when you give charity you could do so with a great show, and likewise when you speak out and explain holy truths to other people. In all this, you could be a hypocrite; or you can choose to perform them holily and well, without any fuss.

"But see, daughter, how I have loved you so that I have kept you from becoming a hypocrite. You will be wasting no second of your time, when you are performing all these things; if anybody is thinking well, then they are unable to sin at the same time. The devil cannot read these holy thoughts I give you. Nor is there any man alive who really knows how well occupied you are with me and how holily you are engaged. You cannot even describe to yourself all that you feel in me. In this way, daughter, you conceal your holy thoughts from both the devil and the world. It would be very great folly indeed for worldly people to judge your heart. No man may know that, but God alone.

"Because of this, daughter, I tell you in all truth, you have as much reason to rejoice and be merry in your soul as any lady or maiden in the world. My love for you is so great that I may never take it from you. Daughter, no heart may think nor tongue tell the great love I have for you. And on this I call as my witnesses my blessed mother, my holy angels, and all the saints in heaven, who all praise me for their love of you. Equally, I shall be worshiped on earth for your love. I will have the grace I have given you on earth known to the world, so that people will wonder at the goodness that I have shown to you, a sinner. Because I have shown such mercy and grace to you, many others throughout the world shall not fall into despair, however sinful they may be, for they too may have mercy and grace; they have only to ask it for themselves."

85

nce as I was praying, kneeling in front of the altar of the Cross, my eyelids became heavier and heavier with my need to sleep. At last I couldn't help myself, but closed my eyes and slept. At once I saw an angel appear, clothed all in white; he seemed just like a little child. And he carried a huge book in front of him. So I said to this apparition—was he a child or in fact an angel?— "Oh, so this must be the Book of Life." I could see in the book the name of the Trinity, which was written all in gold. And so I asked the child, "Where is my name written?"

The child answered, "Here is your name, written at the foot of the Trinity." And at that he was gone, I could not tell where.

A little later, our Lord Jesus Christ spoke to me and told me, "Daughter, make sure now that you are true and steadfast in the faith. It is true, your name is written in the Book of Life. It was an angel that gave you that promise. Therefore, daughter, you must be very merry. I am busy each morning and afternoon, drawing your heart to my heart. You should keep your mind continually on me, and then your love of God will grow strong. If you follow God's will and counsel —that is, to be humble, and patient in charity as well as chastity—you cannot go astray."

On another day, I lay at contemplation in the chapel of our Lady, with my mind on the passion of our Lord Jesus Christ.

Then I thought I saw a true vision of our Lord in my spiritual sight; he stood in his manhood, with his wounds still bleeding freshly as though he had just been scourged before my own eyes. Then I wept and cried out with all the strength I had in my body. My sorrow had been great enough before I had this vision, yet afterward it was far greater, and more love for our Lord grew with it. I marveled greatly that our Lord had wanted to become man and suffer such terrible pain for me, when I was such an unkind creature toward him.

On another occasion, I was in Saint Margaret's Church, in the choir, when I knew great sweetness and devotion with many tears. Then I was prompted to ask our Lord how I might best please him. He answered me in my soul, saying, "Daughter, never forget your own wickedness, always think of my goodness."

So then I prayed these words, over and over again: "Lord, for your great goodness, have mercy upon all my own wickedness. Yet my wickedness can surely never have equaled your goodness, even if I did my worst, for you are so good that you can be no better. Therefore it is hard to believe that you would allow anyone to be parted from you forever."

Then I lay in the choir, weeping and bemoaning my sins, and suddenly I fell into a kind of sleep. And immediately I saw with my spiritual eye our Lord's body lying before me. His head seemed to be very close, and his dear face was looking upward. He was the most handsome man that might ever be seen or imagined. Then, as I gazed, someone with a dagger cut this precious body right along the length of his chest. So I wept incredibly bitter tears, and I had more understanding and compassion and pity for the passion of our Lord than ever before. As each day passed, my thoughts and my love of our Lord grew. And so too did my sorrow for the sins of the world.

Again, one time I was in the chapel of our Lady, weeping bitter tears as I recalled the passion of our Lord, together with other graces and goodness that our Lord had sent me.

After awhile, I could not say how long, I fell once again into some kind of sleep.

Immediately, in my soul's sight I saw our Lord standing directly above me. He was very close to me so that it seemed that I reached out and touched his toes with my hand; and they felt just like real flesh. Then I thanked God for all his goodness. These kinds of spiritual sights drew my love wholly to the manhood of Christ and toward a vivid memory of his passion, until the time when our Lord was pleased to give me some understanding of his ineffable Godhead.

As I have already described, these were the kinds of visions and feelings I began to have soon after my conversion. From then on my mind was set, and I firmly intended to serve God with all my heart and strength. I left behind all worldly things and spent most of my day in church, where I went morning and afternoon. Throughout the whole of Lent I was even more diligent in this. And then I persuaded and obtained my husband's permission to live chaste and apart from him, and before going to Jerusalem, I prepared myself with a great deal of corporal penance.

But after taking my vow of chastity, which my husband and I both agreed about, as I have already told, I went to Rome and Jerusalem where I suffered much contempt and rebukes for all my weeping and crying fits. But our Lord, in his mercy, drew all my affections into the Godhead. And this was a more fervent love and subtler in understanding, and greater in desire, than for his manhood. Thus as the fire of love grew within me, my understanding was more enlightened and my devotion more fervent than before, when my meditation and contemplation had their center only in the manhood of Christ. And also, I no longer had the habit of crying out loud; my feelings were more subtle, softer, and more easy for my spirit to bear. Yet my tears were as plentiful as ever.

One day I visited a Dominican house and was in their Lady chapel standing at prayer. My eyelids closed in a kind of sleep when suddenly I saw our Lady. I thought she was the fairest vision I had ever seen. She held a most beautiful white silk scarf in her hand as she asked me, "Daughter, would you like to see my son?"

At this, I saw directly that our Lady held her baby son upon her arm and was covering him very gently with her scarf. And I watched as she did so. I knew a fresh spiritual joy, a deep comfort in my soul; it was utterly marvelous, yet I could never describe it exactly as I had felt it deep within me.

86

n one certain day, our Lord spoke to me, and addressed my soul at his pleasure: "Dear daughter, I will give you new joys and more comfort in heaven for all the many times you have received the Blessed Sacrament of the altar with so many holy thoughts, more than could ever be counted. And also, daughter, you will know in heaven only the true sum of the days of high contemplation you have experienced through my gifts on earth. Although these gifts and graces come from me, your reward in heaven will count them as your own. That is because I have truly given them to you.

"And I thank you highly, daughter, that you have enabled me to work my will in you. That you have let me be so homely with you. Nothing you could do on earth would please me better than allowing me to speak to you in your soul. At those moments, you come to know my will, and I understand your will. And also, daughter, you call my mother to come to your soul, and you ask her to take me in her arms and to suckle me at her breast.

"And, my daughter, I also recognize the same holy thoughts and aspirations that you have when you receive my precious body within your soul. Also that you call Mary Magdalene into your soul to welcome me. My daughter, I know exactly how you think. You think she is the best person to be with your soul. You count most on her prayers, next to my own mother's. And well you may, for she is a great mediator for you in the bliss that is heaven. And sometimes as you receive me, I have seen it, you feel that your soul is wide enough to invite the whole court of heaven there so as to welcome me. I have heard you when you say, 'Come now, all twelve of you apostles, who were so loved by God on earth, you must welcome your Lord into my soul.'

"You also pray to Katherine, Margaret, and all such holy virgins to welcome me into your soul. Next, you pray to my blessed mother and to Mary Magdalene, to all the apostles, martyrs, confessors, and again Katherine, Margaret, and all holy virgins that they should decorate your soul's chamber with many fair flowers and sweet-smelling spices, so that I may come and stay with you.

"Again, I know, dear daughter, that you will sometimes fancy that you have a cushion of gold, another that is velvet red, a third of pure white silk; these are all in your soul. And you imagine that my Father sits upon the golden cushion, for in him resides both might and power. You see me, the Second Person of the Trinity, your love and joy, sitting upon the cushion of velvet red. This is because I bought you so dearly that you feel you may never return the love that I have shown for you. Yet you have thought of being killed a thousand times in a day, supposing that were possible, just for my love. That is why you would like me to sit on a red cushion, in honor of the blood that I shed for you. And lastly, you think of the Holy Spirit sitting on a white cushion, for he is full of love and purity. His white cushion is the symbol of him as source and giver of all holy thoughts, especially the gift of chastity.

"Daughter, I know your mind very well.[122] You think you do not worship the Father unless at the same time you also worship the Son; then you feel, if you are worshiping the Son, that you also worship the Holy Spirit. Then at other times you begin to dwell on the Father, how he is mighty and all-knowing, all grace and all goodness; and you pass on to think the same of the Son, that he too is almighty, all-knowing, full of grace and goodness; then you move to the Holy Spirit, finding in him the same, that he too is equal with the Father and the Son for he proceeds from them both and so he shares equally all that they are.

"Moving on from this, you also believe that each of the Three Persons of the Trinity contains in the Godhead all that the two other Persons have; you are right to believe this. There are three distinct Persons, yet only one Divine Substance. Each Person knows what the others know, each is able to do what the others do, each desires exactly what the others desire. This, my daughter, is the one true and only faith, and it belongs to you only because I have chosen to give it to you.

"Therefore, daughter, when you truly think about it, you have every reason to love me and open your heart totally to me. Then I will be at home there, as has always been my purpose. And if you allow me to come home to your soul on earth, you shall find your homestead with me in heaven without end.

"And so, my daughter, do not be surprised that you weep so bitterly when you receive Communion and take my blessed

---

[122] This may not carry the reader as much as it appears to move Margery; but this important passage should be examined with her two preliminary remarks in mind. She has already told us that her prayer has moved away from the manhood of Christ to the Godhead; but that when she comes away from such contemplation, she has little to say about the ineffable mystery she feels she may have encountered. Perhaps this passage is included by Margery to offer formal evidence of her orthodoxy to future readers.

body in the form of bread. Before you take Communion, you pray to me in your mind: 'Since you love me, Lord, make me free from all sin, and give me grace to receive your precious body worthily and so pay you full honor and reverence.'

"You may be sure, daughter, that I hear your prayer, for you could not say a better prayer than to speak so surely of my love for you. For then I may fill you full of my grace and give you many holy thoughts. So many, it is not possible to tell all. And because we are so close at these times, you are right to ask grace for yourself, for your husband, your children;[123] and it is good that you feel every Christian, man or woman, is a child of your soul for that moment and that you want as much grace for them as you ask for your own children. You also ask mercy for your husband, and you are grateful to me for having given you a husband who let you live a chaste life although he was still fit and virile. In every way, daughter, you have so many reasons to love me all the more.

"If only you knew how many wives there were in the world who would love me and serve me if only they, like you, might be free from their husbands, then you would realize how much you owe me. They do not get their way and so they have much to put up with, yet they will be rewarded in heaven, for I take every good intention as if it had been acted upon.

"Sometimes, daughter, when you communicate, you grieve for your confessor's sins and ask that they be forgiven as fully as your own. It is I that prompt you to pray in this way. And at other times, you ask with your tears that his preaching will change many hearts and that my holy words might strike him more keenly and mean as much to him as they do to you. And you beg a similar grace for all good men who preach my word, that it might profit all those who reflect upon it.

"Again when you receive my precious body, you often ask

[123] Margery never mentions her fourteen children or any domestic detail. Her sole intention is to give a record of her spiritual graces and visions.

for grace and mercy for all your friends, as well as all your enemies who ever shamed you or abused you, scorned or mocked you because of the grace I work within you on behalf of the whole world, young and old, when you weep so many bitter tears. I know full well how much of this shame and abuse you have had to endure, yet your bliss in heaven will be very great.

"Daughter, do not avoid me when I wish to give you my grace; then I will not avoid you. And you will be received into the bliss of heaven where you will be rewarded for each good thought, every good deed, all your good words, those many days of contemplation, and every good desire you ever had in this world. Because of all these, you shall be with me for always as my beloved darling, my blessed spouse, my holy wife.

"So never be afraid, daughter, when people are curious about your weeping so much; if they only knew what grace I am giving you in those moments, they would begin to wonder why your heart did not burst apart. And so it would, if I did not hold back; then, as you know when you receive me into your soul, you feel nothing but peace and tranquillity, your sobbing dies away. This may amaze other people, but you need not marvel for you know that I am behaving then just like a husband who would love his very own wife. Once he marries his bride, he is sure of her, no man will take her away. Now they may go to bed together without fear or the objections of other people and sleep and rest together in their love. And thus it is between you and me every week, and especially on a Sunday. Then you have great fear and trembling in your soul over how best to make sure of my love. How, with great reverence and holy dread, you may best receive me, the Savior of your soul. You behave then with all manner of meekness, humility, and love, just like any worldly wife anxious to welcome her husband home when he has been long away from her.

"My dearly loved daughter, I thank you for all the people

you have cared for in their sickness in my name. For all the
kindness you have done them, however small, you shall have
the same reward with me in heaven as if you had nursed me
when I was on earth. Also, daughter, I thank you for the
many times you have bathed me, within your soul, in the
secrecy of your chamber at home, just as if I had been present
in my manhood. I know well enough, daughter, all these holy
thoughts that you have in your mind. And also, daughter, I
thank you for all the times you have sheltered me and my
blessed mother in your own bed.

"For all these good thoughts and many another and all the
good deeds you have thought about in my name, and performed in my love, you shall enjoy with me and my mother,
my holy angels, my apostles, martyrs, confessors, virgins and
holy saints, all manner of joy and bliss that shall last without
end."

87

I lay completely still in church as I heard and understood all these lovely words being spoken within my
soul, just as if I were listening to the voice of my
closest friend. And when I realized the special promises our
Lord made to me, I thanked him with much weeping and
sobbing. With many holy and fearful thoughts I prayed
within my mind, "Lord Jesus, blessed may you be, for I never
deserved any of this from you. But I only wish I had already
come to that place where I may displease you no more."

With many like thoughts—more than I could ever write down—I worshiped and told of the greatness of our Lord Jesus Christ for his holy visitation and comfort. And for more than twenty-five years, I experienced visitations and contemplations similar to this, as I have already described; they went on for all this time as my own my life was itself sustained by our Savior Jesus Christ, yet they were more subtle and of a higher order than can ever be related. By the time this book came to be recorded, they had continued week by week, day by day, and were interrupted only if I were caring for some sick person or else attending to some other urgent business of my own or of my fellow Christians. At such times they were withdrawn, as is understandable, as they may be had only in great quietness of soul sustained through long practice.

In this habit of speaking and conversation, I was made robust and strong in the love of our Lord. My faith was fortified, and I knew far more humility and charity and other worthwhile virtues than I had known before. I firmly and steadfastly believed that it was God himself who spoke in this way within my mind, rather than any evil spirit. For in such conversing with him, I enjoyed the most strength, the most comfort, and the most growth in grace and virtue—blessed be God.

I often fell ill, so ill that I was fully expected to die. That is what everyone said, but I was told in my soul that I would not die but make a full recovery once more. And so it always turned out. It was sometimes our Lady who would talk to me when I lay sick, and then she would comfort me. Sometimes Saint Peter or Saint Paul would come to me; or again Saint Mary Magdalene, Saint Katherine, Saint Margaret, or whichever saint in heaven I would think of. By God's will and his design, they would speak in the understanding of my soul and teach me how to love God, and how best I could please him. They would answer any question I cared to put to them; and I was always able to know who it was that gave me comfort by the manner of the reply.

Our Lord too, in his mercy, visited me so frequently and so generously with holy conversation and talk of love that quite often I did not know where the day had gone. I would sometimes imagine that, say, five or six hours had been but an hour. It was all so sweet and full of consolation that I might have been in heaven. It never seemed to be a long while; I did not feel that time dragged—it simply passed, without my noticing. If I could have lived for a hundred years in this way (supposing that were possible), I would have preferred it to a single day in my former lifestyle.

I would often say to our Lord Jesus, "Dear Lord Jesus, because it is so good to weep for your love on earth, now I know for sure it will be pure bliss to be with you in heaven. And so I pray you, Lord, let me have no other joy on earth than mourning and weeping for your love. I even believe that if I were in hell itself, I could weep and mourn for love of you just as much as I do here; hell would not bother me, it would turn into a kind of heaven. That is because your love does away with all fear of our spiritual enemy. And I think I would far rather be there and please you, than be here in this world and offend you. But, my Lord, only as your will may it be done."

88

As we began to write this book together, I stayed at home with my secretary. And so I neglected such duties as the rosary more than I had done for many years; but this was simply to get the task done as soon as possible. And I found that when I did go to church, whether it was to hear mass or to say matins or perform my customary devotions, my heart was full of distractions and I found it hard to meditate or even say the rosary. Then I was afraid of displeasing our Lord, but he spoke in my soul: "Do not be afraid, daughter. As many beads as you would wish to say, I will count them as said. Your efforts to get down in writing an account of all the graces I have shown you pleases me greatly. I am pleased, too, with your scribe. Even if you came to church and wept as much as you did before, you would still not please me as much as you do with your writing. Daughter, through this book, many people will turn to me and come to believe.

"Daughter, can you think of a better prayer, I ask you, than to pray to me with your heart and your thoughts? When you pray to me in your mind, then you yourself understand what you ask me; and you can tell what I am saying to you, you know what I promise to you and to yours, as well as all your confessors. And with regard to your regular confessor Master Robert, I have granted you what you asked, that he should have of half your tears and half your good works, a half-share of the merits I have worked in you. And so he will be rewarded for your tears, just as if he himself had wept. And, my daughter, be confident that you shall both be very merry in heaven together at last; you shall bless the times you got to know each other.

"And, daughter, you will always bless me for having given you such a true confessor. He may have been sharp with you at times, but that has only helped you. Without that, you would have become too close to him, too affectionate. When he behaved harshly to you, you would turn to me in agitation and say, 'Lord, I have no one to trust, but only you.' And then you prayed, 'Lord, for the sake of your painful wounds, gather all my love into your own heart.' And, daughter, I have done just that.

"You often think this is a great thing I have done for you. It seems like a miracle, that I have concentrated all of your love to myself, because you have often been very attached to someone else. Indeed, you were so attached to him that you believed it was impossible to withdraw your affections from him. And afterward you wondered if, had it pleased me, he could have dropped you for love of me, and no longer been on your side. And you felt that without him, few would have taken you seriously. You knew that once he had dropped his support for you, that would be the greatest blow you ever had to bear in public. Yet you were willing to put up with such a catastrophe, according to my will, to show your love for me.

"Yet when you were full of these anxious thoughts, your love toward me grew; and, daughter, I took these thoughts and fears for deeds done. I know very well how sincerely you love this friend of yours; and I have often told you that he would be very pleased to reciprocate your love for he would recognize that it is indeed God who speaks within you, and certainly no devil. Besides, this same person has pleased me by often excusing your weeping and your shrieks in his sermons. Master Aleyn has done the same; and they shall both be well rewarded in heaven. I have often told you, daughter, that I would sustain your weeping and crying by sermons and preaching.

"I can tell you in addition, daughter, that I am very pleased that your confessor Master Robert tells you how you must believe that I love you. I know you have great confidence in his advice, and that is sensible because he is never one to flatter you. He also pleases me when he says that you must sit still and give your heart over to meditation and entertain such holy thoughts as God will put in your mind. I have often given you the same advice, yet you will hardly do anything about it without a good deal of grumbling.

"But I do not blame you, daughter; I have often told you that I am pleased however you pray, with your mouth or in your heart, whether you read or listen to something being read to you. Yet I will tell you, daughter, if you will only listen to me, mental prayer is best for you. That is how you will best come to grow in your love of me. And the more homely you allow me to be in your soul on earth, it is only right and fitting that I myself should be more homely with you in heaven. Therefore, daughter, if you will not listen to me, follow the advice of your confessor; for he gives you the same advice as I do.

"Daughter, when your confessor tells you that you are not pleasing God, you believe him implicitly; then you are sad and upset and you weep bitterly until you return to a state of grace once more. But at these times, I too cannot let you suffer for long without wanting to make things right. That is why I frequently come to you in person to comfort you and tell you how much I truly love you. I tell you with my own lips that my love for you is real and immovable, for it is grounded in my Godhead: nothing on earth that you can see with your own eyes is so firm and secure as my love for you.

"Therefore, daughter, return the love of the one who loves you. Do not forget me, for I never forget you, daughter; my eyes always look at you in mercy. My mother, who is full of mercy, knows this truth; and she has often told you the same, and so have many of my saints.

"Therefore, daughter, you have every good reason to love me with your whole heart and all your affection. If you will listen to my will, daughter, I will attend to yours—this is the truth, rest assured."

89

et at times while I was busy dictating this book, I would often be overcome with holy tears and much weeping. And often I would feel a flame just like fire in my breast, yet even as it enfolded me, it was utterly pleasurable. My scribe, too, would sometimes be overcome by tears.

As the task continued, I would often go to church to find our Lord Jesus Christ with his glorious mother and many saints alongside them. They came to my soul and thanked me, saying that they were very pleased with the writing of my book. I also would hear the sweet singing of a bird close to my ear; and there were other sweet sounds and melodies that I am quite unable to describe. But I fell ill many times as we worked at this book; yet as soon as the work began again, then, quite suddenly, I would be hale and hearty once more. For very often I had to be ready to work at a moment's notice.

One day in Advent, shortly before Christmas, as I lay at

my prayers in church, the wish came into my heart that God would make Master Aleyn preach a sermon, the finest he possibly could. And as soon as I had this thought, I heard our Sovereign Lord Christ Jesus say in my soul, "Daughter, I know very well what you have just been thinking about Master Aleyn; I tell you the truth, he shall preach a very great and holy sermon. Make sure you believe firmly in every word he utters. Think that it is I myself who says these things to you, for they shall be words of great solace and comfort to you. I myself shall be speaking in him."

As soon as I heard this, I sent for my confessor, together with two other priests who were my closest confidantes, and told them. But when I had done so, I felt immediate regret. I feared lest Master Aleyn's sermon would not live up to my expectations—for such revelations are often hard to discern. Sometimes the ones that people judge to be revelations turn out instead to be mere tricks and illusions. And so, rather than give ready credence to every seeming inspiration, it is better to wait steadfastly to test whether they are sent from God. But in spite of my fears, this particular feeling turned out to be real, and all my fears and my heaviness of heart gave way to great spiritual consolation and gladness.

I was often very depressed about such feelings. I would go for days without knowing precisely how they should be discerned. I was very aware of the danger of being misled and deluded. Then I would simply wait until such a time as God, in his goodness, enlightened me—I would rather have lost my head from my shoulders than take any other course.

This anxiety about discerning my innermost feelings was the greatest scourge I have had to put up with on earth: sometimes, for instance, what I took to be understood physically was meant as a spiritual metaphor. It was especially worrying at the start, but at least this anxiety kept me humble. For I could take no joy in any such feeling until my experience showed me whether it was true or not. But may God be blessed forever; he gradually increased the power and

strength of his love and the dread I felt for him. And as I
progressed, so he helped me grow in virtue.

This book ends here, for God took to his mercy the man
who wrote the original draft of what has been copied out
again here. He did not write at all clearly nor was he accurate
in recording, in any kind of exact detail, what had been told
to him; moreover, his handwriting and his spelling made very
little sense. So now here at last, with God's help and the
efforts of she who felt and experienced all these happenings,
is a faithful account all contained and set down in this little
book.

BOOK 2

1

As I have already explained, our Lord took to his great good mercy the man who first wrote down this book, and so then a priest made a fresh, legible copy as well as his simple talents permitted. And once this task was done, he judged it an appropriate honor to the blessed Trinity and to the Holy Name that people should also hear some other holy works of God—at such time as it pleased him.

Accordingly, he began to write on the feast of Saint Vitalis, April 28, in the year of our Lord 1438; at my dictation he began to record some, but not all, of the graces that our Lord bestowed on a simple soul during the years since the first account was finished.

To begin with, there is an important matter that the first account fails to mention. It started soon after I had given up my business affairs and had firmly turned to God insofar as human weakness allowed. I had a son, a tall young man, who lived with a prosperous burgess in Lynn and who often sailed abroad on business. I tried to save him from the dangers of this sad world, but I could not find the right words. Whenever we met, I would counsel him to leave his worldly career and follow Christ. But in the end he avoided me, and so we rarely met.

But one day, in spite of himself, he happened to meet me. And as was my habit, once again I advised him to leave the dangers of the world and not be so caught up in his business affairs. He disagreed with my advice and answered me back sharply. I was upset by his attitude and told him: "The least you may do, if you will not leave the world, is to keep clear of women until you find a wife in obedience to the law of the church. If you fail to do even this, I pray that God may punish you and make you sorry for it."

We left each other, and soon afterward he went abroad on business once more. Led astray by evil company, as well as his own foolishness, he wallowed in the sins of the flesh. Almost at once he lost color and his face was covered with spots and sores, almost as if he had leprosy. When he returned to Lynn, his master dismissed him—not for something he had done, but simply assuming that he did indeed have leprosy.

My son told everyone that he must have been cursed by his mother; he thought this could be the only reason God had punished him so grievously. One of his friends came and told me that I had done evil, and that because of my prayers, God had punished my own child. I ignored this, but let it be known that I would do nothing for my son until he came to ask me himself. Finally he realized that this was the only remedy. He came to me and told me about his misdeeds; and he promised to obey God and do as I wished, making amends for his failings. He added that, with God's help and as far as he was able, he would turn away from such temptations in the future.

He begged me for my blessing and earnestly asked that I

pray for him to our Lord, that in his mercy he would forgive his sins and so take away the malady which made everyone shun him as though he were a leper. He still imagined that it was because of my prayers our Lord had sent such a punishment; so he trusted that if, of my charity, I prayed for him, he would be cured. I realized his sincerity and felt exceedingly sorry for his condition; even so, I chastised him once more for his folly, before promising to pray, God willing, for his recovery.

I made my meditation, mindful of the fruit of my womb, and begged God to forgive him his wrongs and free him from the complaint that our Lord had sent him, providing this was according to God's will and would profit my son's soul. I prayed long and hard, and he was completely cured of his illness. He lived for many a long year, and married happily, having met his wife in Prussia, and was blessed with a child.

When I heard the news from abroad that my son had married, I was overjoyed. I thanked God with all my heart that now at last he would be able to live a clean, chaste life according to the laws of marriage. Presently, in God's good time, they had their child, a beautiful little girl. He sent word of this to England and told me how graciously God had treated both him and his wife. I prayed in the Lady chapel, thanking God for his grace and goodness to my son; wishing to see him again, I was answered that I would surely see them all before I came to die.

I wondered at my joyous feelings, but doubted them too, as I had no intention of crossing the sea again to where they were as long as I lived. Yet I trusted to God that nothing is impossible. And so I trusted my feelings, and knew that this would come about when it was God's will.

2

ome years after he had been married, my son returned to England to see his mother and father;
and we were taken aback at the change. Whereas
before he had dressed in the best fashion, his clothes all
slashed,[124] and would speak in a very showy manner, now he
was dressed very soberly and spoke most virtuously.

Amazed at this complete change, I asked him, "Son, bless
you, how have you changed so?"

"Mother," he told me, "I think due to your prayers our
Lord has called me. So by God's grace I intend to listen to
your advice more than I have in the past."

When I saw the marvelous way in which God had drawn
him to himself, I thanked God with all my might; at the same
time, I watched my son closely for fear that he was merely
pretending. Yet the more I observed him, the more reverent
he appeared. Then I was sure that he was indeed being attracted by our Lord's mercy and I was overjoyed. I could not
stop thanking God for his grace and goodness.

I wanted to encourage him and also offer him some idea of
where our Lord was leading him, so I opened my heart to
him, telling him how our Lord had guided me by his mercy. I
revealed the way in which I had been called, and told him

---

[124] High fashion, which was to become even more pronounced in Elizabethan times, dictated that the outer garment be "slashed" or cut to reveal the undergarment—in contrasting
color.

how many graces I had been given; although my son, for his part, told me he was not worthy to hear any of this.

Afterward, he went on pilgrimage to Rome and many other holy places in order to obtain pardon; but he always came back to his wife and child, as was his duty. He often spoke of me to his wife, so that at length she decided to leave her own mother and father and her native country in order to come to England and meet me. My son was pleased at this idea and sent word to me in England to tell me of his wife's wish. He wanted to know whether they should come by sea or take the overland route [as far as Calais]. He trusted my advice implicitly, for he believed it to come from the Holy Spirit.

When I received his letter with this request, I began my prayers so as to discover what God counseled or told us to do. As I prayed, I learned that my son would arrive safely whether he came by sea or by land. So I wrote him letters relating my feeling that whether he came by land or sea, he would arrive safely by God's grace.

On receiving my advice, he asked about suitable ships for England; he booked a passage on one for his belongings and his wife and child, as well as himself, planning to make the crossing to England all together. But as soon as they were on board, such a storm blew up that they were too afraid to sail and disembarked again. Leaving their daughter behind in Prussia with some friends of his wife, they then took the overland route to England to come at last to his father and mother. When they arrived, I was glad in our Lord because I had been right to think that whichever way they traveled, they would arrive safely. May God be blessed.

They arrived on the Saturday in very good health. But the very next day, while we were having our Sunday midday meal with a group of friends, my son was taken ill. He had to leave the meal to go and lie down. His illness laid him low for about a month, when finally, after living in good grace and with his faith firm, he gave himself up to the mercy of our Lord. So the truth of the saying, "He shall come home in safety," came about in both body and spirit. He had come home not just in his body to this mortal land but he had also reached the land of the living, where death shall never appear again.

Not long after this, his father also went the way that every man must go. Meanwhile my son's German wife decided to stay on with me for another eighteen months; but then her friends urged her to return home, writing letters begging her to go back to her native Germany. Wanting to please her friends, she told me about their invitation and how she felt she ought to do as they suggested, but she was anxious to know whether I minded her going back to Germany.

I gladly gave my consent, and she began to make her preparations to sail as soon as she found a suitable ship. It was not long before we learned that a German ship was due to sail out of Ipswich with some of her own countrymen on board. We both agreed that it would be good for her to sail with them, rather than with strangers. So she went to her confessor for absolution; and as she was with him, I stayed waiting in the choir. And I began to think, "Lord, if it is your will, I would ask my confessor's permission to make the crossing with her."

Our Lord replied in my mind, "Daughter, I know that if I told you to go, you would go without a second thought. Therefore I do not want you to breathe a word to him about your idea."

I was glad to hear this and greatly relieved not to have to think about crossing the sea. For I had experienced its terrible dangers once before, and I had determined never again to sail across the open sea, if I could help it.

When my daughter-in-law had finished her confession, the good priest, who was also my own confessor, came and talked with us. He asked, "Is there anyone else to go with your daughter-in-law and wait with her until she takes ship?" A German man had come to escort her to the coast, but the priest was concerned for her, saying, "It is not right that she should travel such a distance with a young man in a strange country where neither of them is known."

So I spoke up, saying, "Sir, if you tell me to go, I will accompany her myself as far as Ipswich, where her ship lies. There she will meet up with her own countrymen and make the crossing with them."

But my confessor replied, "How can you accompany her? You hurt your foot recently, and you are not yet fully recovered. And besides, you are an old woman. You are too old to travel."

"Sir," I replied, "I trust that God will help me perfectly well."

But he insisted, questioning me about my return journey; who was to see me back home?

So I told him, "Sir, the hermit belonging to our church here. He is an energetic young man; I think he might, for the love of our Lord, agree to be my companion and see me safely home again. If you would give your leave?"

So it was agreed that I should take my daughter-in-law [the sixty miles] to Ipswich and afterward return to Lynn. We set off and it was Lent. Some six miles outside Lynn, we came upon a church where we stopped to hear mass. And all the while we were in church, I wanted tears of devotion, yet none would come. All I could feel was the continuing command in my soul to cross the sea with my daughter-in-law. I kept trying to put this from my mind but it always came back again, indeed so promptly that I had no peace or quiet of mind. All I had was this continual nagging and bidding to cross the sea. I thought this was a harsh burden for me to face. And I tried to excuse myself to our Lord in my mind, saying, "Lord, you know my confessor has not given me his leave, and I must obey him. So I cannot do this without his say-so."

Yet I was answered in my thoughts, "I tell you to go in my name, Jesus, and I stand above your confessor. I shall allow you, I shall guide you and bring you home again safely."

I would still have liked to excuse myself, if only I could have found a way. So I said, "I have far too little gold or silver to travel, and I know my daughter-in-law would prefer me to stay at home. In any case, it is doubtful if the ship's master will let me ship with them."

Our Lord answered, "If I am with you, who shall be against you? I shall provide and find friends to help you. Do as I say, and no one on that ship shall resist you."

So then I realized there was no helping it; I must set out at God's bidding. But first, I thought to go to Walsingham[125] and make an offering to honor our Lady. And as I made my way, I heard news that a friar was to preach in a small village slightly out of the way. So I came to the church where he was to give his sermon, and there was a large audience come to hear him since he had a great reputation for preaching. And in his sermon he repeated many times the words, "If God be with us, who shall be against us?" Hearing these words, I was more resolved than ever to obey God's will and follow my decision.

Having been to Walsingham, we went on to Norwich, traveling all three together, my daughter-in-law, myself, and the young hermit. When we arrived at Norwich, we met a Franciscan Gray Friar, who was a considerable scholar, indeed a doctor of divinity. He had heard from me previously of my way of life and my interior feelings; and so he warmly welcomed me and talked with me as he had done when we met before. But he noticed that I was sighing a good deal and wore a gloomy expression that told of my hidden worries. And so he asked me what was the matter.

"Sir," I told him, "when I left Lynn with the permission of my confessor, I planned to escort my daughter-in-law to Ipswich. She is due to take ship there and, by the grace of God, sail across to Germany. And then I proposed to return home to Lynn accompanied by this hermit who had joined us for this very reason. That was what he expected. But when we

---

[125] This famous East Anglian shrine (which is still in use today) was second only to Canterbury as a place of pilgrimage. It comprised a holy well, the slipper chapel (where pilgrims took off their shoes before entering the shrine), and the Holy House, a reproduction of the house of Loretto, supposedly where Mary had received the Angel Gabriel's salutation. Margery does not make it clear if this is her first visit; but that would be surprising, as it was so close to hand.

were no more than six miles outside Lynn, we turned into a church to pray. There I was bidden to cross the sea with my daughter-in-law. But I know well enough that she would prefer that I stay at home, as indeed I would if only I dared. But my soul was so moved, and I knew no rest of soul or spirit until I agreed to follow my inner feelings. And that is why I am so fearful and heavy-hearted."

The good priest told me, "You must obey God's will. I am sure it was the Holy Spirit who spoke to you, and so you should follow this movement of your soul in the name of Jesus."

His words gave me much comfort, and so I took my leave of him and traveled to the coast with my companions. When we arrived, the ship was ready to sail. I asked the master if I too might sail to Germany, and he received me on board most kindly. And my fellow passengers were all in equal agreement at my joining their passage. No one had any word to say against me, save for my daughter-in-law, the one person who should have been on my side.

Then I said good-bye to the hermit who had journeyed with us. I paid him for his trouble and asked him to make my excuses to my confessor as well as to my other friends when he arrived back at Lynn. I assured him that as I left Lynn I had not had the slightest intention of making another sea crossing as long as I lived. "But I must obey the will of God."

The hermit left us with a long face and set off back to Lynn. He passed on my message of apology to my confessor and my other friends. He explained my sudden and unexpected journey, saying he had had no idea that we were going to be separated so suddenly.

When they learned this news, they were all very surprised; and they all had their own explanations. Some said it was just how a woman's mind worked; they maintained it was madness for an old woman like me to risk my life at sea, just for my daughter-in-law, entering a foreign country where I had never been before, not knowing how I would ever return. Others judged it very kind of me to see my daughter-in-law home and help her rejoin her own friends, whom she had left behind when she and her husband first set out to make their visit. And there were others who knew better; realizing how I lived, they thought and believed it to be the will of Almighty God acting for the greater glory of his name.

3

My companions and I went on board our ship on the Thursday of Passion Week, and God gave us good wind and weather on that day and the day following. But on the Saturday, and especially on Palm Sunday itself, our Lord, letting go his hand as it pleased him, put my faith and fortitude to the test. He sent such terrible storms and high seas that we all believed we were about to die. The storms lasted night and day; they were so extreme and terrible that it became no longer possible to work the ship. All we could do was to put ourselves and our ship in the hands of our Lord. The crew, despairing of their seamanship, gave the vessel her head, leaving our Lord to drive us where he would.

I had my fill of terror and fear; I think I have never known anything like it. I cried out as loud as I could to our Lord to save me and everyone on shipboard. I thought to myself, "Lord, it was for love of you I came, and you have so often promised me that I would never perish on land or at sea in a storm. People have often cursed me for the grace you work in me. They wished on me a dreadful death that would be full of pain, and now it looks as if they will have their way. Lord, make haste to still these storms, and show us your mercy, or else I will be cheated of the promises you have so often made me. My enemies will gloat and I will be put down, if they have their way and I am deceived in my end. Blessed Jesus, now is the time to remember your many mercies. Make good your promises to me. Show me that you are the true God and that no evil spirit that has brought me here into these perilous seas. I have always trusted and followed your promptings for many years; and I shall continue, through your mercy, if only you deliver me from these deadly dangers. Help us, Lord, come to our aid before we perish or despair. We cannot last much longer without your mercy and your help."

But our merciful Lord, speaking in my heart, blamed me for my fear, saying, "Why are you so afraid? What is there to fear? Am I not as mighty on the sea as on land? Can you not trust me? I shall make good every single promise I have given you. I shall never let you down. Suffer quietly for now; trust in my mercy. Hold fast in faith, for without faith, how may you please me? You have only to trust and to put away your doubts, and you will have great peace in your soul. Then you will be a great comfort to your companions, whereas now you are all in a great panic and grief."

It was with such words, and many more too high and holy to repeat, that our Lord comforted me. Blessed may he be. I called upon the holy saints, and by our Lord's grace they answered me with words of great comfort. At last our Lady came and said, "Daughter, all is well. You know I have always told you the truth. Put away your fear. I am telling you in truth, these winds and storms will soon die down. Fair weather is on its way."

So it happened, blessed be God, that in a little while our ship was driven in safety toward the coast of Norway. And there we landed at last on Good Friday, staying and resting there for Easter Eve, Easter Day, and Easter Monday. And on Monday,[126] we all took Communion together on that ship.

On Easter Day, the ship's master led most of us as we went to mass in the church. Now it was the custom of that country to raise the cross on high at noon. And as they did so, I made my meditation with much devotion so that I wept and sobbed just as I might have done at home. For God did not stint his grace either in church or back on the ship; whether we were at sea or wherever I journeyed it was the same. He was always present in my soul.

And when we had all received Communion on the Monday, as I have described, our Lord sent a following wind that blew offshore and carried us all the way to our intended destination, Germany. I made good friends with the master of the ship; for his part, he provided me with food and drink and indeed anything else I needed, all the time I was on his ship. He behaved as gently toward me as if he were my own mother. He gave me warm covers from his own locker; otherwise I think I might have perished from the cold as I was not prepared for the voyage like the others. But I had set out at my Lord's bidding and therefore he, who had told me to go, provided for me as well as any of my companions. Honor and praise to our Lord for all of that.

---

126 "We all took Communion together on that ship": The symbolism of the ship as a figure of the church cannot have been lost on Margery, especially since it had nearly foundered yet reached the shore in safety, in time for Easter Day. Since Communion was only rarely given, the ship's master too must have been anxious about continuing the journey and made special arrangements with the priest to "housel" all the ship's company as they set out.

4

stayed on in the German city of Danzig for some five or six weeks. And there I was warmly received by many different people, all out of their love of our Lord. Yet there was none so much against me as my own daughter-in-law, quite the opposite of her proper filial duty which should have been to look after me. In spite of this, I was pleased in our Lord at the welcome shown to me by so many people for love of him, so that I was of a mind to stay with them. Yet, at the same time, our Lord prompted me in my soul to leave their country.

Therefore I was at a loss as to how to follow our Lord's bidding, which I never for a moment intended to resist. Yet the problem was that I had not one single traveling companion, neither man nor woman. And whenever I came in sight of the sea, I turned back again out of pure fear, remembering all we had put up with on our crossing. Worse still, there was a war going on at the time, so that traveling by land was very risky. Considering all these problems, I became thoroughly miserable and did not know who to turn to.

But at last I found a church and went in to pray; I asked our Lord, as it was he who had told me to set out, if he would now send me help and traveling companions. All at once, a man came up to me and invited me to make a pilgrimage to Wilsnack. He told me that it was a good way off, in Brandenburg; he told me that apparently, some years earlier, the church had been burned down but in the ruins they had found three hosts, preserved but bleeding. So that now many people came from far and wide in order to venerate the precious blood of our Lord Jesus Christ.

I replied that I would be more than happy to go with him, provided I could find some honest person willing to escort me from Wilsnack back to England. He agreed that after fulfilling his pilgrimage to Wilsnack, he himself would guide me safely back to the coast from where I might set out for England. There I would be sure to meet up with some trustworthy fellow countrymen. We also agreed, at the same time, that I would pay his expenses for this second leg of our journey together.

Then he managed to charter a small boat that would take us to our pilgrim destination. But because I was English, I was told I could not leave port until I had permission from the Teutonic Knights;[127] but all I met with were obstacles and endless difficulties. At last our Lord caused a merchantman from Lynn to hear of my plight. He found me and promised that he would do all he could to get me away, aboveboard or in secret. Eventually, after a great deal of trouble, he succeeded in obtaining permission for me to travel.

So, at length, I went on board the ship that my new companion had chartered. And God sent only a light breeze, so I was relieved that there were hardly any waves to speak of. But the ship's company declared they were making no headway and began to grumble and complain. I prayed to our Lord, who then sent a much stiffer breeze so that we fairly scudded along; but I noticed the waves beginning to rise and fall alarmingly. My companions were now thoroughly de-

---

[127] The Teutonic Knights was originally a religious military order formed by German crusaders. By Margery's day, they had become the Hanseatic League, a powerful alliance of the mercantile city-states of northern Europe—in which Danzig played a prominent part. The local war to which Margery refers was an incursion by a Polish army of Hussite mercenaries into Pomerania (hence the decision to pilgrimage by sea). The League was also at odds with England over the king's refusal to pay sums due under a previous agreement; it was busy levying counter-charges against English merchantmen sailing out of Danzig.

lighted, but I was having a bad time because of the waves. Then our Lord spoke to my soul and told me to lie down so that I would not be able to see the waves anymore. And I did just that. But even then I was still very apprehensive, and everyone blamed me for being afraid. Until, at last, we came to a place that they called Strawissownd [Stralsund].

(No one must mind if these place-names are not correctly spelled. I was more concerned to say my prayers than with taking down the name of every place we came to. And my scribe cannot be blamed for such inaccuracies, for he never even went near them.)

5

Having landed at Strawissownd, we did not stay long but quickly set out for Wilsnack. We were frightened by the many dangers that might lay ahead of us. For there was open war between England and the country we were crossing, and I continually begged my companion not to leave me in such a hostile land where everyone we met seemed against us. The war increased my fear, so it was far more than it usually was on a pilgrimage, but our Lord kept saying in my heart, "What are you afraid of?" He would insist, "No one is going to harm you or anyone who travels with you. You must tell your companion that nobody will hurt him or do him any mischief as long as he is with you.

"Daughter, you know from your own experience that if a wife loves her handsome husband, she will go wherever he wishes to take her. And, my daughter, there can be none so handsome, so good as I; therefore, if you love me, there is nowhere you will fear to go with me. Daughter, it is I that have brought you here, and I shall bring you home again to England in perfect safety. Never doubt it, always believe in me."

When I held such holy conversations, I found that I sobbed convulsively and wept a great deal. And the more I behaved in this way, the more my companion was irritated at having to be with me. Then he would scheme to get rid of me and leave me on my own. He would begin to walk so fast that I found it almost impossible to keep up with him. He would start saying how much he was afraid of enemies and thieves; he was sure they would take me away from him and beat him up, and rob him in the bargain. I tried to cheer him up as best I knew how, by telling him that I was certain no one was going to attack or rob us or even say a harmful word against us.

At one point, as soon as I had said such a thing, a strange man suddenly appeared out of a forest. He was a tall fellow, well armed and, so it appeared to both of us, only too ready for a fight.

My companion took great fright and asked me, "Look at him, what are you going to say now?"

"Trust in our Lord God," I told him, "don't be afraid of this stranger."

The apparition simply came past and said not a word to us; and we carried on along our weary way to Wilsnack. At my age, I could not walk nearly so far in a day as a man might, but he didn't give me a second thought and never even waited for me to catch up to him. So I just struggled on as best I could, until illness prevented me from going a single step further. Yet I felt it was almost a miracle that a lame woman in her sixties should have kept going for days alongside a healthy man whose only idea seemed to be to lengthen his stride.

On Corpus Christi Eve, we came by chance on a small inn

which was a long way from any town. The only bedding they could provide was a pile of straw. I lay resting there all that night and throughout the next day until evening came. All this while, our Lord sent almost continuous lightning, thunder, and rain; and so it would have been quite impossible for us to continue on our weary way. I was secretly relieved because I felt really unwell and knew that if the weather had been better, my companion would have gone ahead without me. I thanked God for giving him good reason to stay where he was, although he was all for starting out again.

Because I felt so unwell, a wagon was found and I was carried, albeit in great discomfort and penance, to see the Holy Blood of Wilsnack. Along the way, the local women would take pity on me; they kept on telling my companion that he should be ashamed of himself for the way he treated me. But his only thought was how to get rid of me; and he never listened to them or seemed to care about my plight. Such was the journey, with all its mishaps and trials, that brought me at last to Wilsnack. And there I saw the miraculous Sacrament of the altar with the Precious Blood oozing from it.

6

e did not linger in Wilsnack but set off by wagon without delay for Aachen. Presently we came to a busy ford and there we met up with a whole group of travelers; some were heading for Aachen, others to different places. Among them was a monk, a very careless, dissolute man who was traveling with a crowd of young merchants.

Both the monk and the merchants knew my guide well, and hailed him by name. Once over the ford, we formed up together, they in their wagons, and we in ours. And when we came to a house of Friars Minor, they all said they were thirsty. Then they decided that I must go in to the friars and ask for some wine. But I told them, "Sirs, if this were a convent, I would be perfectly happy to do so. But since they are men, I'm sorry, but I won't."

One of the merchants went instead to fetch a jar of wine; and presently a monk came out and invited us in to adore the Blessed Sacrament in their church. This was during the octave of Corpus Christi and they had the sacrament exposed in a crystal stand for all to see.

The men followed the monk inside to visit the sacrament. And then I too followed them in, changing my mind because I wanted to pray before the Blessed Sacrament. And as soon as I saw it, our Lord gave me so much sweet devotion that I wept and sobbed with surprising bitterness, and could not contain myself. The monk and all the men turned on me angrily on account of my tears. And when we got back to the wagons they went on at me again, calling me names and complaining that I was a hypocrite and heaping many wicked words on me. I tried to defend myself and even quoted the Bible and quotations from the Psalms, *"Qui seminant in lacrimis"* and again *"Euntes ibant et flebant"* and other similar sayings. But that merely made them all the more angry. They said they no longer wanted to journey with me and even persuaded my guide to go along with them.

I begged and pleaded as humbly as I knew how that they would not leave me on my own in a strange land where I knew nobody. Only with great pleadings and prayers was I able to keep riding with them, until at length, on the octave of Corpus Christi, we came to a decent-sized town. But once we had arrived, they were adamant that they no longer wanted my company. Even the man who had agreed to be my guide, and to escort me safely back to the coast for my crossing to England, handed me back my gold and other valuables that he had in safekeeping for me. Then he offered to lend me extra money if I happened to be in need, and told me firmly that I was now on my own.

"John," I told him, "I never wanted your money. In these foreign parts it's your friendship that counts far more than gold. And I want to tell you that I think you would please God more if you stayed with me, as you promised when we were in Danzig, than if you went on foot all the way to Rome."

That was how they walked out on me and left me to find my own way home. My parting words to the man who had been my guide were, "John, the only reason you are leaving me is because I weep when I see the Blessed Sacrament or call to mind our Lord's sufferings. You are deserting me because I follow God. I have never known him to let me down, so I am sure he will see to all my needs and keep me safe on the way home. Blessed may he be."

Then they went off and left me utterly alone. Night came and I was very miserable. I was completely by myself and did not even know how I would spend the remainder of that night or with whom I could continue my journey on the following day. I found lodgings, but there some local priests accosted me and called me English tail;[128] they spoke many obscene words in my hearing and cast indecent looks in my direction. They asked me if I wanted them to be my escort. And because of all this, I was terrified for my chastity.

So I went to the woman who owned the house and asked her if I could have two maids to sleep in the room with me that night. She found two such, but I was so concerned that I hardly slept at all the whole night long. I prayed for deliverance and to be saved from all uncleanliness, and asked God to find me some new companions who could help me on my way to Aachen in the morning. I was answered by an impulse to go to church early the next morning, where I would meet with some fellow travelers.

Accordingly, I paid my bill early the following day and asked if they knew of anyone heading for Aachen, but I was told they knew of no one. I took leave of them and went off to the church to meditate and discover whether my inner prompting had been true. As I arrived, I noticed a group of poor people. So I went up to one of them and asked where they were going. He told me Aachen, so I asked if I might join him.

"Woman," he asked me, "have you no man to walk with you?"

"My man has left me," I replied.

That was how I came to join company with these poor folk. They were so poor that when we came to a town, I would look to buy some food while they set about begging something for themselves. When we were out in the country, they would often take off their clothes and sit quite naked while

 128 This was an old German joke against the English, claiming they had tails.

they picked the fleas from each other. But I was forced to put up with them, although it slowed down my journey and thus cost me far more than I had anticipated. In traveling with them, I too became infested with their fleas, but I felt too shy to take off my clothes like they did. I was sorely bitten, especially at night, until such time as God sent me different companions. But in spite of the discomfort and all the delays, I stayed in their company, although I still felt uneasy until we could manage to get to Aachen.

7

hen we finally reached Aachen, I met a monk on his way from England to Rome; it was a great comfort to talk, after such a long time, with someone who spoke my own language. We stayed together for something like ten or twelve days, in order to see our Lady's smock and several other holy relics which went on display on Saint Margaret's feast-day.[129]

While we waited, a respectable woman chanced to come from London. She was a widow and was accompanied by several servants; she had also come to see the relics and ven-

 [129] The so-called Four Great Relics were held to be our Lady's smock, worn at the birth of Jesus; his own swaddling clothes; the cloth that received the head of John the Baptist; and the loincloth worn by Christ on his cross. The silver shrine in which they are still kept dates back to 1238. Margery was fortunate to arrive in Aachen at this precise time, since the relics were only put on public display every seven years for two weeks following the Feast of Saint Margaret, which was then on July 20, 1433.

erate them. So I called on this lady and told her of my difficulty in having no one with whom I could make my return
journey. She was kind to me and promised to give me everything I needed; she also invited me to eat and drink with her
and was very friendly in every way possible.

But once Saint Margaret's feast was come and gone and
they had seen the holy relics, the good woman suddenly left
Aachen together with her large party. I felt that my plans had
suddenly collapsed, because I had counted on traveling with
her, and as a result I was very downcast. So I quickly took
my leave of the monk I have already mentioned, the one who
was on his way to Rome; and traveling by wagon with some
other pilgrims, I set off as fast as I was able. I hoped that in
this way I would perhaps be able to overtake this good lady,
but it was not to be.

Then I met up with two Londoners who were making their
way home. They told me they would look after me, but, as
they were in a hurry, they insisted that I would have to go at
their pace.

And so I hurried along behind them with great difficulty,
until we reached the next large town. Here we met another
group of English pilgrims who had been visiting the court of
Rome and were also returning to England. I begged that I
might join them; but they gave me short shrift, telling me that
since they had been robbed and had hardly sufficient money
to reach home, they must make the best possible time, and
they didn't really want to be held up by me. But they eventually agreed I could join them, on the one condition that I go at
their pace.

I had little alternative but to join this group and see how
long I was able to keep up with them, so I left the two Londoners and joined this fresh group. When we went in to take
our first meal together, everyone ate heartily. But I noticed
one man who was lying down full length on one end of a
bench. When I asked who he was, I was told he was a friar
who also belonged to their party.

"So why doesn't he eat with you?"

"We were all robbed and so was he. Now it's every man for himself."

"Well," I answered, "he shall share such money as God sends my way."

I knew that our Lord would provide for both our needs. And so I asked him to eat and drink with me, which cheered him up greatly. But as soon as we all resumed our journey, I quickly realized that I could not keep up with them. I was just too old and feeble to match their pace; I tried trotting along so as to go a bit faster, but I simply did not have the energy to keep it up.

So I decided to ask the penniless friar who had eaten with me if he would be willing to travel with me as far as Calais. I added that I would pay his expenses and give him an offering on top of this. He was more than happy with my offer and accepted it. So having agreed to this plan, we let the other travelers go on ahead, while we settled for a pace we knew we could keep to.

Presently, the friar declared that he was very thirsty and went on to explain himself. "I know this road quite well for I have often come along here on my way to Rome. There is a good inn not far from here. We could stop there and have a drink."

I was quite happy at this suggestion. And when we arrived, the good wife of the house turned out to be very sympathetic toward us. But in her opinion, she declared, I ought certainly to be traveling on a wagon with other pilgrims rather than be walking alone with a friar. So I explained to her how I had planned to travel with a certain good lady all the way to London, and how I had been mistaken. By the time we had rested and this conversation was concluded, sure enough a pilgrim wagon came trundling past. The good wife, who knew the driver, ran after him even though they had already gone past her house. She pleaded that I might join them and so speed my journey. And so it was agreed and I was able to climb aboard. And when we came to the very next town, I suddenly caught sight of the good lady from London.

So I asked the good pilgrims to excuse me and let me pay for my share of the journey. I told them all about the English lady who I had seen and how we had made an arrangement when we first met in Aachen that we would travel back home together to England. And so I left them, and they set out on their way once more.

I went across to the English lady fully expecting to be greeted warmly. But quite the contrary; she was sharp and very blunt with me: "Who do you think you are? I'm not having you coming along with me, I don't want to know you."

I was at a loss at this outburst and didn't know what to do next. I knew nobody in sight, and no one knew me. I had nowhere to go. I didn't know what had become of the friar who had agreed to be my escort, and whether or not he would soon be coming my way. I was very confused and terribly upset. I was at my lowest point since leaving England.

But all the same, I trusted God's promise and remained in town until he sent me help. It was almost evening when I saw the friar arrive. I hurried up to him and told him how badly I had been snubbed by the lady I had trusted. The friar did his best to comfort me, saying that we would fare no better or worse than God ordained. But he added that he was unwilling to spend the night in that town because he knew the people there were not to be trusted. So we set off into the dark, our mind beset with all our problems, the chief among them where we were going to spend the night.

We came to a forest and took a path along the edge of it, all the while keeping our eyes open for a place to spend the night. And, exactly as our Lord disposed, we presently came across one or two cottages. We hurried up to them and discovered that a man lived there with his wife and two children. But they did not run an inn nor did they usually put people up for the night. But I spied a pile of bracken in an outhouse and persuaded these people, with some difficulty, to let me sleep there for the night. The friar, after more negotiations, was shown a barn, and we felt ourselves well enough served just to have some kind of roof over our heads for that night. The following morning, we paid them for our shelter and took the road toward Calais once more.

The going was getting harder all the while, as now we found ourselves trudging through deep, shifting sand dunes, and, moreover, the path seemed to go up and down all the time. It took us two more full days before we arrived, and we suffered great thirst and weariness for there were hardly any villages and we could find only the meanest of lodgings.

It was at night that I was most afraid, above all of my spiritual enemy; I was in constant fear of being raped or violated. I dared trust no one; whether I had reason or not, I was constantly frightened all the time. I hardly dared sleep at night for fear of some man raping me. And as a result, I hardly shut my eyes unless I was able to find a woman or two to sleep beside me. Yet by the grace of God, there was usually a young girl or two willing to lie by my side where I stopped to rest, which went some way to help ease my mind.

As a result of all this, as we neared Calais, I was so tired and exhausted that I thought each step would be my last as we tramped along our way. And so at last we arrived at Calais, myself and the good friar. He had been so kind and gentle with me on our journey together that I rewarded him for his generosity as well as I could; and he seemed well pleased. And after that we said our farewells to each other.

8

n Calais I met with much kindness from many different men and women, yet all of them were complete
strangers. For example, one woman made me at
home in her house and not only offered me a good wash, but
even gave me a new smock, which was a great comfort. Others invited me to eat and drink with them. And since I had to
wait three or four days for a ship, during that time I met up
again with a good number of people I already knew; they
were all courteous and warm in their conversations with me,
but as we waited to embark their kind words were the only
thing they had to offer me.

The only thing I wanted was simply to sail with them to
Dover, but they were unready to offer me the least help; they
would not even tell me which ship they intended to sail in.
But by keeping my wits and asking around, I managed to
guess their plans and settle for the same ship. But no sooner
had I loaded my things aboard, imagining that these people
were about to sail—although I was still unsure of their exact
arrangements—they suddenly changed to another ship. Why
they did this, I had no idea.

But by God's grace, I guessed that they were on the point
of sailing. So, leaving my things behind in the first boat, I
managed to get a place for myself aboard their new vessel.
And there I noticed the smart lady from London who had
refused to let me join her party. And so at last we all set sail
for Dover together.

I could tell from the looks I got and the people's general attitude toward me that they had little affection for me. So I prayed to God that I would not become seasick and so make myself even more unpleasant in their sight. My prayers were answered; although plenty of other people were soon violently seasick, I myself felt perfectly well. Indeed, I found I was even able to move around the ship and help those who were in distress, which seemed to be a surprise to everyone. The London lady was the worst afflicted of all, and I was most attentive to her. I tried to look after her out of love for our Lord, for I had no other reason to care for her.

We sailed on until we reached Dover. Then it was clear that everyone had companions to travel with, except myself. And I could find no one. So I had to set off for Canterbury alone; again I was feeling generally sorry for myself but especially miserable as I did not even know the way.

I got up early the next morning and knocked on the door of a poor man's cottage. He was still pulling on his clothes and struggling with his buttons and ties, but he came to the door and asked what I wanted. I asked him if it was possible that he had a horse and if he would perhaps help me get to Canterbury. I made it clear to him that I was ready to pay him well. He was only too pleased to help me in our Lord's name and agreed at once to escort me all the way to Canterbury.

I was overjoyed in our Lord, who always sent me help and support at times such as these. So I thanked him with many devout tears and much sobbing and weeping; for it was the same in every place I had been to, so many times that it was impossible to tell, on this side of the sea or on the other, always the same whether on water or dry land. Blessed may God be.

9

rom Canterbury, I traveled up to London. And I
was still wearing my canvas sailor's jacket that had
kept the weather out all the time I was abroad.[130]
When I reached the city, I wasn't dressed properly as I was
more than a little short of money. I realized there were plenty
of people who might recognize me before I had a chance to
borrow some money, so I was wearing a handkerchief across
my face. But in spite of this, some good-for-nothing spotted
me and, recognizing Margery Kempe of Lynn, shouted out by
way of insulting me, "Ho-ho, 'False flesh, you shall never eat
good meat!'"

I refused to stop and pretended I had not heard these
hoary old words. I had never spoken any such words. How
could I? They were certainly not from God nor indeed from
any good man's mouth. Yet for a long time now, it had been
said everywhere that I had coined them. And as a result, I
suffered a great deal of shame and embarrassment everywhere I went. The father of lies—the devil—was their source
and they were spread and savored by his servants. These
were false people, envious of the way I lived my life, whose
only weapon against me was to wag their lying tongues.

No man or woman living could prove I had ever spoken
such words. Yet everyone believed the tale purely and simply

---

[130] This somewhat unusual garment may have been a wind-cheater given to Margery by the
sea captain on her outward passage (see Chap. 3, Book II).

on the word of liars, who went on repeating what they had heard. It was thanks to the devil's work that this kind of evil story made its rounds.

It had all begun just shortly after my conversion when the devil persuaded one or two people to concoct the following tale about me: I was said to have been sitting at some good man's table one Friday fish day. And there I was served all kinds of fish, so the story went, including red herrings, a nice steak of pike, and so on. Then I was supposed to have said, "You false flesh, you would like the red herring, but you shan't have your way." Having said that, I was supposed to have pushed the red herring to the side of my platter and attacked the pike.

There were other versions as well of what I was supposed to have said. But this one in particular, "False flesh, you shall eat no herring," became a kind of catch phrase that people would use at my expense. These same words kept being repeated, although there was no truth in the original story, and so they would be passed on and end up in places where no one had even seen or heard tell of me.[131]

While in London I visited the home of a good widow where I was made welcome and kindly received for love of our Lord. And in many other places there I was strengthened and encouraged by people in our Lord's name, may God reward them all. There was one good lady in particular who afforded me very special charity, both in offering me food and drink and giving me many other benefits.

I dined with this good lady on one occasion when there was a large gathering present. I did not know anyone, and equally, I was unknown to them; although someone pointed out to me several people who were from Cardinal Beaufort's

§ [131] Margery tells this story against herself. It is a fascinating example of the rapid, almost contagious spread of an anecdote or *bon mot* that catches on. There is always a vestige of truth or the story would never have begun. In twentieth-century Britain, one famous instance is recorded of a playground jingle sung by children to a hymn tune: "Hark the Herald Angels sing, Mrs. Simpson's pinched our king." This spread by word of mouth from Kent to Lancashire in a matter of weeks, a tribute to the joy of word play. While children knew the truth, the English press chose to remain silent about the impending crisis.

household. It was a very fine feast and soon everyone was very merry.

As the party got going, more and more jokes were made and soon I heard someone repeating the famous words: "False flesh, you'll have no more good meat . . ."

I sat quite still and suffered in silence. Everyone had their say in making more fun of the foibles of the joke's victim. When their jesting had run its course, I asked them if they had any idea who the person was who supposedly coined this phrase.

They said, "No, not at all. But they say there is one such false hypocrite in Lynn who delights in saying such things. She leaves the coarse meats to one side, only to pounce upon the best to be had on the table."

"Listen to me, sirs," I offered, "don't you think you should say no worse than you know to be the truth about other people, and not exaggerate as much as you can? As a matter of fact—may God forgive you—you are out of your depth. I am the person in question. I know what I'm talking about. I've grown used to putting up with the embarrassment by now. But I swear to God, there is not a grain of truth in any word of it."

When they realized that I wasn't angry with them but merely wanted to set the record straight in a friendly way, they were reduced to silence by my directness and did their best at once to make amends.

It was the same all the while I was in London. I often spoke my mind quite fearlessly. I would rebuke people who swore or cursed or lied, and any other such malicious people; I spoke out too against the pompous fashions of men and women. I never spared them or flattered them, not even when they may have given me gifts of food and drink. And I strongly believe that my speaking out in this way helped a good many people.

Whenever I came to church, our Lord sent me very high devotion, thanking me for not being afraid to check sin in his name; and also because, as a result of this, I often suffered mockery and rebuke for his sake. He promised me much grace in this life, and, hereafter, his joy and bliss without end.

I was so comforted by these sweet communings with our Lord that I could not control myself or check my spirit as I would have liked, and certainly as others would have wanted. But it was our Lord himself who was in control, prompting all of it himself, the violent sobbing and copious weeping for which I suffered a great deal of slander and blame, most especially from the curates and priests in those London churches. They often turned me out of the church, so that I went from one to another in order to cause them less of a disturbance. Yet many ordinary folk praised God on my account, firmly of the belief that it was God's grace that worked in my soul.

10

From London I went [a little way down the Thames] to Sheen [Syon Abbey], three days before the Lammas Day pardon [on offer there], which I hoped to obtain through the mercy of our Lord. And when I was in the church, I had great devotion and much high contemplation. I remembered the bitter pain and suffering of our merciful Lord Jesus Christ, how much he suffered in his blessed manhood. And those who witnessed my weepings and heard my loud sobbings were full of curiosity and wondered what could be eating at my soul.

One young man, who had observed my changing face and manner as I prayed, was moved by the Spirit. Once I had composed myself, he came to me on his own initiative, fed by an inner hunger to understand for himself what might be the cause of such tears.

He asked me courteously, "Mother, please I beg you, tell me the root of your tears. Never have I seen such tears, nor heard anyone sob so. And, mother, I may still be young but I long to please my Lord Jesus Christ and follow him to the best of my powers. And I intend, with God's help, to take the Carthusian habit at Sheen[132] and therefore I beg your help. Be like a true mother, for I trust you. Tell me what you can."

As gently as I could, humbly yet with great joy of spirit, I told him something of the cause of my tears: how I had many times been unkind to my maker and offended his goodness; also that my great hatred of sin made me sob and weep. Then too, the great and immeasurable love of my Redeemer, whose power through suffering, his shedding of blood, brought me back from everlasting pain. So that now, trusting to inherit his joy and bliss, I was made to sob and to weep: Why was anyone surprised! I told this young man many good words of comfort which seemed to urge him on to attain his great ideal. And afterward we ate and drank together during my stay and he was very glad of my company.

Come Lammas Day, the day of pardon, I entered the church at Sheen [Syon] and caught sight of the hermit who had escorted me from Lynn when I journeyed to the coast with my daughter-in-law, as I have already told. I went over to greet him at once and welcomed him with all my heart.

"Reynald, welcome, it is so good to see you. I am sure our Lord sent you here: for I hope that, just as you led me out from Lynn, you will take me home again at last."

132 Margery has told us that she went to the site of the two powerhouses of English spirituality some ten miles down the Thames from London: the Brigittines of Syon and (on the opposite bank) the Carthusian Charterhouse of Sheen. In her account, she not only confuses the two; but she meets this ardent young novice wishing to join the nuns! Syon certainly had a pardon on Lammas Day: the Carthusians would certainly not have opened their doors to Margery.

But the hermit scowled at this; he seemed not the least inclined to take me home to Lynn as I fully expected.

"You had better know," he answered shortly, "that your confessor has given you up for lost. You went abroad without saying a word to him. You asked his leave merely to take your daughter-in-law to the coast, no further. None of your friends know what you've been up to. So I doubt very much if they will want to know you on your return. You must find another traveling companion this time: I got all the blame when I was last with you. Now I've had enough."

I coaxed him, begged him for the love of God not to be vexed with me. I told him that anyone who had loved me truly, for God's sake, when I had left, would still love me, in his name, on my return. I offered to pay his way on the journey home. And at last he relented. He came with me back through London, then home to Lynn; to God's worship and the great merit of both our souls.

As soon as I came home to Lynn, I went obediently to my confessor and humbly sought his penance. He was very fierce with me, telling me that I had undertaken my journey without his knowledge. In particular, he stressed that his anger with me was due to my lack of obedience. But with our Lord's help, I soon was back in charity with him as well as with all my other friends, just as I had been before my departure. May God be praised. Amen.

THE PRAYERS OF

MARGERY

KEMPE

For many years it was my custom at prayer to begin in this manner: Whenever I entered church I would kneel before the Blessed Sacrament to worship the Blessed Trinity—Father, Son, and Holy Spirit: one God and three Persons; also the glorious Virgin, Queen of Mercy, our Lady Saint Mary; and the twelve apostles. Then I would say the holy hymn, *Veni creator Spiritus,* saying each verse slowly and asking God to enlighten my soul as he did with his apostles on the day of Pentecost. I asked for the gifts of the Holy Spirit, the grace to know his will and carry it out, the grace to withstand the assaults of my spiritual enemies, and the grace to avoid every kind of sin and wickedness.

When I had completed the *Veni creator,* with all its verses, I would continue: "I take for my witness the Holy Spirit; our Lady, Saint Mary, the mother of God; all the holy court of heaven, and all my confessors here on earth—that even supposing it were possible that I might enjoy all knowledge and understanding of God's secrets through the word of some devil from hell, I would refuse.

"And as surely as I would never wish to know or hear, to see, feel, or understand in my soul more than God willed, just so may God help me in everything I do, in all my thoughts and in everything I say, whether I am eating or drinking, asleep or awake.

"And since it will never be my intention to worship any false devil instead of my God, nor to follow any false faith or untrue beliefs, I renounce the devil, all his lies and everything I have ever done through his influence while believing that I had been following God's promptings and the influence of the Holy Spirit. For you know and see the inner workings of everyone's heart. And inasmuch as I have done wrong, have mercy on me and grant me a well of tears, a constant source with which I may wash away my sins through your mercy and goodness.

"And, Lord, bless me in your high mercy so that all these tears may increase my love for you, build up merit in heaven, and help and strengthen my fellow Christians alive or dead. Good Lord, do not spare these eyes that are in my head, any more than you spared the blood from your own body which you shed so plentifully for man's sinful soul. Rather grant me so much pain and sorrow in this world that I may not be prevented from your bliss, and may see your glorious face when I shall go from here.

"As for my crying, my sobbing, my tears, Lord God Almighty, you know what scorn, humiliation, contempt and blame they have caused me. You know it is not within my power to weep out loud or in silence, whatever feelings of sweetness and devotion visit me, for all these tears of mine are the gift of the Holy Spirit. Since this is the case, Lord, justify me before the world so that people come to recognize that this is your work and your gift, given only to make your name known and to increase men's love for you, Jesus.

"And I pray you, Sovereign Lord Christ Jesus, that as many men may be turned to you by my crying and weeping as have been angry with me, until the world comes to its end, if this be your will. And as for human love, I would have no other love than yours, my God, to love you above all things and to love all things for God and in God. Therefore extinguish in me all lusts of the flesh, and also in all those whose human form has revealed the beauty of your own blessed body. And put your holy dread into our hearts, for the sake of your terrible wounds.

"May my confessors also fear you and love you in me; and may the whole world have sorrow for their sins on account of the grief you have put into my heart on their account. My good Jesus, make my will your will and your will my will, so that I may have no other will than yours.

"Good Lord Christ Jesus, I pray you have mercy on all Christian lands; on the pope and all his cardinals, on all archbishops and bishops, and on all the order of the priesthood; on all professed religious and especially on those who work to save and defend the teachings of the Holy Church. Lord, bless them in your mercy and give them victory over their enemies and good success in all they do to accomplish your kingdom. And for all those that are in grace at this time, send them perseverance until their last day, and make me worthy to share in their prayers and them in mine.

"I cry for mercy, blessed Lord, on the king of England and on all Christian kings, all lords and ladies throughout the world. Lord, help them to use their authority to please you best so that they may one day be lords and ladies in heaven without end. I cry for mercy, Lord, on the rich of this world who have your goods in their hands; give them your grace to use them in your service. And I cry your mercy, Lord, upon the Jews, the Saracens, and all heathen peoples. Good Lord, remember all the saints in heaven who once lived as heathens on earth; so generously have you extended your mercy across the whole earth.

"Lord, you have said that no one shall come to you unless first you call them, nor shall anyone be called unless you call them. Therefore, Lord, if there is someone who is not called, I pray you call them. You have called me, Lord, although I never deserved your call. It was through your mercy alone. If anyone knew of all my sins, Lord, as you do, they would wonder at your mercy and such great goodness. I wish that everyone could thank you for your goodness to me; but this is your way, to make worthless creatures good. So make the whole world worthy to thank you and give you praise.

"Lord, have pity on all heretics and believers in falsehoods, on all tax dodgers, thieves, adulterers, prostitutes, and criminals; Lord, of your mercy, spare them. If it be your will, may my prayers help them to be delivered speedily from their misdeeds.

"I cry out to you, Lord, for all those who suffer temptation or are under siege from their spiritual enemies. Of your mercy, give them grace to stand firm against these temptations, and save them from their tests as you think best.

"Have mercy too on all confessors. Pour into their souls as much grace as I would have you give me. Have mercy on all my children, those born of my body as well as my spiritual children, and on everyone living in this world. I would consider all their sins as if they were my sins, and, by true contrition, I ask you to forgive them as earnestly as I plead forgiveness for all those sins that I have committed.

"I cry out for your mercy, Lord, for all my friends and for all my enemies. And I pray especially for the sick, for all lepers, for all sick men and women confined to their beds, for all who are kept in prison, for all creatures in this world who have spoken well or ill of me, or shall do so, until the earth ends. Have mercy on them all and give your grace to their souls, just as I would ask you to give your grace to my soul.

"And to those who have said anything evil against me, in your great mercy, forgive them. And to those who have spoken well, I beg you, Lord, reward them for their own good charity rather than for any merit I may have. Yet you would not be unjust to me if you let the whole world hate me and turn against me for the offenses I have caused you.

"Have mercy too, Lord, on the souls in Purgatory as they await your final pardon and the prayers of the church. Surely, Lord, these are numbered among your chosen souls. Be as tender toward them as I would ask of you if I were even now suffering their pains.

"Lord Christ Jesus, I thank you for good health and for the wealth of this world; I thank you for poverty, for sickness, for contempt, for every humiliation, and for all wrongs. I thank you for every misfortune that has come my way or is still to come as long as I shall live. I thank you truly for letting me suffer even the smallest pain in this world to atone for my sins and add to my store of merit in heaven.

"Lord, hear all these prayers of mine, as I truly have so many reasons to thank you. Yet even if my heart could contain all the hearts and souls known to God from a time without beginning who will dwell in heaven without end; and as there are drops of water, both fresh and sea-salted, chips of gravel, stones great and small, grass blades growing in every part of the world, corn seed kernels, fish, fowl, beasts, leaves on the trees of summer, feathers on birds and hairs on beasts, seeds in plants or in weeds, in flowers, both on land and in water wherever they are most abundant, or as many as have ever been on earth, are now and shall be and could be in the might of your power; and as there are stars and angels in your sight, and all other kinds of good things which the earth brings forth; and if each soul were as holy as our Lady Saint Mary who bore Jesus our Savior, and if it were possible that each of these could think and speak with as great reverence and praise as our Lady Saint Mary herself did while she was here on earth and even now does in heaven and shall do without any end—I could still think in my heart and speak with my mouth at this time in praise of the Trinity and of all the court of heaven, to the great confusion of Satan, who fell from God's presence, and of all his wicked spirits, so that every one of these countless hearts and souls could never thank God sufficiently nor fully praise him, bless him to his full deserts, reverence him as he truly needs for all his great mercy that he has shown me on earth. This I cannot do and may never achieve.

"So I pray my Lady, who alone is the Mother of God, source of all grace, flower and fairest among all the women that God made, the noblest ever seen or heard by God; and because of your surpassing merits, amiable lady, humble lady, loving lady, with every reverence that lasts in heaven, and with all your saints, I pray you, Lady, please offer thanks and praise to the blessed Trinity for love of me, asking mercy and grace for me and for all my confessors, and seek our perseverance in living our lives to please him the most, until the end of our lives.

"I bless my God in my soul, and all you saints in heaven. Blessed may God be in you all, and you in God. Blessed be you, Lord, for all your many mercies poured upon us who are already in heaven or still upon your earth. And in particular, Lord, I thank you for Mary Magdalene, for Mary of Egypt, for Saint Paul and for Saint Augustine. As you showed mercy to these your saints, give your mercy to me and to all who seek your mercy. That peace and rest you once gave to your disciples and all those who loved you, may you give this same peace and rest to me on earth and in heaven without end.

"Remember, Lord, the woman taken in adultery and brought before you, and how you dismissed all her enemies as she stood alone; so in the power of your truth dismiss all my enemies from me, enemies of my body and my soul, so that I may stand alone before you. Make my soul die to all the joys this world has to offer, and make it come alive so that I hunger for the highest contemplation of God.

"Remember too, Lord, Lazarus who lay dead in his grave for four days. As I myself once visited the holy place where you lived in your holy body, where you were crucified and died for man's sins, where too Lazarus was raised from death to life; as surely as any man or woman may be dead through mortal sin at this moment, if any prayer can help them find new life, hear my prayers for them and make them live without end.

"I thank you, Lord, for all those sins that you have saved me from falling into. All those sins I have not done. I thank you, Lord, for all the contrition that you have given me for those that I have committed. For these graces, and for all other graces that I need and that all men on earth need.

"And for all men who trust in my prayers, all those who will come to believe and trust until the world's end, I ask you, Lord, to grant them, of your great mercy, every blessing in soul and body that they shall ask for and that may be to the good of their souls. Amen."